Learning to Read in the Late Ottoman Empire
and the Early Turkish Republic

Learning to Read in the Late Ottoman Empire and the Early Turkish Republic

Benjamin C. Fortna

Senior Lecturer in the Modern History of the Middle East,
School of Oriental and African Studies, University of London, UK

palgrave
macmillan

© Benjamin C. Fortna 2011

All rights reserved. No reproduction, copy or transmission of this publication may be made without written permission.

No portion of this publication may be reproduced, copied or transmitted save with written permission or in accordance with the provisions of the Copyright, Designs and Patents Act 1988, or under the terms of any licence permitting limited copying issued by the Copyright Licensing Agency, Saffron House, 6-10 Kirby Street, London EC1N 8TS.

Any person who does any unauthorized act in relation to this publication may be liable to criminal prosecution and civil claims for damages.

The author has asserted his right to be identified as the author of this work in accordance with the Copyright, Designs and Patents Act 1988.

First published 2011 by
PALGRAVE MACMILLAN

Palgrave Macmillan in the UK is an imprint of Macmillan Publishers Limited, registered in England, company number 785998, of Houndmills, Basingstoke, Hampshire RG21 6XS.

Palgrave Macmillan in the US is a division of St Martin's Press LLC, 175 Fifth Avenue, New York, NY 10010.

Palgrave Macmillan is the global academic imprint of the above companies and has companies and representatives throughout the world.

Palgrave® and Macmillan® are registered trademarks in the United States, the United Kingdom, Europe and other countries.

ISBN: 978–0–230–23296–9 hardback

This book is printed on paper suitable for recycling and made from fully managed and sustained forest sources. Logging, pulping and manufacturing processes are expected to conform to the environmental regulations of the country of origin.

A catalogue record for this book is available from the British Library.

Library of Congress Cataloging-in-Publication Data

Fortna, Benjamin C.
    Learning to read in the late Ottoman Empire and the early Turkish republic / Benjamin C. Fortna.
        p. cm.
    ISBN 978–0–230–23296–9 (hardback)
        1. Reading – Turkey – History – 19th century. 2. Reading – Turkey – History – 20th century. 3. Education and state – Turkey – History – 19th century. 4. Education and state – Turkey – History – 20th century. 5. Turkey – History – Tanzimat, 1839–1876. 6. Turkey – History – 1878–1909. I. Title.

LA941.7.F68 2011
418′.40710561—dc22   2010034129

10 9 8 7 6 5 4 3 2 1
20 19 18 17 16 15 14 13 12 11

Printed and bound in Great Britain by
CPI Antony Rowe, Chippenham and Eastbourne

for Sarah

Contents

Figures

Preface

This book is the result of a doubtless foolhardy effort to trace the untraceable, namely, what happens when young people learn to read. Like a ship moving through the sea, reading leaves behind little to mark its passing. This lack of evidence is a source of frustration for historians because, as we all know instinctively, reading affects the reader profoundly, even if the impact may not leave any physical trace.

My first book, *Imperial Classroom: Islam, the State, and Education in the Late Ottoman Empire*, attempted to demonstrate some of the ways in which the spread of education both reflected and in turn engendered important changes in late Ottoman society. The focus on institutional public education meant that the book was largely confined to the realm of the state. The book drew largely on governmental archival sources and the writings of individuals closely connected with state-supplied education. It proved difficult, although not impossible, to plumb the ways that education was experienced by its most important constituency, children.

In this book I deliberately set out to try to focus on an important aspect of education that was influenced by the state but hardly dominated by it. Learning to read and reading has, I hope, allowed me to achieve a better balance between state desiderata and individual experience. I have deliberately avoided a dependence on archival material and other state records, trying instead to rely on a variety of sources, chiefly textbooks, magazines and memoirs that inform the practice of reading in the late Ottoman Empire and the early Turkish Republic. This book necessarily draws on state-based materials for many of the children's texts analyzed here, many of which were written by teachers, pedagogues or bureaucrats and therefore mostly within the sate orbit. But these are, I trust, balanced by recourse to some of the growing literature that was independent of state patronage or direct control. Memoirs proved important to recovering the way all these texts were experienced by young readers.

I wanted also to cross the chronological barrier between empire and republic. To do so I had to go beyond my own training and research comfort zone but I took inspiration from a number of colleagues carrying out research in the early Republican period. I don't pretend to match their command of the period but I do hope that this modest attempt to move across the divide in order to trace the development of reading will prove helpful to others.

BCF
London, October 2010

Acknowledgements

I am indebted to many individuals and institutions that helped me while I was researching and writing this book. Funding from the Spencer Foundation, Chicago, and research leave from the School of Oriental and African Studies allowed me to visit a number of libraries and archives in Turkey. Among them were the Atatürk Library, the Beyazıt State Library and the Prime Minister's Ottoman Archives, all in Istanbul, the National Library in Ankara and the Seyfettin Özege Rare Book section of the Atatürk University Library in Erzurum. I would like to thank librarians and colleagues in each of these institutions for their helpfulness in locating the sources referred to in this book. I would also like to thank a number of colleagues who generously offered help and advice: Ali Akyıldız, Bill Blair, Nazan Çiçek, Peter Colvin, Burcu Akan Ellis, the I.T. Department, Şükrü Hanioğlu, Bora Keskiner, Klaus Kreiser, Carol Miles, Cüneyd Okay, Şevket Pamuk, John Parker, Nader Sohrabi, Adam Waite, Rob Whiteing and Philipp Wirtz. Michael Strang and Ruth Ireland at Palgrave Macmillan merit special thanks for their professionalism and encouragement. Will Fortna deserves all credit for making my sorry images presentable. I also thank the anonymous reviewers whose comments strengthened the manuscript. Naturally, all shortcomings are my own.

Special thanks go the members of my own family, including my sons Will, Nick and Benjy for making me proud and keeping me smiling in their own very different ways, and most of all to my wife Sarah, a stellar teacher of reading and prodigious reader. This book is dedicated to her, with love.

Abbreviations

BOA	Başbakanlık Osmanlı Arşivi (Prime Minister's Ottoman Archives)
CSSAAME	*Comparative Studies of South Asia, Africa and the Middle East*
IJMES	*International Journal of Middle East Studies*
REMMM	*Revue de mondes musulmans et de la Méditerranée*
TC	Türkiye Cumhurityeti (The Republic of Turkey)

Transliteration, Dates and Surnames

Writing about the Ottoman Empire and Turkey presents challenges with respect to a number of markers of historical change, including transliteration, place names, calendar conversion and naming patterns. For the sake of uniformity I have rendered Ottoman Turkish according to the system followed in *Redhouse Yeni Türkçe-İngilizce Sözlük/New Redhouse Turkish-English Dictionary*, 12th edn. (Istanbul, Redhouse Press, 1991). Place names common to Western readers have been given in their usual forms, thus Istanbul (and not İstanbul) and Salonica (not Selânik). I have assumed that publication dates of works that appeared before the Turkish Republic's adoption of the Gregorian calendar in 1926 are in the Rumi (i.e., Ottoman solar calendar) normally used in publishing unless otherwise stipulated. I have referred to author's names as they were published at the time, giving later surnames in brackets. Thus the works of the educationalist Ahmed Cevad [Emre] are alphabetized under Ahmed and not Emre. No system is perfect but I hope to have been consistent with this one.

1
Introduction: Reading Empire, Reading Republic

In the modern world the importance of reading is everywhere apparent. In today's society we are continually confronted with a swirling array of things demanding to be read. Making sense of them is critical to our engagement with the world and implicitly synonymous with modern existence. The range of texts and images with which we are confronted is prodigious and seemingly ever expanding. In fact, the imperative to read is so great that it is frequently taken for granted or, to use a common English expression, taken "as read."

From our first encounters with picture books and ABCs as small children to the school primers and textbooks that teach us the rudiments of literacy and then serve as the primary tools in our education, we spend more and more time with texts. By the time we are adults the proliferation of texts intensifies. Now we are consuming them on a daily if not hourly basis. It is estimated that the average white-collar adult spends more time reading than anything else except for sleeping.[1] We have become reading animals.

The fare is varied, seemingly changing all the time, reflecting the pulse of technological change and market behavior. In a typical day it is not uncommon for an urbanite to engage in continual reading from morning to night (atypical days present their own types of reading materials: the voting ballot, the roadmap, the hymnal, the playbill and so on). At breakfast there is often a newspaper to be perused or, for those still groggy with sleep, the nutritional information from the cereal box which focuses the only partially comprehending attention. On the way to work, perhaps a newspaper, one's own or that with the more salacious headline over the next fellow's shoulder that proves so difficult to ignore. Others turn to that stalwart of the modern age: the novel, probably a paperback, inexpensive, lightweight and handy.

Still others flip through the pages of a magazine, glossy and alluring. Meanwhile, a range of texts competes for attention: street signs, route information, billboard advertisements. Our own movement makes this assortment of text appear ambient, mobile; some text is actually moving as signs rotate, blink or flash. We can now summon the infinite textual resources of the Internet on a variety of electronic devices and even read electronic "books." Sometimes the commuting reader is interrupted. Is it a mobile phone call? Perhaps it is only a "text" message: more reading matter, but this time sent invisibly, in a sort of high-tech pidgin, and landing in one's hand.

It is now time to work. This usually means more reading, whether of the printed page (letters to sort and decipher, reports to digest, papers to file or grade or write, instructions to absorb or ignore, forms to fill in, surveys to suffer through) or, again, the electronic.[2] These last can take many of the old textual forms but also throw up a few modern variations (e-mail, web-pages, the circulated joke, the Nigerian get-rich scheme, mortgage offers or worse). Perhaps it is time for a meeting but that does not usually mean text-free conviviality; there are the agenda and minutes to absorb, more reports to wade through, and perhaps a few charts or graphs to attend. On the way home, the process repeats, still plenty of textual opportunities to contemplate. Back home, we might encounter more mail to sift through, a recipe to decode, perhaps someone needs help with their homework. You could check the sports scores in the paper you could not possibly finish earlier in the day, or maybe "catch up" on your e-mail. There are countless web and teletext pages for the desperate. Now it is time to relax, put up your feet and "read a good book." It's a wonder we can keep our eyes open, that we do not drown in this sea of text.

But it was not always this way. For most of recorded time the ability to read (and write) was the preserve of a small elite who controlled access to their knowledge, their texts and their shared language of references and symbols. The lion's share of reading was linked to the perpetuation of statecraft, organized religion and literary traditions. How, when and why reading ceased to be a privileged phenomenon and became instead a popular one is central to the shaping of the modern world, central in fact to what it means to be modern. This link between literacy and modernity operates on a number of levels, that of the individual, paragon of modernity itself, that of groups of individuals who come together for a variety of reasons (religious, social, economic, familial, cultural, political and so on), and that of society at large, of readership in the aggregate.

Texts have become such a basic feature of modern society that it is frequently difficult to imagine contemporary life in the absence of reading and literacy. That the relationship between humans and texts has only recently intensified in the ways that are the subject of this book is easy to forget. It is a useful reminder that the colossus of the modern educational system, upon which so much in today's society depends, was built, over centuries, around the basic tasks of learning to read and reading. British students "read" a particular subject at their universities where the position of Reader is a vestigial reminder of a calmer past more conducive to reading than today's heavily bureaucratic incarnation.

Widespread reading is synonymous with modern society. Economists have adduced a clear link between education and economic advancement.[3] Students of the nation have flagged the connection between the emergence of not only common readership, mainly of newspapers, but also of fiction, occasionally serialized in the papers themselves, and the coalescing of nationalisms. For arguably the most influential of these, Benedict Anderson, the emergence of "print capitalism" and the literacy upon which it depended, was the *sine qua non* of national coalescence.[4] For a modern nation to exist meant having a language and a literature; to deny a nation these attributes was tantamount with denying its very existence.[5] But the primacy of reading is also clearly a feature of the pre-modern era when, because of its very scarcity, it was valued all the more. Paradoxically, the more widespread literacy has become and the more intense the relationship between readers and texts, the more its power has become taken for granted, and the more its champions need to emphasize its importance. Whatever the case, it is clear that reading bears an iconic quality for the individuation of society in the modern period. Both the widening access to literacy and the increased emphasis on individual as opposed to collective reading has had profound implications in the political, religious, economic and social fields.

Yet for all of its crucial importance, reading is still relatively little studied and even less understood as a culturally and historically conditioned practice. In spite of considerable attention to the mechanics of reading, there remains something surprisingly ineffable, almost mysterious about the process of learning to read and reading. As every parent or teacher knows, there comes a point when a child will simply start to read. He or she has been helped, coached, perhaps even been subjected to phonics methods of various sorts, but in the end there is a liminal leap when, like learning to ride a bicycle, a child becomes a reader and is able to venture forward on his or her own.

The young reader now enters a new territory, a new world. This book is about what young readers experienced when they came into the new country of reading in the late Ottoman Empire and the early Turkish Republic. It is intended as a modest contribution to a broader literature on reading and learning to read that has focused almost exclusively on the Western experience. This book is about this process of learning to read and childhood reading in a society on the periphery of the West, influenced by it to varying degrees but formed by its own particular historical, cultural and geographical context, namely, that of the late Ottoman Empire and the early Republic of Turkey that partially succeeded it. It is the story of how reading became widespread in a society of unprecedentedly rapid change against the backdrop of warfare, invasion, famine, the dissolution of an old, multi-national empire and the creation of a number of nationally organized states in its wake. It focuses on the relationship between one of these, the Turkish Republic, and the Ottoman Empire in spite of the fact that are not directly comparable by concentrating on reading in the Turkish language. The transition from one to the other offers certain advantages for the history of reading. The normal way of approaching this transition has been to emphasize the break between empire and republic. Yet a remarkable series of continuities – of language, of the attention paid to expanding both education and literacy, of the attempts at social indoctrination and discipline, of many individual lives and careers across the putative border of 1923 – all attest to the fact that in many ways the core of Ottoman literary and cultural life carried on under the republic. Of course, this transition often entailed change, both superficial and profound, and it would be wrong to deny any number of important modifications between imperial and republican culture. For this study, the interplay between the continuities and the changes makes for a particularly rich mix, especially when, as will soon become apparent, the successor state insisted in its early years on painting its predecessor in a largely pejorative light.

In other words, this is a history of the transition from Ottoman Empire to Turkish Republic as seen through the lens of learning to read and reading. This rich but almost completely unexplored angle offers a fresh perspective on the relationship between the Ottoman Empire and the most important of its successor states. By looking at the way children's reading was approached, first in the late Ottoman Empire and then in the Turkish Republic, this study offers a new perspective on the fraught historical – and historiographical – relationship between the two eras, focusing on both the continuities and the disjunctures that have characterized the history of Turkey in the modern era. The coming of an unprecedented degree of literacy in the Ottoman lands effected change on a vast scale. The new educational system which did so much to bring it about and the growth of new commercial and career opportunities that it occasioned were perhaps the most readily observed of the changes that literacy induced. Harder to discern but in many ways more important were such phenomena as the challenges to established authority in many of its forms, political, social, cultural and economic. While the displacements and readjustments of the modern era appeared across the globe, it is important to remember that there was nothing preordained or teleological about this process. It carried with it surprises alongside its more expected outcomes. For example, it is possible to see the increase in literacy as an important step toward breaking down authoritarian structures, and the fragmentation of religious and political authority.[6] But it is also the case that, when harnessed in particular ways, it served to reinforce and even increase the sway of dominant power relations. It is therefore best to regard literacy as a neutral set of practices, attitudes and technologies that could, under a variety of conditions be put to a number of quite different ends. It is also necessary to observe that the spread of literacy and the various messages it conveyed could often proceed by chance and without, and indeed at times in opposition to, the wishes of dominant social and political forces.

Expanding literacy played a crucial role in the transformation of "traditional" society. Reading on a wider scale made possible the individuation of modern society but also facilitated the coalescing of individuals in common cause, whether in the form of its specific associative affiliations and groups or in the general sense of an Andersonian imagined community. The common sharing – and disputing – of ideas associated with the rise of the public sphere, described by Jürgen Habermas as "the sphere of private persons come together as a public,"[7] is virtually impossible to ponder in the absence of a shared literate culture. The rise of the state in its modern form is likewise extremely difficult to imagine without the coming into existence of a large body of bureaucrats trained to create, control and consume texts. The opening up of career options necessitated by the growth of the modern state and its ancillary fields such as journalism, law and education radically scrambled the socioeconomic horizons for new generations and complicated the relationship between public and private. The concomitant inroads made by new actors into society's elite likewise owed much to the new literacy and the institutions that generated and sustained it.

Texts, once the preserve of specific groups organized around religious, administrative and literary pursuits, increasingly branched out to cover a new range of concerns. Reading was more and more a popular and less an elite preserve. Authors responded to this change by producing a wider range of texts, increasingly diverse in both genre and purpose. Texts began to appear in new places and for new reasons. Advertisements, street signs, paper money and graffiti all testified to the broadening of textual culture. The proliferation of a variety of texts in new forms was transforming the texture and meaning of everyday life in the late Ottoman Empire.[8] The change from traditional textual economy where meaning was embedded in a distinctly religious reading environment – "a world in which writing was reserved for the religious learned, news was delivered primarily by voice and urban geography was communicated through oral culture rather than by signs" – to a modern one where texts proliferated beyond their usual confines to appear on a variety of surfaces underpinned the new approach to reading in the late nineteenth and early twentieth centuries. As Wallach cautions, this dichotomized view is useful only as a model; in practice life was much messier. Reading and textual practices frequently blurred and overlapped the lines between these idealized extremes; reading was both an indicator and a cause of modernity:

> …the transformation of public text was not merely a symptom of social changes, but also a potent tool employed to achieve these very changes. Through the display of certain texts and the withdrawal of others, a new order was being negotiated and pursued. In this sense, public text emerges as an important agency of modernity. Public texts were used by writers – the state, local elites, and grassroots communities – to promote their vision and their interests; they were also used by readers, residents… to negotiate their notions of identity and geography, as part of everyday life.[9]

Reading thus needs to be seen as integral to both the ruptures and the continuities between traditional and modern times. An ancient practice, reading persisted in its old ways but also adapted to new modes, new texts and new places. In this study we will see how the proliferation of new reading materials, mostly textbooks and children's magazines, changed the practices associated with reading in a period of imperial-to-national transition.

Changes in text – and inevitably in language – were gradual and anticipated the nationalist turn, rather than being triggered by it. In the case of Turkish there were many important late Ottoman precursors to the Republican "language revolution." But it was not simply language that was now subject to change and displacement. Again Wallach's recent research is instructive, showing the parallels between the surface plasticity of the new texts and the changes associated with modernity. "What characterized modern public text most of all, and made it into such a useful tool, was its dematerialization and its transformation into a detached signifier."[10] Whereas previously public writing had tended to be carved in stone, engraved in metal or carefully painted or penned by hand, new texts were increasingly mass produced, appearing on cheaper materials; manuscripts, precious metals and stone made way for posters, lithographs, newsprint and even graffiti in the life of public texts.

This book explores the important connection between the accessibility of text – increasingly visible on posters, billboards and banners and available as relatively inexpensive books and magazines to be held and even owned, in contrast to the more deeply inscribed and inaccessible texts of "traditional" Ottoman cultural production – and the created, superficial aspect of nationalism that, paradoxically, demanded a belief in its purportedly eternal, permanent effect. New roles for texts and therefore reading were crucial to the arrival of modernity in the Turkish context. But the roles reading played in this transition to modernity were neither simple nor uncontested.

Chapter overview

By focusing on the importance of learning to read and reading during the transition from Ottoman Empire to Turkish Republic, this book addresses this increasingly literate society. This introductory chapter sets out the main questions addressed in the book, delineates its chronological coverage, roughly speaking from 1880 to 1930, discusses the main contours of the remarkably limited historiographical treatment the subject of learning to read and reading has received so far, and identifies the political agenda inherent in much of the prevailing accounts of literacy and education, in particular the extent to which the early Republic of Mustafa Kemal, later Atatürk, used literacy and reading as a political instrument to denigrate Ottoman achievements and trumpet the Republic's advances. This chapter establishes the book's comparative approach by drawing on the relevant literature on comparable historical cases, in particular those of France, Russia and China, all apposite for different reasons, and then links them with the main themes to be raised in subsequent chapters.

Chapter 2 begins the exploration of these themes by paying attention to the many and varied ways in which reading was represented in late Ottoman and early Republican society, and to the ways it was subsequently remembered. It focuses on the ways reading was modeled because they reveal the intentions and agenda underlying the increase in reading in this period. Representations of reading also point out the many tasks with which reading was freighted. Young readers were encouraged to approach their texts for reasons of religion, morality, imperial or national uplift, careerism, personal improvement or simply for entertainment or escape. Interspersing examples drawn from children's reading material itself with accounts of learning to read and reading that appear in memoirs, this chapter sets out the many and at times contradictory modes and valences attached to reading against the backdrop of dramatic change.

Pushing further in the direction of reading content and the messages that sustained it, Chapter 3 selects four thematic tensions or binary pairings prevalent in the reading process and reveals the range of possibilities facing young readers. Each of these pairings – the religious and the secular; the family and the state; the new and the old; the global and the local – affords the opportunity to highlight the tensions and ambiguities as well as the often stultifying didactic certainties facing young readers. The chapter shows not only the range of genre, politicization, humor and even parody available in this rapidly expanding literature but also the extent to which readers' choices were beginning to be dictated as much by the market as by the pedagogical demands of the state, whether Ottoman or Republican.

Chapter 4 turns to the basic but until now surprisingly understudied questions surrounding the mechanics of reading, publication and illustration. Beginning with an examination of the various elements inherent in the physical act of reading, such as deciphering script, recitation and vocabulary acquisition, this chapter moves on to discuss official concerns with the pedagogy of reading, including rote memory, parroting, "reading" without comprehension, as well as the personal pleasure or even, according to one source, the addiction that reading could induce. The discussion takes in both poetry and prose and situates Turkish texts within the wide variety of languages available in the Ottoman and Turkish context. The analysis moves from textual considerations to encompass the increasing prevalence of the image in conjunction with text. Especially important in attracting and sustaining the attention of young readers, and increasingly affordable due to technological changes, illustrations in the form of engravings, drawings, cartoons and photography, gave reading an entirely new look and a new appeal.

The increased attention paid to the appearance of reading materials leads to the question of commodification and the market, the subject of Chapter 5. Following recent research on the relationship between commodification and modernity, this chapter addresses the hidden but crucial socioeconomic aspects of reading and literacy. The new-style education responsible for the expansion of literacy had replaced an essentially consumption-free educational apparatus, based on oral transmission and writing on erasable surfaces, with one requiring that books and other teaching materials be purchased on a vast scale. The seemingly insatiable demand for teachers and textbooks meant that many could now make, or substantially augment, a living by writing. On the other side of the equation, the growing ranks of young readers constituted a market that publishers were quick to exploit. In the attempts to set their offerings apart from the competition, the publishers of children's literature were soon tempted to resort to poking fun at the stiff didacticism of state supplied education, especially as symbolized by its main target, the teacher. The chapter concludes by demonstrating the extent to which this new literature, that the state had done so much to create, began to undermine state authority in the interest of sales.

Chapter 6 looks at the history of learning to read and reading from a biographical perspective. It focuses on the ways reading was assimilated into daily lives and affected individual careers, in short how reading became a way of life and in some cases even came to organize the way people lived. Drawing on the examples of both well-known and relatively obscure authors, the discussion turns to follow the ways in which these readers became writers, how they were drawn first to consuming and then producing texts for their fellow readers. Here again the variety of experience is remarkable, transcending divisions in class, gender, politics and, of course, the historical and historiographical division of the Ottoman the Republican eras. In contrast to the usual attention to reading as a social or group phenomenon, I emphasize individual reading as key to understanding the development of the modern person. A brief conclusion reflects on the relationship between reading and modernity.

The Ottoman/Turkish case in comparative perspective

The history of reading in the late Ottoman Empire and early Turkish Republic was of course unique in many respects. No other historical case offers the same pattern of linguistic, cultural and political influences as those acting on the place and period chosen here. The literary scene of the late Ottoman Empire was especially varied, given the range of ethnic groups involved and the variety of both languages and literary genres in use. It is important to note that this study concentrates only on the Turkish-language aspect of that dynamic and multilingual scene. Literacy in Turkey, whether Ottoman or Republican, has been the subject of Western observation for a long time, with results almost as varied as the Ottoman reading scene itself. On the one hand, an Englishwoman writing in the 1830s observed, "Perhaps, with the single exception of Great Britain, there exists not in the world a more reading nation than Turkey... Nearly every man throughout the Empire can read and write, and there are, at this moment, upwards of eight thousand children scattered through the different schools of the capital."[11] On the other hand, an early twentieth-century informant of the German observer Martin Hartmann baldly declared that, "The Turk thinks he is educated when he can prattle a bit in French; he does not read."[12] The Englishwoman's perhaps hyperbolic comments on Turkish literacy – accurate literacy rates are difficult to obtain for the middle of the nineteenth century but the consensus places them in the single digits; more information about literacy figures appears below – are tempered by her less than gracious views on the utility of reading the Qur'an but nevertheless provide an indication of the attention lavished on reading and writing well before the boom years of publishing that were to follow later in the nineteenth and the early twentieth centuries.

Reading in Turkish was of course only one part of the larger Ottoman literary constellation. The late Ottoman reading scene was remarkably varied, the product of a range of foreign and domestic authors publishing a variety of material in an array of languages that included Albanian, Arabic, Armenian, Bulgarian, English, French, Greek, Hebrew, Ladino, Persian and Turkish among other tongues.[13] Equally interesting is the fact that at the start of our period the one-to-one correspondence between language and ethnicity or, indeed, between language and script was nowhere near as fixed as it would become in the era of the nation state. Thus Turkish was written mainly in the Arabo-Persian script but was also produced using a number of other alphabets, including most notably Armenian and Greek. In fact, the "first Turkish novel" was composed in Armenian letters in 1851.[14]

Although this study concentrates on reading in Turkish, and its main sources are the textbooks and magazines produced for young readers of Turkish, it is important to note the remarkably varied lïnguistic environment of the late Ottoman period. Texts appeared to help children navigate the polyglot linguistic waters. For example, an anonymous pamphlet entitled *Kitab iftitah al-qira'at* (Introduction to reading) appeared as early as 1848 to provide children with a simplified, synoptic approach to Arabic, Turkish and Persian, the tripartite spirit nicely encapsulated by the Persian expression *"lafz lafz-e Arabest * Turki hunerest * Farsi shekerest"* (which might be translated as Arabic is language; Turkish is skill; Persian is sweetness) which appears on the back cover.[15] One can occasionally find copies of Ottoman Turkish primers in which marginal and interlinear notes reveal traces of a cross-language commitment to reading. In one such example, an unknown Greek hand has penciled in transliterations in Greek letters of several of the words in a text entitled "To the Children of the Nation" (*Evlad-i vatan'a*).[16] The inside cover of this booklet contains two crude pen drawings showing soldiers or perhaps military cadets in Ottoman uniform with fez and sash, which would be highly interesting if they were drawn by the same non-Muslim hand. Books designed specifically to teach non-native speakers of Turkish, such as Armenians and Jews, the official language of the empire and those intended to teach those acquainted only with the Arabic script to write Turkish in other scripts (such as Armenian and Greek) used both relevant scripts on the same page, visible symbols of the empire's multilingualism.[17]

Such crossover was also apparent in the varied types of reading material on offer in the late Ottoman period. Original and translated works vied with one another in a lively and innovative world of literary production. Within each linguistic sphere there existed a productive tension between older, more established styles, genres and subjects and their more recent rivals. New, imported forms of expression such as the short story, the novel and free verse, encouraged by the rapidly growing press, appeared alongside the traditional narrative and poetic forms deriving from both the Arabic and Persian traditions that were central to high Ottoman literary culture and the more "popular" Turkish bardic repertoire.

But for all of the particularity of the Ottoman/Turkish experience it is important to place it in a broader context. There are unmistakable similarities to be found in other parts of the world and the comparisons they suggest allow us to see the Ottoman/Turkish case in a wider perspective and not as an isolated case. We are now fortunate to have several histories of reading that approach the topic from a global perspective, useful both for pointing toward the cultural specificity of reading practices around the world and for underscoring many of their common features.[18] Reflecting the preponderance of the material available, these studies favor the Western experience in general and largely ignore the Ottoman/Turkish case in particular – Fischer notes the conquest of Istanbul and the initial Ottoman reluctance to embrace the printing press – especially in the modern period. But they provide a useful long-term chronological and a broad geographical background against which we can situate the story of reading in Turkish and note the many parallels with reading elsewhere.

Historians have noted many such parallels between reading in the Islamic and Christian worlds at all levels of learning. Western hornbooks performed a similar function to reading boards and erasable slates in the East.[19] Ariès's discussion of instruction in the medieval European school draws an explicit parallel with Qur'anic schools in the Islamic world:

> The pupils learned what they needed to know in order to say and sing the offices, namely the Psalms and the Canonic Hours, in Latin of course, the Latin of the manuscripts in which these texts had been established. Thus the instruction was predominantly oral and addressed to the memory, like the instruction given at present in the Koran schools in Moslem countries: anyone who has heard the alternating recitation of the verses of the Koran in the great mosque at Kairwan [sic] will have an idea of the medieval school ... The pupils all chanted in unison the phrase spoken by the teacher, and they went on repeating the same exercise until they had learnt it by heart. The priests could recite nearly all the prayers in the office from memory. Henceforth reading was no longer an indispensable tool of learning. It only served to aid their memory in the event of forgetfulness. It only allowed them to 'recognize' what they already knew and not to discover something new, with the result that the importance of reading was greatly reduced.[20]

The shared origins of higher learning that link East and West are well known.[21] These parallels, however, are often overshadowed by a tendency to juxtapose pre-modern institutions in the West with modern-era, often extant, counterparts in the Islamic world, creating a chronologically lopsided comparison. The underlying assumption is that while the West has moved on, the East remained mired in medieval practices and mentalities. It is therefore important to emphasize the many contemporary parallels between East and West – including, among others, the late nineteenth-century arrival of state-supplied schooling, the hopes invested in education generally and reading in particular for national progress and uplift and the increasing role of market forces in shaping the culture of reading despite the obvious and therefore more frequently observed differences in economic development, literacy rates, etc. This study highlights both the shared and divergent traditions between East and West.

Ariès perceptively points to a critical distinction between old and new approaches to reading, one that is usually missed in the context of the traditional-to-modern shift. This is especially the case in Turkish Republican critiques of old-style, that is to say, religious education, which was often ridiculed as impractical, meaningless parroting (Arabic, like Latin in the West, performing the role of the outmoded language belatedly declared an impediment to progress, and personally detested by those who found it difficult).[22] What these critiques (which often read like bitter vendettas) frequently fail to comprehend is that the difference between the two types of schools – the poet Yahya Kemal describes leaving one and entering the other as a move from Asia to Europe – was not simply one of technique or pedagogical method. The very *raison d'être* of education itself was almost diametrically opposed; once centered around religion, schooling – and the reading that sustained it – was now increasingly geared toward imparting "useful knowledge" and discovering "something new," a shift in underlying purpose from otherworldly to practical that is not sufficiently understood, a shortcoming which would continue to inform discussions of education and religion in the Turkish Republic in later years.

* * *

From the late eighteenth century onwards literacy was on the rise across the globe. The expansion of state education served as the main catalyst for this trend but readership quickly expanded beyond the confines of the classroom. We are perhaps most familiar with the developments in Western Europe where state-driven literacy initiatives have been well documented, France in particular. Schools in medieval France did not teach reading in the way that modern schools would later approach it. Local languages and dialects did not figure in education; students had to learn their native tongue at home and in the workplace. As in the Islamic world where Qur'an schools focused on Arabic, schools taught the ecclesiastical language (Latin) instead and were strongly geared toward theological, i.e., scholastic, pursuits and, another similarity, rote memorization dominated.[23] The subsequent expansion of readership and the shift in reading material from religious to secular content has been strongly linked with the changes that led eventually to the French Revolution, not least by undercutting the myths and symbols of the monarchy.[24] In fact, printing and reading has been front and center in scholarly attention to the creation of modern France, both in Paris and in the provinces.[25] Another area of enquiry has focused on whether or not a "reading revolution" took place in the late eighteenth century.[26] Defining such revolutions has proved difficult but it is clear that in the late Ottoman Empire, as in Western Europe, reading practices were undergoing a sea change. The French example was vitally important in other respects as well. Like France, the Ottoman/Turkish history of reading involved a major societal investment in literacy. Similarly, this "one way ride" occurred within the contested context of a dynamic between state and religion with far-reaching implications and across multiple lines of linguistic and socioeconomic demarcation.[27] Moreover, France in general and Paris set Ottoman trends in a number of fields, ranging from governmental reform to literature to fashion. The Ottoman Ministry of Education and later its Republican successor were modeled on the centralizing French paradigm and in some cases school buildings were based on French architectural plans. The pull of French culture was strong among many Ottoman urbanites; French fashions were widely copied and French novels were popular with many from the sultan on down.[28] So in terms of both actual influence and historiographical parallels, the French case is particularly relevant.

Russia was closer to the Ottoman Empire both in terms of geography – equally struggling with its Euro-Asian identity – and its conflicted relationship with Western European models. Although late Ottoman literacy rates were lower than those of Russia, a similarly linked trajectory of popular reading in Turkish and change is readily apparent.

As Jeffrey Brooks has shown, reading was integral to the formation of popular culture in the late Tsarist period. As the old Russia yielded to the new with the emancipation of the serfs, urbanization and industrialization, popular literacy emerged hand in glove with a new array of inexpensive reading materials. These chapbooks, magazines and novels opened new horizons and challenged older political, social and cultural assumptions. A new Russian identity was coming into being, in large part due to common – in both senses of the term – reading matter.[29] Stephen Lovell's work takes the story into the twentieth century and thus allows us to note many parallels with the Ottoman/Turkish case. In particular, print culture was crucial to the emergence of a new reading public, a concern with progress, contested notions of the correct way forward for empire/nation and a new emphasis on deploying reading materials to effect political, social and cultural change, all features that resonate with developments in Turkey.[30] Indeed, the Soviet model had a particularly powerful effect on the early Turkish Republican period; from its five-year plans, to its industrialization campaign, its adoption of a new script (parallel to the alphabet reform in contemporary Soviet Central Asia) and its use of propaganda, Soviet inspiration clearly influenced the public persona of the single-party period.[31]

Reading in China manifested several comparable attitudes with the Ottoman Empire. Recitation, vocalization and physicality all played important roles in learning to read Chinese texts in the late imperial period and into the communist era.[32] The specific relationship between orality and textuality typified the Ottoman and Chinese cases; memorization and the oral, performative aspects of reading were pronounced in both societies. Another common feature was the persistence of mothers as teachers of reading alongside the more traditional male instructors.[33] Furthermore, Chinese schools, like their Ottoman equivalents, were noisy places. Mechanical memorization was crucial to entering what one scholar of the Chinese language referred to as "an empire of text," a phrase equally suited to the Ottoman Turkish reading landscape.[34] As in the Ottoman/Turkish context, reading in China was linked to political change and the cultural shift from empire to republic. Literacy was an important vector linking nationalism and revolutionism in China in the 1910s and 1920s.[35] Chinese reading primers, like their Ottoman and Turkish Republican counterparts, mixed morality and ideology with a newly practical attention to the mechanics of learning to read.[36]

This geographical tour could go on indefinitely. Throughout the world universal education and literacy were the vehicles through which the state was to pursue its aim of both creating and then shaping national identity and loyalty.[37] The specific tools employed were the teacher and the textbook. Of the two, the printed pedagogue was easier for centralizing authorities to control. School texts therefore represent extremely useful indicators of the state's stance toward its citizens/subjects. They tell us how state functionaries who vetted, approved and in many cases also wrote the texts conceived of their young audiences and attempted to influence them. The attitudes they convey with respect to morality, social roles, class and the nation all come through clearly in the pages of the texts designed for young readers. But we should be wary of an exclusively functionalist or utilitarian approach to state education and the textbooks it produced. Beyond the specific requirements of the state, these humble texts also inevitably convey the aspirations and anxieties of the age. The strong sense of the moral, however crudely didactic its presentation, speaks as a response to rapid change and the fears it provoked, and an attempt to redress what was frequently felt to be the backwardness of the nation to which they were addressed. As was the case in Western Europe where the widespread appearance of state education also only really appears from the 1880s onwards, Ottoman and later Turkish children were becoming a crucial point of contact between state planners and its citizenry. They were also fast emerging as an important segment of the book market, as we shall see, providing another parallel with Western European trends.[38]

But as important as they were, the states of the period were certainly not the only actors in this field. The trend was much larger than even that which the rapidly expanding state bureaucracies of the period could accomplish. In many respects the most important changes were occurring away from state, in the private recesses of society where a combination of new vehicles for learning and reading were matched by a growing taste for reading. Here the role of the market was crucial. Although created in large part by the expanding apparatus of the state and monitored and censored by state institutions, this burgeoning market for reading materials quickly outstripped the capability of the state to control it. It was thus able to provide an array of texts that drew readers away from the agenda and strictures associated with the state approaches. As a result a vibrant Ottoman/Turkish penny press similar to that which Brooks describes for Russia facilitated a breakdown in the elite's monopoly over the written word akin to that traced in France by Furet and Ozouf.[39] While I have been unable to find more than anecdotal evidence for the persistent involvement of religious organizations in the spread of literacy and reading in this period – something similar to the efforts of the sufi literacy campaigns in Saharan Africa – it may be that future research will bring this and the activities of other non-state actors to light. In any case, it is clear from even a cursory examination of the broad and eclectic textual production in this period that the state sector, powerful though it was, was being challenged and indeed surpassed by market forces.

In light of the until recently dominant historiographical tendency to assume a teleological development in the shift from late Ottoman

Empire to early Turkish Republic, this eclecticism needs to be emphasized. The expanding array of reading materials should not necessarily be seen as a vector for homogenization. Selectively viewed, this body of materials can indeed provide evidence for a number of changes normally associated with this period, for example, secularization, nationalization, Westernization. A more careful examination, however, suggests that the reading material accurately reflects a much broader spectrum of beliefs, tendencies and approaches. In this crucial period of transition from empire to republic it is important to note that the reading materials and practices to be investigated in this book do not fall neatly into the binary roles they are often assumed to play. William McNeill, for example, sees printing and literacy as a force either for splitting a culture, as in the case of Western Europe, by juxtaposing traditional (pagan, Christian) learning "with a flood of new and often incompatible information about the wider world. Or printing could, as in the case of China where printing originated, serve to consolidate traditional literary and intellectual culture by assuring wider access to Confucian and other classical texts."[40] The late Ottoman/early Turkish case probably lies somewhere in between these two extremes: it produced, or at least greatly contributed to, profound changes but not, in my view, the sort of social schism that has often been theorized. It represents more of an ongoing attempt to assimilate, supplant and emphasize a number of different cultural bases, including those of the Western European, Perso-Islamic and Turkic traditions. Eclecticism ruled. Even the powerful *dirigisme* of the Kemalist state could not impose a lasting turn away from non-Western traditions. To succeed, the Kemalist "revolution" had to adapt to the popular base of the nation, revealing a grudging realization of the limits of imposing cultural change from the top down.[41] Acknowledging the varied set of impulses – so apparent in the reading materials from this period – is integral to understanding the different forces at work in Turkish society today.

In spite of its critical and, indeed, its constitutive role in modern society, the study of reading has been remarkably neglected. Although it sometimes receives lip service in terms of its transformative function in society, it is more usually taken for granted. Ironically its very centrality to modernity may be part of the reason it is overlooked. For all of its importance, reading is difficult to study; it is an activity that largely remains unseen to the historian, its silent and largely traceless nature making it difficult to analyze and assess.

Part of the difficulty stems from the fact that learning to read and reading depend upon an intricate complex of overlapping functions and attributes. It varies according to context, the types of text engaged, the physical locale in which the reading takes place, the intention given to reading, whether sacred, didactic or diverting, the language of the text in question, the sorts of message being conveyed, whether the text is accompanied by illustration, the physicality of the experience – the concept of "bookness" is important in many cases – and the phase or stage in the life of the reader in question. These and many other vicissitudes of reading both make it difficult to generalize about the subject and ensure its importance for a number of fields that attempt to get to grips with human experience. They are the main issues to be addressed in the rest of this book.

The nearly traceless nature of reading makes this kind of investigation an inherently difficult if not foolhardy task, but there are nevertheless important advantages that flow from this kind of study. First and most accessibly, reading serves as a window on the issue of continuity and change from empire to republic. It shows both how quickly and radically the dominant narrative, presented in such simple fashion for young readers, could shift, creating as it did a national mythology and suppressing an imperial identity which had itself only recently been "invented" in the late nineteenth century and how many other features of that late Ottoman narrative were retained, blending almost seamlessly into the new, national mix, despite its insistence on novelty and change.

Following the important work of Michael Meeker,[42] this book attempts to supply further evidence, drawn from a different context, for the persistence of Ottoman-era institutions, practices and concepts in the establishment and of the Turkish Republic amid the many changes it effected.

Hence the importance of focusing on the 1880–1930 period, a chronological delineation that while slightly unusual – most studies accept 1923 as the defining watershed – affords certain advantages. The periodization employed here is organic in the sense that it follows the emergence of children's reading materials linked with the arrival of widespread schooling and the related creation of a market for children's reading matter. By the early 1930s the mechanisms of the republic were sufficiently established to suggest new directions and, in any case, a 50-year period is no doubt an overly ambitious period of time for a detailed study such as this. Learning to read and reading afford an opportunity to overcome some of the historiographical obstacles posed by the presumption of a stark divide in 1923. This study follows some constructive steps in this direction. For example, Elizabeth Frierson approaches the period 1876–1928 as one era with three major changes of regime, highlighting the reform-minded impetus after 1923. Following Şükrü Hanioğlu, she sees all leaders in this period, from Abdülhamid II to the Committee of Union and Progress to Mustafa Kemal as linked by a politics based on the rhetoric of the public good.[43] In the field of education, Mehmet Ö. Alkan has demonstrated the importance of tracing the continuities across the late Ottoman and early republican periods.[44] Straddling conventional periodization inevitably raises difficulties but in my view they pale beside the gains to be reaped from the more natural chronological definition suggested by the sources themselves.

Secondly, thus chronologically defined, this topic provides a means of moving beyond the discourse defined and dominated by the state, which has been a problem in the field of Ottoman and Turkish history. There are historical reasons for this tendency, including the richness of the state archives, the strong extent to which elites were linked to state (i.e., what we would today call the public sphere historically occupied a relatively small space), the dominance of the centralizing tendency in all periods from the late eighteenth century onwards and the huge state interest in, some might say obsession with, image control. Reading was naturally important to the state but also went far beyond even its rapidly expanding grasp. Exploring the relationship between children and their varied reading materials allows us to follow it both in and out of the state's orbit.

Thirdly, children's reading provides a lens that allows us to see a number of important changes taking place in this period in especially stark relief. Most broadly, it allows us to track the shift from multi-ethnic, multi-cultural, multi-linguistic environment to one increasingly resembling monoculture – a development most obviously associated with the Turkish Republic but also evident in the latter years of the empire – and to do so from the simplest of perspectives, namely, through the eyes of children. Against these large-scale shifts and aligned with them, we can also trace a number of developments affecting the practice of reading, including the shift from communal reading, manuscript culture and erasable surfaces to individual reading, print culture and consumable texts. These changes were important in opening literacy to larger numbers, in emphasizing the individual over the collective, with important implications for the development of social and particularly religious thought,[45] and also rendering it subject to the whim of the market-driven economy. Against the trend toward a mass reading market we can also discern the variety, indeed, the eclecticism of reading materials, audiences and contexts that were not always aligned with the dominant trends.

It is perhaps also necessary to say something briefly about what this book does *not* intend to address in detail. It is not primarily about the alphabet change, or the "language revolution," of 1928. That important and heavily symbolic development has been well studied.[46] In the context of reading, the change in script from Arabo-Persian to Latin seems to have affected the process of learning to read much less than might be expected given its symbolic importance and the attention it has attracted. In fact, it may well have retarded reading efforts in the short term and certainly imposed a rupture that broke up textual and generational continuity. But the larger point I would like to make here is that in many respects the attention garnered by the alphabet change has obscured the important developments that were already in train in the late Ottoman and the very early Republican periods. In other words, emphasizing first 1923 and then 1928 masks the Ottoman-to-Republican continuities and uncritically adopts the Kemalist public relations efforts aimed at claiming improvements in literacy for the Republic alone. One reason I end this study just after the language "revolution" is to demonstrate how relatively unimportant it was in the larger, ongoing context of learning to read.

This book is also not primarily concerned with tracing the development of the publishing industry or the spread of literacy although both are clearly crucial factors affecting reading. Publishing and book culture in the late Ottoman period have been well examined by scholars such as Johann Strauss and Frédéric Hitzel. I attempt to complement their work insofar as I address issues relating to the practice of reading in general and the consumption of reading materials in particular, but always with a focus on young readers. Counting or estimating the share of the population that was "literate" is a thorny problem however that notoriously tricky term is defined due to marked differences across regional, gender and class lines. There are a number of often wildly conflicting estimates available for literacy in this period, reflecting dissimilar methods of counting, age restrictions and so on. Some have posited a literacy rate as low as 2 per cent in the 1860s and most estimates remain at or under 10 per cent until the late 1920s. Perhaps the most careful attempt posits an average across the Turkish Republic of just over 10 per cent on the eve of the language reform of 1928 but notes important differences between city and countryside and male and female.[47] Kemal Karpat has produced statistics that, while speculative, suggest considerably higher literacy rates across the empire in the 1890s, particularly in the capital.[48] My view is that trying to arrive at a more precise counting is not terribly helpful beyond establishing that literacy rates were in the process of rising dramatically from the early nineteenth century to the twentieth and that, as Karpat notes, this was a topic that increasingly attracted attention.

Of much more interest to me is what literacy meant, how it was achieved and the ways in which it was presented and represented to the young. This study therefore focuses on the possibility of re-writing the transition from Ottoman Empire to Turkish Republic. It holds that reading was key to both Ottoman and Republican approaches to political, cultural, social and economic mobilization, given the possibilities that literacy offered in terms of both mass communication and commodification, two hallmarks of modernity.

In short, reading in the Ottoman/Turkish context is situated at the confluence at some of the most important changes of late nineteenth and twentieth centuries. It thus offers an excellent vantage point from which to examine the shifts that have defined the modern period. But it also serves as a necessary reminder of the need to look for the frequently ignored continuities between periods and to seek out the silences and tensions embedded in the birth of the modern. The rest of this chapter previews the centrality of reading to the transition from empire to republic and the way it has been characterized in both primary and secondary materials.

Reading, change and continuity from empire to republic

The history or reading is particularly well suited to the task of reconsidering the continuities and changes inherent in the transition from Ottoman Empire to Turkish Republic. The prevailing wisdom has depicted this as a story of rupture, emphasizing the newness of the Republic, the radical nature of Mustafa Kemal's reforms, and reveling in the contrast between the putatively outmoded nature of the Ottoman past and the self-conscious modernity of the newly imprinted national state. But the received wisdom has been heavily influenced, if not largely created, by the Republican agenda itself. Like a number of other newly independent states in the neighboring Balkans and the Middle East, the early Turkish Republic found it convenient to draw stark contrasts with the *ancien régime* even, or perhaps especially, when the degree of continuity was actually quite profound. It also engaged in sometimes quite breathtaking bouts of historical amnesia as it attempted to dispense with over six centuries of Ottoman and nearly nine centuries of Islamic inheritance, in many instances simply by ignoring it. The young republic attempted to portray itself as both rational and progressive, ushering in a series of reforms that would convert what it deemed to be essentially a backward society into one paradoxically both modern and authentic, insisting on its authenticity in spite of its clearly *arriviste* status, a quandary which led, contradicting its rationalist impulse, to some remarkably outlandish and ill-advised attempts at concocting linguistic and historical theories in the attempt to solidify its shaky self-confidence.[49]

Literacy, reading and education were central to the projection of the image of the modernizing republic. Perhaps the ultimate expression of the identification between the state and literacy came in 1928 when Mustafa Kemal famously toured the country with chalk and blackboard in a campaign to promote the abandonment of the Arabic script in favor of the Latin alphabet. But well before the "language reform" – a rather gentle translation of the Turkish term "language revolution," (*dil devrimi*) – and even before the republic had been established the embryonic nationalist government in Ankara had turned its attention to educational matters. In July of 1921, before the decisive battle of Sakarya that turned the Greek invasion into a retreat, the provisional government organized an educational congress.[50] In that period the nationalists emphasized a strong Islamic component as central to the process of inculcating the principles of the unity and indivisibility of the nation.[51] With Mustafa Kemal's appearance as a sort of Educator-in-Chief, the Republic signalled its intentions in the field of education. The Unification of Education law (*Tevhid-i tedrisat kanunu*) of 1924, instituted at the same time as the abolition of the Islamic theological colleges (*medrese*), announced just how radical republican educational intentions would be and how determined the fledgling state was to impose its monopoly over the field. But the irony here is that, apart from the relatively short-lived village institutes (1940–1954), the educational policy of the early republic essentially carried on with program that the late Ottoman state had already initiated. It carried on the expansion of the state educational system along lines spelled out in the Ottoman Education Regulation of 1869 and continued to teach a largely secular-ized curriculum but one that syncretically imparted a heavy dose of Islamically grounded morality and religious instruction, especially in the early years of the republic until imposing the "*lâiklik*" that was such a critical if ultimately fairly short-lived aspect of education in the new state. Even then religious instruction continued to be taught in Turkish schools until the late 1920s, and then reappeared in the 1940s. At the same time, the early republic drew selectively on Ottoman history qua Turkish history but in a way that justified the existence of the superior republic.[52]

In many ways the usual periodization obscures the continuities linking the late Ottoman and early Republican periods. The Hamidian, the "Young Turk" and the early Republican eras all shared a profound faith in reading as an instrument for political, social and economic change, in short, for progress. Efforts at engendering change, whether in the form of the Hamidian-era school texts, the smuggled counter-propaganda of the anti-regime activists, the proliferation of periodical literature in the Young Turk era or the revamped state-supplied texts of the Kemalist period, shared a common faith in the power of reading that transcended the antagonisms of their individual agendas. Robert Darnton's depiction of the role of printing in the broad array of changes that swept in the French Revolution have resonance for the Ottoman/Turkish case: "At every stage of this [revolutionary] process, they use the same basic tool: the printing press."[53]

Beyond the largely superficial breaks claimed by the republic, continuities abound, even in such vital areas for the republic's propaganda as literacy and state education. Even the vaunted language revolution built on the efforts of textual and alphabetic experimentation of the late Ottoman period. Indeed Mustafa Kemal's own party soon abandoned many of the alterations effected in the heady years of the early Republic. The Republican People's Party eventually rescinded its own earlier ban on religious instruction, an ultimately unsuccessful ploy to try to steal a popular issue from the more conservative opposition Democrat Party, in the run-up to the first freely contested elections of the republican era after World War II. In the event the Democrat Party won anyway and began reversing the Kemalist policy on Islam in schools, a struggle that continues down to the present day in such central issues as the Turkish-Islamic synthesis, the question of how the state should approach the education of religious officials (the *imam-hatip* schools controversy), the headscarf debate and ongoing discussions about place of religion in an avowedly secular state.

Republican state control over education displays striking parallels with its approach to women, another area key to republican image management. There was a strongly gendered approach to this agenda, one directly identified with literacy and reading. Kemalists portrayed the late Ottoman woman as secluded, illiterate and passive, in direct contrast to the enlightened, active, confident woman promoted by the Republic.[54] Mustafa Kemal's policies with respect to women are particularly fascinating because he managed to succeed in developing an image of the republic and himself in particular as the great emancipator of women.[55] The party line was essentially that the Ottoman period had repressed women because it was inherently autocratic, retrograde and beholden to religion. By contrast, as the propaganda had it, Mustafa Kemal liberated the women of the republic and provided them with education, the vote and roles in building the new society. While there is certainly a factual basis underlying this foundation myth – women were given the franchise in 1934 and enjoyed for a time a level of female representation in parliament that would make many Western campaigners envious – revisionist research has shown that Kemalist policies toward women were built on an existing tradition of women's activism and inclusion dating from the late Ottoman period, were generally patronizing to the women involved, and supportive only insofar as the relevant women maintained an uncritical and indeed sometimes a blatantly propagandistic stance toward the regime. In this sense, Kemalist policy toward women was ironically not dissimilar to that practiced by Sultan Abdülhamid II whose patronage of women's publications and fostering of female education seem to stand very much in line with later Kemalist practice.[56]

The Kemalist policy of using the "women question" as a means of furthering its own agenda has clear parallels in the realm of reading. The myth of the modern republic as an enlightened vehicle sweeping away backwardness, superstition and illiteracy relied heavily upon short-term historical amnesia. Considerable evidence has shown that literacy rates, while not high, were rising in the late Ottoman period, thanks to a concerted, sustained effort to increase educational provision and the emergence of a dynamic publishing market, including an impressive list of titles devoted to reading children.[57] In fact, it could be argued that the Kemalist reforms set back the cause of literacy by insisting on the alphabet change and "purification" of the language. Certainly it has wreaked havoc with the ability to communicate, particularly across generational lines.[58]

Ironically it was the more superficial changes effected by the early Republic, such as the naming and dress laws, the alphabet and language changes, and the creation of the iconographic cult around Mustafa Kemal Atatürk, that tended to produce the more enduring changes. Running deeper under the surface were a number of trends in which republican policy aligned itself with Ottoman practice in spite of the propaganda to the contrary. The problem was that the Republic's official stance *vis-à-vis* the empire prevented it from acknowledging this legacy directly. In fact, one could almost argue that the tremendous size of the debt that the republic owed the empire made it impossible for the self-styled modernizing Republic to admit the source of so much of its inheritance. Given the fragility, or to use Navaro-Yashin's phrase, the "flimsiness" of the project of Turkish modernization,[59] the Republic sought to emphasize its strength, thus generating another parallel with the late Ottoman state. To a large extent this was effected by creating or heightening the impression of contrast with the Ottoman Empire. Several overlapping traits were used to draw these contrasts, and literacy played an important role alongside such themes as the rights of women and the supposedly retrograde nature of religion.[60]

The Republic was remarkably successful in creating this contrasting set of images. For their own sets of reasons, both international and domestic audiences bought into the Republican mythmaking. The language reform became a largely self-fulfilling prophecy as the generations raised on the Latinized script were taught, whether subtly or unsubtly, to disparage the old script as an unsuitable vehicle for rendering the Turkish language. From this perspective the grammatical forms of Ottoman Turkish were mocked as outmoded, even though some of the most treasured texts and speeches of the early Republic, including of course those of Mustafa Kemal himself, were naturally written, spoken and recorded in the former idiom.[61] The choice of the new script turned not on the question of linguistic suitability – as students of languages written in another alphabet know, the script is the least of their problems – but rather on the political and cultural wish of the Kemalists to break the links with the Ottoman and Islamic past and reorient the young country to the West. As an exercise intended to cut the people off from their literary and religious hinterland it was, in the words of Geoffrey Lewis, a "catastrophic success."

Kemalist policy toward reading and education was of a piece with the broader republican agenda aimed at forging a unified, or perhaps monolithic, nation. By focusing on one script, "simplifying" the Ottoman Turkish language, and emphasizing an unwaveringly patriotic message, the young republic was taking the statist dissemination of its communications to a stage well beyond Ottoman practice. As recent scholarship has shown, this policy had both exclusive as well as inclusive elements. Although the new nation-building messages were directed at all those living within the borders of the new state, the diversity of this population in religious, ethnic or linguistic terms was hardly matched by the unrelentingly one-dimensional approach. Such phrases as "Citizens! Speak Turkish!" and "Happy is he who calls himself a Turk!" were only the superficial manifestations of state policy directed against such peoples as Kurds, Armenians, Greeks, Laz and so on, who found their freedom of expression and use of language much less protected than had been stipulated in the terms of the 1923 Treaty of Lausanne.[62] As subsequent chapters indicate, reading materials aimed at the younger citizens of the Republic rarely even hint at its inherently diverse demography or any of the potential fault lines in the national edifice.

On the ground, little had changed in the immediate aftermath of the creation of the Republic. The customary acceptance of 1923 as a political and cultural watershed has meant that few studies have tried to cross the divide, which is itself another dubious success of the republican myth. Some of those who have attempted to cross this chronological division have even felt it necessary to bend over backwards to explain their reasoning. In fact, one scholar adopted a nearly apologetic tone when he published an article that examined the Ottoman antecedents of Kemalist policies.[63] Thus before moving onto the subject of reading and the transition from empire to republic, it is necessary to address the problematic manner in which this transition has been treated in the existing literature. What I attempt in the following section is to point out the main lines of the continuities and changes that can be gleaned from a history of reading in this period. Since my aim here is to delineate the broad contours of this transition I limit myself to only a few of the sources that will be interrogated more systematically in the following chapters. Given the presumed importance of the founding of the republic for the history of education and literacy in general, I focus attention mainly on the immediate aftermath of the events of 1923, before returning to the late Ottoman period in order to provide the necessary background and context. The point here is not to be exhaustive, but rather to identify the broad strokes of the transition as far as children's reading is concerned.

It has been noted that the children's literature showed very few signs of change occurring between the periods before and after 1923; in the eyes of children, little had altered. In fact, readers of some children's periodicals from the early 1920s would not have been aware of any change in the adult world. While some children's literature, as we shall soon see, was keenly attuned to political developments, others seem to have been almost stubbornly oblivious. A glance at the publication *Bizim Mecmua* (Our magazine) from 1922 until, say, 1925 offers no evidence of any change at all. Its size, its format, its features, its illustrations and its content all remained the same, blithely indifferent to the changes that had taken place in the political, and ostensibly at least, in the social and cultural arenas. It is only in 1927 that its format changes, but this seems to have had no relation to politics. Four years on from the Turkish "revolution," the journal still carries no picture of Mustafa

Kemal or even mentions his name.[64] But other children's publications were quick to reflect the arrival of the new regime, a sign of the varied approaches to be found in the children's reading material in this period.

The history of reading in the late Ottoman Empire and early Turkish Republic therefore requires that we break away from the realm of the state. The fact that a periodical such as *Bizim Mecmua* (and there are many others like this) appears serenely oblivious to the purportedly epochal events associated with 1923 ought to serve as a useful reminder that in many ways it is precisely in unofficial spaces that we find evidence of the important changes and continuities of the modern period. For all of its transformative power and its critical role in setting the agenda – and for all the scholarly attention it has received – the realm of the state is inherently limited. For reasons discussed above, this is often difficult to remember. In subsequent chapters we will return to look at such topics affecting reading as the increasingly vital link between text and image, the role of the market, individual lives in the worlds of reading and writing and so on, in order to get at the history – ultimately perhaps the more important history – that lies beyond the purview of the state. For the time being we stay with the state in order to establish the extent to which it was trying to forge its own agenda and to ascertain its role in defining the parameters of the historiographical discussion. In any event and as we shall soon see, key figures connected with the state were themselves involved in the production of reading material for children in this period, making it difficult at times to distinguish the state from the non-state.

Children's literature suggests that it was 1908 or perhaps 1911 rather than 1923 that proved to be a more important turning point. As the threats to the empire's existence seemed to multiply and to take on increasingly ominous portents during the Young Turk period, literature produced for children, like that written for adults,[65] not surprisingly reflected an increasingly strident tone, particularly after the Italian invasion of Ottoman Tripolitania (Libya) in 1911. Its tenor was militant nationalism and, as one observer has put it, it did not forget the children.[66] In fact, the young republic, carrying on with the approach adopted by the empire, made a concerted and high-profile effort to deliver its message directly to the young through the medium of school textbooks and reading primers. In the late Ottoman period, a host of nationalist-minded authors, including such important names as the leading ideologue of Turkish nationalism Ziya Gökalp, the Turkologist, historian and, later on, prominent Turkish politician Mehmed Fuad

Köprülü, the nationalist poet Mehmed Emin and the author Ömer Seyfettin, wrote children's books designed to mould young readers into nationally-minded Ottomans ready to fight – and die – for their country.

Thus what 1923 brought in the way of children's literature was not so much a new tone – that had been achieved in the preceding era – but rather a relatively slight adjustment in orientation. Instead of rallying the young subjects to defend the empire against the depredations of Western "civilization," the young citizens of the republic were to be encouraged to disparage the now jettisoned Ottomanness of the old regime. Depicted as reactionary, old fashioned and perhaps worst of all, failed, the Ottoman state was quickly subjected to a savage demonizing campaign. This is most easily seen in some examples of reading material composed for children. The first example is taken from a children's reader produced in the early years of the Republic by none other than Mehmed Fuad Köprülü.[67] This book, entitled *Cumhuriyet Çocuklarına Yeni Millî Kıraat* (The new national reader for Republican children), gets right to the point. The book's frontispiece features a soldier in full battle dress prominently holding a rifle, with affixed bayonet, that reaches from the ground all the way to the level of his ear. This image establishes a clear martial context in which the business of "national" reading is meant to take place. The book's first passage, titled simply "The Republic of Turkey," begins as follows:

> Until recent times the Turks were the slaves of the Sultans. These Sultans, living in ornate, august palaces, following their pleasure from morning to night, and feeding thousands of retainers in their palaces, supposed themselves to be the personal owners of the country.[68]

The rest of the entry is devoted to explaining how the "poor, hungry, and naked" Anatolian Turks eventually woke up and threw off their "blood-sucking oppressors," their "greatest enemies," the sultans. The blatantly propagandistic nature of this sort of writing is unmistakable.[69] It is interesting to note that the Greeks, who were the more typical object of resentment due to their invasion of Western Anatolia that precipitated the War of Independence, are here nowhere to be found. They would eventually receive harsh treatment in children's literature,[70] but for now all of this text's venom is devoted to disparaging the Ottomans. The young readers are given a national hero with whom to identify in direct opposition to the disparaged Padishah, namely "Gazi Mustafa Kemal Pasha."

In spite of this passage's vilification of the Ottoman era, this sort of simplistic, good-versus-bad approach continued the tradition established under the old regime, a subject to be addressed in more detail below. For the time being I would only like to draw attention to the unrelenting denigration of the Ottoman sultans and the creation of a binary but of course unequal opposition pitting Mustafa Kemal against a nameless and hapless Ottoman sultan. This way of representing recent history served several purposes for the Kemalist ideologues. First, it established Mustafa Kemal as the supreme representative of the republic, a position he jealously guarded against the other heroes of the revolution.[71] Secondly, it depicted the sultans as detached, lazy, exploitative, the very opposite, in short, of all the qualities that the republican propagandists wished to be associated with Mustafa Kemal. Thirdly, the demonization of the sultans was done in such a way as to present them as ahistorical cartoon figures, detached from actual events, context and even deprived of their names.

The generic caricature fashioned for the sultans in the service of the early Republic is easily seen in the next example of a text written to present the Ottomans as reactionary. The author of *Cumhuriyet Çocuklarına Türkçe Kıraat* (A Turkish reader for Republican children) was Ahmed Cevad [Emre], a transitional late Ottoman and early Republican author of textbooks whose work reflected the changes occurring in state education from the Ottoman to the Turkish period. The first in this series features a skit entitled *"Yaşasın Cumhuriyet"* (Long live the Republic).[72] Its action centers on two children, Osman, a bossy would-be Padishah, and the heroic Turhan (an old Turkish name meaning chief or nobleman). The names are not chosen by accident, of course, but rather to accentuate the difference between Ottoman imperial past – Osman is the eponym of the Ottoman (Osmanlı) dynasty – and the Turkish nationalist aspect of the Republic. Unsurprisingly, it is Turhan who emerges as the guardian of Republican values against this reactionary Ottoman usurper. Each protagonist is surrounded with a crowd of anonymous partisans, who seem to represent factions in broader society. Here is a taste of the dialogue from the opening lines:

Osman: (rifle on his shoulder, with a contingent of children behind him, sternly): Look sharp! Come here all of you and let me see you.
(The children stop their playing and look on in astonishment.)

Turhan: (bravely): Are we supposed to come on your order?
Osman: Yes, on my order. Leave your games and come here! (He aims his rifle at them, and so do his confederates.)
Turhan: What do you want from us?
Osman: You will give me all of your toys and all of your playthings.
Turhan: Hey, mister! Who do you think you are? You are acting like the evil padishah who robbed the nation. That day has gone, my dear.

Eventually, of course, Turhan and his faction of Republicans win the battle. Turhan's last line is: "Let's all shout together, 'Down with the Sultan; Long live the Republic!'"

School textbooks and the children's press of the late Ottoman and early Republican period were invariably didactic, reflecting an authoritarian approach to pedagogy that has proved difficult to dislodge and modeling the types of behavior intended for their readers to emulate. But the need to draw such a stark line between empire and republic must have been partly due to the well-attested instinct for successor states of the nationalist stripe to denigrate their immediate predecessors and partly due to the fact that, from a child's perspective at least, much less had changed than the rhetoric had suggested.

The persistence of a fairly high share of poetry was another feature of the children's literature that underscores the continuity between empire and republic. The poetic tradition was the highest form of literary expression throughout centuries of Ottoman literature. In the late Ottoman period, poets began to move away from the established meters in favor of a more direct style better suited to the emerging nationalist tendency. Gökalp's poetry is the prime example: "each of his verses became slogans, easy to memorize and became delicacies of young students who shouted them out loud, standing firmly on two legs in military style."[73] Gökalp's poetry appeared in many children's publications in this period. When he died in the autumn of 1924 *Yeni Yol* published his photo with a poem dedicated to his memory.[74]

Having traced some of the continuities and changes across the transition from empire to republic, we can now push further back into the late Ottoman period to consider the context of an emerging market for young readers. The expansion of education by the Ottoman state was the engine for the creation of a growing demand for children's reading materials. This worked both directly through the state's role as commissioning the publication of reading material, mainly school textbooks, and indirectly through the creation of a new educational system and the expansion of literacy in the first place. The students who had been taught to read in the state schools were already exposed to a variety of reading materials. Whether they, or perhaps their parents who might be the ones paying for them, actually liked them or not is hard to determine, but it is perhaps telling that many of the emerging children's periodicals in this period identified their product as being closely linked to the curricular program of the state schools.

Another factor likely to encourage the development of a market for reading was the fact that unlike the religiously based schools where pedagogy was typically communal, oral-aural and organized around a shared text or more often an erasable board,[75] their new state counterparts encouraged reading as an individual pursuit that, in turn, encouraged the purchase and possession of individual copies of the required textbooks, a development with crucial economic and cultural repercussions. In Chapters 2 and 3 we shall see how this new reading was modeled for children and parents in the new literature. A principle feature of the new reading milieu was commodification, the subject of Chapter 5

The content of these texts in the late Ottoman period was fairly predictable. Emphasis was placed on a mutually reinforcing cluster of concepts and values. Discipline, obedience, loyalty, hard work, cleanliness, family, the state, geography and morality all featured heavily in this literature, just as they did in many places around the globe in the nineteenth and twentieth century, the period of *Self Help* by Samuel Smiles in the English-speaking world, Bérenger's *La Morale en action* in the French and so on. In the Ottoman context, the prevalence and repeated printings of such texts as the Stories of the Prophets (*Kisas-i Enbiya*), a variety of catechisms (*ilm-i hal*) – that produced by Ahmed Cevdet Paşa was in much demand – and a very wide range of books devoted to morality (*ahlâk*) reveal the strong connection between reading and improvement. Literacy was considered inherently meliorative; the path to progress, both personal and societal, ran through the pages of books.

The tone and content of this literature was overwhelmingly didactic, moralizing, and replete with normative messages, whether bluntly or subtly delivered. Imparting knowledge and the correct way to live a modern life were prominent themes in this literature, revealing its roots in the educational project with which it was closely associated. As we shall see, almost all of the reading primers from the late Ottoman period equate school-taught literacy with moral, intellectual and economic development. One of the most popular reading primers has as its first text a passage entitled "Attending School" which emphasizes the benefits that the well-mannered child derives from going to school and learning to read:

> I am a little child. I don't know anything yet...I am a student. I have teachers. They are the ones who teach me how to read and write and educate me. I must obey them. I must work hard at my lessons...I go to school happily.[76]

Tellingly, the most prolific moralizing author of the late Ottoman period, the strongly didactic Ahmed Midhat Efendi, has been likened to a schoolmaster and described as the "teacher of ordinary people."[77] His stories, some of which will be referred to in subsequent chapters, presented a clear moral compass, often with a "good" character depicted in stark contrast with the "bad."

But while it was moralizing and normative, this literature was nevertheless also remarkably eclectic. Alongside the persistently didactic, moralizing texts occurred others simply created to divert and entertain. Still others began to poke fun at some of the most earnest symbols of the state's educational endeavor, including its foremost vanguard, the teachers themselves. As we shall see in later chapters, signs eventually appeared that this reading material was beginning to deviate from state's agenda in search of new readers *cum* customers. This marked the start of an important development related to the market, which carried with it the potential to undermine the official line, whether Ottoman or Republican.

Because the thematic content had changed so little across the Ottoman-Republican transition, only a relatively superficial effort was needed after 1923 to realign the literature produced for young readers with the republican realities. Or rather with republican foundation myths, because much of the thrust of republican image projection bore little resemblance to what had gone before. In many ways the real novelty in republican policy was its series of reorientations. Apart from the denigration of things Ottoman centering around the image of the sultan and against a steady backdrop of children's tales on subjects familiar from the late Ottoman period (animals, right from wrong, advice, bromides, tales from overseas, Nasreddin Hoca stories, the seasons, filial piety and so on), a number of other shifts were required. These included: the reorientations from the Ottoman world to that of the specifically Turkish; from Islamic society to the emphatic laicism of the single-party period, with an emphasis on the pre-Islamic history of the Turks; from the urban to the rural as

Anatolia was emphasized at the expense of Istanbul; and from the elite to the populace.

The means for effecting these changes included institutions devoted to the production and consumption of texts, such as the People's Houses, the Turkish Historical Society, the Turkish Language Society and Public Reading Rooms. The Kemalist state even went so far as to launch a campaign, however ultimately unsuccessful, to rewrite folk literature in order to bring it into line with what it saw to be the requirements of the modern age.[78] Although, as we shall see, such shifts were often mere projections and operated on a rather superficial level, they represent a clear intention on the part of the young Kemalist state to disassociate itself from the immediate past. Some of the clearest signs of the newly constructed world appear in children's literature.

The skit featuring Osman and Turhan discussed earlier is a good example of the idealized, wishful contrast between the old regime and the new. It also points to the symbolic role that personal names would play in the Republic. Well before the family name law of 1934 was put into effect, the children's literature of the early Republican period began to exhibit signs of such a trend. While old-style names of course persisted in many children's texts just as they did in real life, giving new names to the characters in readings set for children was a relatively simple option. Emphasizing the Turkic character of the new state while downplaying the Islamic nature of Ottoman-Turkish society was easily accomplished through the act of naming. Onomastic patterns in the late Ottoman and Turkish Republican periods demonstrate the clear link between the prevailing cultural emphasis of the state and the names given to children at birth.[79] "Islamic" names gave ground to the "Turkic" names after the advent of the Republic. Thereafter the balance shifts back and forth, reflecting the ebb and flow of the dynamic surrounding the tussle between laicist and religious impulses in Turkish society, a problem demonstrating that merely superficial changes would not suffice to alter the underlying socio-religious fabric of the country.

In the aftermath of the Lausanne treaty the new territorial dimensions of Turkey needed to be inscribed in the minds of the young, and there is not surprisingly a strong geographical commitment in the post-1923 literature. This amounted to a continuation of the Ottoman policies with respect to identification with imperial territory albeit on a much reduced scale. The shrunken borders were a big help in this regard. Whereas the Ottoman attempt to inculcate identification with the shape of the Ottoman domains had suffered from the instability of the empire's shrinking contours, the Republic could now take advantage of a relative permanence.[80] It was much easier for school children to identify with a stable shape, and Republican educators made sure that the national cartographic shape was imprinted on the minds of their young charges.

The emphasis on this newly defined territory required a rediscovery of Anatolia, a process that consisted of two elements. One was the shift in attention to the Anatolian hinterland. Ankara, a former provincial center, was selected and then developed as the capital of the new republic, a move laden with symbolic intent. Meanwhile efforts were made to acquaint the population with the geography of Anatolia, its towns, mountains, rivers and so on. The other element in this shift was essentially cultural or even spiritual. This involved the process of identification with the life of the village. The long-forgotten villager was now not only raised to the lofty level of a citizen of the Republic but, rather more important, was appropriated by the state to serve as a symbol of the new Turkey. But this spiritual adoption of the villager was not without problems; the appropriation was selective and shot through with contradictions. On the one hand the choice of simple peasants as repositories of the national culture clashed with the heavily patronizing mode of the state's top-down revolution from above. And of course, none of those in the inner Kemalist circle was from a background that remotely resembled village life. Nevertheless, Kemalist policy privileged and glorified the Anatolian countryside and its rural way of life, and as a result the reading material generated by the Republic showed a marked increase in attention to the rural.[81]

Part of this task was simply geographical. At the same time that their stories were starting to include fictional characters with old Turkish names like Orhan and Turhan, children's publications from the early Republican period began paying attention to Anatolian towns like Adapazarı and Ankara, often providing drawings or, better still, photographs in order to acquaint the readers with these newly validated places.[82] As we will see, children's periodicals were not unaware of the market potential of towns like these; with time many such publications cultivated these readers by publishing letters and photographs from school children in the Anatolian interior in order to boost their sales.

Mustafa Kemal had already begun to pronounce on the educational needs of the new nation when the War of Liberation was still far from over. What he had in mind was somewhat contradictory. As early as 1921 he stated that education as practiced to date was a cause of the retardation of the people and it needed to be replaced with an education conforming to "our national character, in harmony with our history and completely liberated from the superstition of the past, freed from all foreign influence," whether Western or Eastern.[83] He wanted an education in harmony with the people but also noted that every villager would need to be taught to read. In other words, republican educational policy should be based on the villager who had nevertheless been deprived of education. Thus republican textbooks and primers attempted to educate a largely urban audience about the essentially noble qualities of the villagers. At the same time the educational system set about the rather more difficult task of altering their lives. Specifically, this included the much slower process of extending education to the villages and bringing their inhabitants up to speed with such basics as geography, history, religion and morals, as well as the four basic mathematical operations (*âmal-i erbaa*).[84] The newfound interest in rural life focused largely on creating positive images of agriculturalists and their work.

One way of demonstrating the pleasures of the countryside to the still almost exclusively town-dwelling young readers was to provide stories in which a fictional student goes to work on a farm in summer time. Mehmed Fuad Köprülü's reader, which opened, as we saw above, with the selection entitled the "Turkish Republic," turned quickly to embrace the rural idyll. The book's fourth text, after the more or less predictable "Love Your Mother" and an entry in which a boy explains an act of charity, is entitled "The Little Farmer."[85] The protagonist is a young student named Fahri who is depicted in the accompanying sketch illustration in a tunic resembling a school uniform but wearing a large-brimmed sun hat while he watches a man dressed in baggy trousers (*şalvar*) plowing a field behind a pair of oxen. Having done well in his exams, Fahri has been allowed to spend two months on his uncle's farm on the shores of the gulf of İzmid. The location is revealing of the tentative stages of the turn to Anatolia, near enough to be accessible from Fahri's native Istanbul yet sufficiently distant to allow for the pleasing contrast with the city. On the farm "everything he saw seemed beautiful to him. Because even though he has lived in Istanbul for years he has never seen anything like that which there is on the farm." Everything is different from Istanbul. In the end Fahri's uncle teaches him how to plow a field. When he returns for lunch, even the food tastes better, now that he has been in touch with real life, the story seems to say. As if to reinforce the positive contrast with urban life that the countryside provides, the next offering in Köprülü's reader is a poem written by the writer, educationalist, encyclopedist and politician İbrahim Alaeddin [Gövsa] (1889–1949) called simply "The Farmers." The first lines read,

> Far from the these cities of argument and uproar
> On that blessed land whose skies see no mist
> What cheerful lives they lead, the good-hearted farmers...[86]

While the paean to the countryside was largely generic in these early republican children's readings, it is not difficult to see that they could lead to the more specific homage to Anatolia that would come later. In this regard, the readers from this period share the same mixture of generic and contextualized passages with their late Ottoman predecessors.

The momentous events of the period between the Libyan War in 1911 and the defeat of the Greek invasion in 1922 provided the context that allowed for the foregrounding of a specific historical setting for children's stories. Of the readings for which a context is provided, the most common is that of the recently fought War of Liberation. Occasionally these passages do double duty, both praising the virtues of the rural population and focusing on the heroics of the wartime struggle. One such example is given in the last entry in Köprülü's reader. Entitled "The Virtue of the Villager" (*Köylünün fazileti*) the selection describes the spontaneous generosity of a villager who leads an officer in search of fodder for his animals to his own lush fields.[87]

Other examples are still more historically grounded. Staying with Köprülü's reader, we can find a poem that asserts the unanimity of the national response in the face of the destruction witnessed in the burning of Izmir.[88] The first lines read,

> The enemies were in İzmir; the country was burning !
> The traitors thought the nation was ruined!
> But the faith of this nation is great.
> Great and small, all wanted it to be saved...

There is also an entry devoted to the famous battle of İnönü, a turning point in the Greek invasion and the site from which Mustafa Kemal's colleague and successor İsmet Paşa drew his surname, and a lesser known incident concerning Antepli Şahin Bey, a hero in the national struggle against French forces in southeastern Anatolia.[89]

While it was in many ways natural for the Kemalists to draw upon this struggle to provide heroes for its young audience, what is more surprising, and perhaps ultimately more revealing of their underlying ethos, is the extent to which the processes of learning and reading were infused with a military flavor. The militarization of learning is, as we have already noted, a process that began in the Young Turk period in the aftermath of the Italian invasion of Libya in 1911. What the republic did was to give the military bearing a more conspicuously national dimension, going much further in attempting to inculcate an ethos of the soldier in every young reader, not merely those attending military schools.[90] As examples in later chapters will show, both Ottoman and Republican periods produced a consistently gendered approach to reading. Boys were meant to become soldiers and girls to become mothers and support their martial menfolk.[91] Returning to Köprülü's reader, we find Mehmed Emin's poem "Mektepli," which might be translated as "The Schoolboy."[92] It is accompanied with a small illustration depicting a child wearing a sailor suit and seated at a table reading a large book. The sun is rising over the mountains in the background, and a drape with the star and crescent of the national flag pulled rather conspicuously across the upper third of the picture. A small notation tells the child readers that they are to learn by heart and recite (*ezber ve inşad*).

Friend!	*Arkadaş!*
I am a little soldier:	*Ben bir küçük askerim:*
I have that blood in my veins;	*Benimde damarımda o kan var;*
My eyes gleam with that fire;	*Gözlerim o ateşle parıldar;*
I also want to wage war;	*Ben dahi cenk eylemek isterim;*
O child, what is your strength	*Ey çocuk, kuvvetin ne?*
– Knowledge!	*– Marifet!*
My pen will be my weapon,	*Kalemim bana silah olacak,*
My book will serve as my fort;	*Kitabım bir kalelik edecek;*
My days will be full of conquests;	*Günlerim futuhatla dolacak;*
In every place I wil be at the front.	*Her yerde benim önüm gidecek.*
O soldier, who is your enemy?	*Ey asker, düşmanın kim?*
– Ignorance	*– cehalet!*

The militarization of reading could also be effected by recourse to more distant historical material. The Republican literature was keen to assert the primacy of a continuum of Turkish, as opposed to, say, Seljuk or Ottoman, history. Yet at the same time it needed to distinguish the Turkish Republic from the rest of the Turkic states. This could be handled, as in Ahmed Rasım's 1926 *Doğru usûl-i kıraat* (The true method of reading), by taking some time to explain the reasoning behind the name of the Turkish Republic. After a passage named after the heavily emphasized republican phrase "The Sovereignty of the Nation" (*Hâkimiyet-i milliye*), an entry called "The Name of Our State" (*Devletimizin adı*) goes to some lengths to encourage his readers to understand why the old, dynastic names such as that of the Seljuks and the Ottomans can no longer apply, and why the state is properly called "Türkiye," as opposed to "Türk," devleti.[93] The reason given is that the name "Türk" in itself would not have been sufficient, given that the Turks, rather exceptionally in this view, were responsible for founding "up to fifty states." A new name was needed, and here the final suffix was chosen on the European model – Russia (*Rusya*), France (*Fransa*) and Germany (*Almanya*) are cited as comparable cases.

Republican reading primers usually associate historical references to the Turks with military triumph. Here again Köprülü's reader is instructive. An entry called "The Unknown Hero" (*Mechul kahraman*) tells the story of the siege of the Balkan fortress of Kanije, and the heroics of an unknown Turkish captive of the Hapsburgs who sacrificed himself in order to blow up the enemy's powder magazine.[94] This self-sacrifice – what today might be termed a suicide bombing – produced such a massive hole in its defenses that the enemy was unable to repair the fortress and, as a result, the Turks were finally able to capture it. What is interesting here is that the passage makes no mention of the Ottomans. The episode is referred to as an example in "Turkish history" of "our," or alternatively, "our ancestors'" great love of the nation, sacrifice and heroism. It is only by inference – and with knowledge not provided in the text – that readers would be aware that this involved the Ottoman Empire. The fact that the author is the leading Ottoman historian of the early Republic only serves to underscore the extent to which the empire's past was suppressed in the service of the new nation. This is a good example of the rather deft appropriation of any number of episodes in "Turkish" history to depict what are treated as the constant features and qualities of "we" the "Turks." This sort of approach allowed the Republic to benefit from the reflected glory of bygone states while carefully avoiding anything that would possibly credit its illustrious imperial predecessors.[95]

Equating martial and educational duties in the service of the nation was embedded in the Kemalist discourse. Mustafa Kemal's speeches and writings and the new school texts were mutually reinforcing. Consider the following passage from the Headteacher (*Başöğretmen*)/Commander-in-Chief (*Başkomutan*):

> Our National Ministry of Education is carrying out its duties of edu-cating and disciplining the nation with the utmost effort, attention and industriousness. Everywhere in the country the children of the light are trying to enlighten the minds of the children of the coun-try. The military is carrying out the same duties as these organiza-tions. The military establishment is a disciplining institution and a school that teaches and educates the mature youth of the nation, not only in military terms but also in cultural terms... [96]

The instrumental nature of the army and the school in the linked tasks of forging the new Turkish nation is unmistakable.

The forceful emphasis on the Turk and Turkishness should be clear from the various aspects of the children's literature we have discussed here, namely, the newly emergent pattern of giving children conspicu-ously Turkic, as opposed to Muslim, names, the growing concern with Anatolia and its villagers, the appropriation of a variety of historical material, pre-Islamic, Seljuk and Ottoman, as primarily Turkic history and the militarism inherited from the Young Turk era, now increasingly grounded in actual historical – especially military – contexts provided by the recent "War of National Liberation."[97] The prominence given to Turkishness in this multifaceted effort is remarkable in that it was a campaign that managed to fashion a strikingly novel and revolution-ary garment out of a variety of essentially pre-existing fragments. Most of these trends had clear antecedents, but the power, perhaps even the genius of the early Republican strategists, was to conjure a new combi-nation from the largely unconnected pieces of the old – and to convince the citizens of the Republic as well as most of the rest of the world of the novelty of this mission.

Controlling what was read by both of these audiences was critical to the success of this project. This study naturally focuses on the internal audience but it also tries to refer to the ways in which Kemalist attention to historiographical developments cultivated important external part-ners in this cause. We need only return to the deference and hesitancy of observers both internal and external in the face of the Turkish national myth to fathom the depths of the Kemalists' "success" in this regard.

The second half of this chapter has offered some glimpses into the importance of traversing the transition from Ottoman Empire to Turkish

Republic in order to appreciate its various continuities and breaks. The year 1923 represents a watershed in many important ways but when seen from the perspective of children's reading materials it is also interesting to see how it fits into the longer continuum of the period ranging from the 1880s to the 1930s. The chapters that follow explore in greater detail the world of children's literacy against the backdrop of change and continuity.

2
Reading Represented

This chapter begins the exploration of the mechanics and meanings associated with learning to read and reading by tracing the many and varied ways in which reading was represented in late Ottoman and early Republican society and the ways in which it was subsequently remembered. It focuses on the modeling of reading practices because it reveals the intentions and agenda underlying the impetus to increase reading in this period. Representations of reading also point to the many tasks with which reading was freighted. Young readers were being encouraged to approach their texts for reasons of religion, morality, careerism, personal improvement or simply for entertainment or escape. Interspersing examples drawn from children's reading material itself with accounts of learning to read and reading that appear in memoirs, this chapter sets out the many and at times contradictory modes and valences attached to reading.

Few of these representations were neutral. Most actively promoted reading in one way or another, situating the act of reading on the side of progress and modernity, and claiming it to be a necessity not just for individual fulfillment and attainment but also essential for the cumulative betterment of first the empire and then the nation. When seen from the perspective of the twenty-first century, most observers find this a natural, indeed positive, development. The author and readers of this book are by definition part of an emphatically literate culture. We assume reading to be an essential, constitutive component of modern life and tend to consider those who cannot partake in this celebrated enterprise as primitive and unfortunate. Our bias in favor and our generally positive experience of reading conditions the way we think of reading historically. It makes it difficult for us to recapture the radical dimension of a society in transition from scant to predominant literacy.

We have to work to summon up the sense of possibility and the unprecedented that expanding literacy generated in the period we are examining here. This sense of novelty helps explain the late Ottoman and early Turkish republican focus on and faith in literacy and reading as transformative.

Many of the representations of reading from this period were intended to do more than merely depict, teach or improve reading; they were actively promoting it as a practice to be emulated and as a concept to be valued. Why this was so is linked to the fact that only a small but rapidly growing segment of the population was literate. So the literature examined here presents reading as both natural, expected and as something empowering, necessary and special. Those making the representations feel that there is simply not enough reading taking place and that what there is is not being appreciated in the proper way. Hence we discover so many examples that instruct, model and inveigh. The drive for literacy was concerned with more than mere mechanics; as always, reading was a vehicle for inculcating certain values, dependent on the politics and the social and cultural agendas of the period. Reading, as presented to children, is contingent on a number of factors, some brutally emphasized, others more subtly imparted as a feature of the ambient background of a newly defined childhood.

The late Ottoman and early Turkish republican periods represented the act of reading in a wide variety of ways. Reading was portrayed for a variety of reasons, some of which are blatantly obvious and some of which need to be teased out from the context and content of the material. Writers, illustrators and publishers in this period seem to have gone out of their way to display, to model, advertise, fictionalize and even invent the act of reading. The various ways in which reading was represented – to the children as primary target, to their parents who were usually responsible in some way for the coming together of child and text, and for the unimagined historian of posterity – were chosen for a variety of reasons, historically contingent if sometimes difficult to decipher. In other words, while the "real" practice of learning to read and reading occurred silently and often without independent witness, the textual and visual representations of reading inevitably distort our understanding of it. Nevertheless, they are the natural, sometimes the only, place to begin a search for its recovery.

The cumulative effect of these depictions was to confront young children with a variety of types of reading and to invest the practice of reading with a range of symbolic meanings. The purpose of this chapter is to recover the variety of ways in which reading was represented to child readers of school texts, short stories, magazines and autobiographical accounts while linking these representations to a number of symbolic and discursive fields in which the practice of reading was embedded. In other words, the point here is to reveal the breadth of the symbolic and contextual associations invested in learning to read and reading across the transition from empire to republic. This sets the scene for Chapter 3 in which several of the most important of these associations are examined in greater detail.

The previous chapter provided glimpses of the ways in which reading was both affected by and constitutive of the political imaginings of young readers. The changes buffeting the late Ottoman Empire and the early Turkish Republic are clearly reflected in the process of learning to read and reading, even if they are not always visible when or in the ways we might have been led to expect. In fact, the authors, educators and illustrators responsible for the children's literature seem to have been keen to make visible the largely unseen practice of reading. As we shall see in Chapter 4, many children's publications gave prominent place to visual displays of idealized children engaged in reading, often placing such images on their covers. But the images presented, usually of children dressed in a modern, often Western way and often in the context of organized schooling, were highly selective. The narrowing of the images modeled for young readers is part of the broader story of reading in this period.

Depictions of reading: Changing environments

Reading involves a complex interplay of physical and mental activity. Both are required to make "sense" out of a text.[1] Reading has meant different things at different times and in different places in the past. In other words, it is culturally and historically conditioned. While there are obviously some immutable aspects to reading independent of a given time period, it would be a mistake to equate today's notion of what reading is or does with what it used to do in the past, or indeed how it might operate in the future. In the transition from Ottoman imperial to Turkish republican society, the purpose of reading, the way it was learned and the value attached to it were all changing, sometimes dramatically and sometimes subtly, almost imperceptibly. What is important here is to gain a sense of how varied the experience of reading could be, in terms of the different contexts in which it took place, the types of materials involved, and, as a result, the diverse modes of reading that were being modeled for children in this period. More often than not, reading was represented to children as an act involving much more than merely deciphering text. Reading was infused with a variety of tensions, causes and agendas that clearly inflected the ways in which children were encouraged to think of it.

In this period, reading, like human life itself, usually began at home. A great majority of those who learned to read in the late Ottoman and early Republican periods gathered their first experiences of reading from close family members. As general literacy increased, it became more usual for children to be inducted into the world of reading through the family as opposed to a member of the religious classes. Fathers, mothers, siblings, aunts and uncles provided the first experience of literacy, according to the autobiographical literature from this period.[2] This meant that although the state would soon intervene in an attempt to dominate the process of reading, more often than not the initial approach to reading, the method of instruction, the language and type of text chosen were all associated in one way or another with "tradition;" reading was usually first encountered in a religious and cultural environment that reflected past practice.

Let us briefly refer to a few autobiographical descriptions of children learning to read. One of these, to which we will return in more detail below, is that of Halide Nusret [Zorlutuna] (1901–1984), who would go on to become an important Turkish writer. Her initiation into the world of reading was infused with a prominent religio-cultural tone. She first encountered reading through her mother, whom she describes as a natural teacher. Reflecting the typical particularities of the late Ottoman linguistic milieu, Halide Nusret's first reading lesson was prefaced by a recitation in Qur'anic Arabic, and not the Turkish of her everyday life. Even the timing of her introduction to reading was determined by tradition: The numerically propitious age of four years, four months and four days.[3] The autobiography of the acclaimed writer Halid Ziya [Uşaklıgil] (1866–1945) begins with a description of a dream sequence in which his mother appears in an old house. Schoolbooks lie scattered throughout the house thereby juxtaposing and linking the familial and institutional aspects of reading and education. He pointedly compares his mother with the Kaaba in Mecca; she was the central figure around which his young life turned and an abiding figure of consolation and comfort.[4]

The family was crucial to introducing children to reading but it did so in ways that were usually at variance with the agenda of state education. While state educationalists tended to denigrate the influences of the home environment, the memoirs describing early experiences with reading generally depict the home as knowledgeable as well as nurturing. A surprising number of the mothers described were literate women. The future poet Nigar Hanım tells of her mother's reciting poetry, while Şevket Süreyya [Aydemir] describes how his mother, whom he describes as his first link with the "life of the mind," read to various people in the neighborhood.[5] The future minor Young Turk figure and author Halil Hâlid recalls his mother "reading aloud from a book of sacred legends,"[6] most probably the *Kisas-i Enbiya* (Stories of the Prophets). For others it was the father who inspired and introduced literacy, usually imbued with a sense of religious piety and the Perso-Islamic tradition. Thus Muallim Naci tells of the support he received from his father who encouraged his reading of the Qur'an and, showing that the melioristic approach to reading was not limited to the state schooling apparatus, implored him to go beyond his limited understanding of the Holy Scripture. "Well done, my son! Strive to read even more beautifully. God willing, you will not end up like me. You will learn well the meaning of the Holy Qur'an."[7] Mehmed Âkif depicts his father as taking on the role of both parent and teacher, something which, as we shall see, the state educational apparatus looked upon with a degree of wistfulness and sometimes outright suspicion. Halid Ziya also links his father with learning and the wider shores of Islamo-Ottoman culture, through his connection to the Persian and Arabic languages and their shared pilgrimage to Mecca. It was his father's best friend who had read the first call to prayer (*ezan*) into the infant's ear and bestowed his full name upon him. Mehmed Halid Ziyaeddin would later become Halid Ziya Uşaklıgil when the secularizing republic promulgated its surname law. The echoes of Perso-Islam and religiosity that first appeared in association with reading would not be so easily expunged.

The rise of modern-style education and the state's appropriation of education from the religious milieu would alter this picture dramatically, with important implications for a number of social dynamics including the relationship between private and public activity and the association between religion and the state. Beginning in the last quarter of the nineteenth century state schools fanned out across the Ottoman Empire. Although not always realized, the state's intention was to provide primary education in every administrative district of every province.[8] Boys' schools were the norm but increasingly girls' and coeducational schools appeared alongside them. Naturally, the increasing availability – and visibility – of education would change the way in which reading was represented, with school-based reading eventually becoming the norm. But there continued to be a substantial difference between the way reading was approached at home and the way it was taught at school. It was thus entirely natural for the authors of textual materials intended for young readers to depict the early experience of reading in a familial environment, but also to try to influence the way in which both settings were perceived. The clearest manifestation of this influence is seen in the almost universal impulse to sanctify the school as the only venue appropriate for the proper teaching of reading. Whether gently or forcefully adumbrated, the message was clear: the home must yield to the school.

Taking an example from a late Ottoman children's primer, we get a glimpse of the ways in which one author, a prolific but unheralded writer of children's texts in the late Ottoman period, represented the initial encounter between child and text in the familial environment.[9] This book, which according to the author's memoirs was written while he was still at school himself and published in the mid 1880s,[10] is a compendium of advice, bromides and stories for children. Among the contents devoted to reinforcing the importance of such subjects as distinguishing between good and evil, effort, and respect for one's parents, comes a story called simply "The Book." This story revolves around a dutiful boy, aptly named Zeki (the name means intelligent, clever) and his mother. One day when they are at home together, Zeki becomes bored and, coming to sit beside his mother, asks her to tell him a story. The mother obliges, relating her account of Fatih Sultan Mehmed, the conqueror of Istanbul, whom she describes as "brave, intelligent, and merciful." Then the child asks, "Mother, do you know Fatih Sultan Mehmed?" The mother replies with surprise that he has been dead for many, many years. The child then asks, with a logical directness befitting his age, "If he is dead, how do you know that he was an intelligent and merciful sultan?" Forgoing the temptation of parental omniscience, the mother explains that she read it in a book, and cites a number of such useful and informative publications.

The story continues. One subsequent day the mother leaves the child alone at home while she goes out shopping. Zeki again suffers from boredom and wonders at the realization that his mother's books seem to contain a trove of beautiful stories. He takes one down and opens it but is unable to see anything apart from some very small black scribbles. He puts the book back, only to try another with the same unhappy result. When his mother returns, he relates his frustrating experience with the printed word to her and asks, "Dear Mother what must I do to understand the beautiful stories that are in your books?" "My son," she replies, "these stories can only be understood by reading them. One cannot do it any other way." The following day Zeki begins school with the desire to learn, and within two or three years, the reader is told, he makes such progress that he is able to read not only his mother's books, but also much more difficult ones as well.

Now, this story does not reveal terribly much about the process of learning to read, but it does tell us something about attitudes toward reading and the ways in which it could be represented in this period. First, it acknowledges the practical difficulties involved. This text confronts what is usually glossed over, namely, the actual problem one faces in learning to work out a correspondence between oral and written language, a subject taken up in Chapter 4. For the majority of children in the late Ottoman Empire this meant learning to read Turkish to which they had been exposed aurally since birth in the letters of the Arabic script. In this story, this attempt is represented by Zeki's stab at deciphering those funny looking "scribbles" on the printed page. Secondly, it suggests that, in spite of the fact that the home is the site of the initial encounter between child and reading – witness the presence of a literate mother, by no means the norm in this period, the availability of books at home, and the awakening of this fictional child's curiosity toward the written word – the text emphasizes that the way to attain the all-important ability to read is through formal education, away from home. As in many texts produced during this period, the home is the place where the child ought properly to receive the first inclinations toward the world of literacy, but the task of actually teaching him or her to read is deemed to be far too important to be left to the family. This author therefore steers the plot line away from its domestic context in favor of formal education; the text uses a private setting to advocate the virtues of public instruction. Significantly it is at school and not at home that the initial interest in reading is validated and where real, measurable success is attained. The lesson is clear: Learning to read can begin through encouraging curiosity on the home front, but the proper venue for reading is the school.

As we shall see, the state-supplied school was held up as the ideal locale for literacy. Here it could be regulated and controlled by the burgeoning educational bureaucracy of the state. Although rarely acknowledged, something was inevitably lost in the transition from home to school. Reading in the context of the family afforded the young more time and space than was allowed in the schoolroom. Whereas the school day was increasingly governed by a rigid time schedule, reading at home was almost timeless. It allowed a fictional child like Zeki or a historical one such as the young Halide Edip the time – and space – to lie down on the floor as she lost herself in the world of books. Zeki knows his mother's books to contain "beautiful stories," and Halide Edip escapes through her aunt's books to Africa and other faraway places. Reading at home also afforded opportunities for questioning and experimentation, as exemplified in the curiosity and directness of Zeki's inquisitive attitude, that were hardly encouraged by the top-down didacticism of organized schooling and the regimented functioning of the school. Learning to read as remembered in the autobiographical literature was by contrast a warm and cozy experience, conditioned by familial love, religious timelessness and a sense of relative freedom, and thus very different from the much more structured reading modeled by literature for children.

Apart from the autobiographical literature, the representations of children's reading that take place in complete independence from organized education are less common. Because most children's publications were either intended for use in schools or written by those involved in the educational infrastructure, reading was hardly ever depicted as something that was to be practiced entirely on one's own. By contrast, in gazettes intended mainly for a grown-up audience depictions of solitary reading are more common, a projection perhaps of parental hopes. Even when we do encounter solitary reading, such as in the case of Zeki in "The Book" or the account of two boys who go off separately to read stories of space travel, found in the children's magazine *Yeni Yol*, to which we return later in this chapter, these are nevertheless confined within the context of school-bound reading. It is mainly in the autobiographical literature that we encounter descriptions of truly independent reading. This points again to the overweening caution shown by pedagogues with respect to untutored or undirected reading, manifested otherwise only in the extreme concern directed toward textual selection and censorship in both the late Ottoman and early Republican periods. As we shall see, privately produced, profit-oriented publications such as children's magazines would adopt a different approach.

Being taught to read outside of the home and away from the family was inevitably more structured and constrained. In formal settings the strict regimen of the clock dictated the process of learning to read, and the choice of reading materials was predictably restricted. But the school experience of learning to read and reading naturally depended on the type of school and the teacher involved. One sort of teacher absent from the materials usually prepared for young children was the private tutor. Affordable only to children from wealthy backgrounds, private tutors were understandably omitted from the textbooks, readers and children's magazines. But they were nevertheless a feature of the domestic pedagogical landscape, as they were in France by the eighteenth century.[11] Although not much is known about the mechanical or financial arrangements for the hiring of private tutors, anecdotal evidence suggests that they played an important if numerically limited role in advancing literacy and education in general. They appear in the autobiographical literature as generally positive figures but given that their educational style and subject matter frequently diverged from that of the all-conquering state school, they represent a connection to a disappearing world. This is especially true insofar as they are remembered across the Ottoman-to-Republican divide. In the changing atmosphere of the new state they are recalled, sometimes painfully, sometimes fondly, as belonging to a different time and an alternative ambience, usually linked to the Perso-Islamic tradition that was so heartily disparaged in the Republican period.

Whether introduced into by a family member or a privately hired tutor, the old world of learning and culture was giving way to a new educational dispensation. Western influence was strong in the new arrangements, but not always decisive. Local desiderata and agenda, whether Ottoman or Republican, were frequently sufficient to dislodge the imported notions, curricula and administrative framework. What does seem to have been appropriated from the West, beginning in the late Ottoman era but picking up intensity in the Republican, was the generally pejorative approach toward the old ways of teaching and, more important, the purpose behind the old-style education. What emerges clearly from the autobiographical literature is inadvertent confirmation of something Dale Eickelman noticed some time ago, namely, that the Western approach was little prepared to appreciate the Islamic system of learning.[12] Its orality, its insistence on direct transmission from teacher to student and its interlinking curriculum all stood in contrast with the ideal form of the modern educational analog. More important than these, however, was the changed conception of the very purpose of education in the first place. The religiously based system performed a number of functions, including training a scribal and bureaucratic elite, providing a measure of upward mobility but it was ultimately predicated on the notion of preparing Muslims for the afterlife. Acquiring skills such as reading and grammar were subservient to a greater theological undertaking centered on learning the Qur'an, committing it to memory if possible. By contrast, the new dispensation was aiming to produce literate, functional graduates who would serve first the empire and then the nation as bureaucrats or leaders in other fields. An instrumental version of morality was seen as a useful adjunct to this greater cause. As such it was altered to fit the political imperatives of the time, appearing in a more Islamic guise in the Ottoman period but adopting a more national dimension in the Republican era.

The new dispensation absorbed many aspects of the old but jettisoned many others. A number of the memoirs from children educated in this period reveal a wistfulness and even a nostalgia for some of aspects of the old ways that were lost in the rush to adopt the new. One dimension of this lost world concerns the religious nature of learning. For all of its having been vilified by the secular republic, the old Qur'an school, the sing-song quality of learning by rote, and even the turbaned hoca himself, to whom I return shortly, come in for some fond remembrances. Another aspect of these memories was the link with the Perso-Islamic past. Poetry is critical here, as is a fondness for the Persian language. Although in the late Ottoman period Persian was taught in the state schools, acting as a sort of semi-indigenous counterweight to French,[13] it quickly disappeared in the Republican era. Yet its appeal remained vivid in the minds of many who made their mark in Republican times. While some were happy to abandon Persian, others were more equivocal. For many who were students during the late Ottoman period, Persian language and literature provided a life-long source of pleasure and meaning. For some this affinity seems to have been produced by the relative ease of Persian grammar as compared with that of Arabic. But even Arabic, frequently mentioned as a source of consternation and, by some, irrelevance, could occasion a twinge of nostalgia by someone like Tevfik Sağlam (1882–1963), a military doctor who would as professor of medicine in Istanbul lead the campaign against tuberculosis in Turkey, who was otherwise fairly dismissive of the old curriculum. But if Arabic could engender some wistfulness, Persian, particularly its poetry, produced much more in the way of affection. Some of this attraction was doubtless due to the fact that Ottoman students generally considered Persian grammar easier to learn than Arabic. But it was also the richness of the Persian poetic tradition and its special place in the poly-lingual schema of Islamicate literature that ensured that it continued to hold sway in late Ottoman and even early Republican cultural life.[14]

If the private tutor – and the lost educational world which he represented – was relatively rare and variously remembered, the second type of pedagogue is a much more unambiguous figure. This was the Qur'an school teacher drawn from the ranks of the ulema. The children's reading material of the late Ottoman period rarely singled him out for special attention. In fact many of the publications from this period simply refer to the teacher, any teacher, whether a member of the ulema or civil officialdom, by the same term, "hoca." In the absence of illustrations, which become more frequent with the passage of time, or specific information about the schools concerned, it is usually impossible to discern the type of school referred to in these children's texts. With time the chance that it was a state school naturally increased. The lack of attention paid to the turbaned hoca doubtless stems from the fact that the ulema were very much part of the educational scene in this period. Both the rapid expansion of state schooling and the emphasis on morality and Islamic education in the curriculum of these new schools meant that members of the ulema were heavily represented in both the state sector as well as in the more traditional Qur'an schools and medreses.[15] Thus one encounters pictures of teachers from the ulema in photographs (see, e.g., the cover photograph of my *Imperial Classroom*) and their names appear prominently on staff lists pertaining to a wide variety of schools in this period, as well as in the commissions used to vet and alter the curriculum of the state schools. In the autobiographical literature these figures were both loved and feared. Many memoirs recall the apprehension associated with being enrolled in a mekteb, at least initially. The well-known phrase with which children were handed over to the hoca – His flesh is yours but his bones are mine (*Eti senin, kemiği benim*) – surely did not help settle first-day nerves. But a combination of peer and economic pressure almost invariably won out. Ahmed Emin [Yalman] (1888–1972) recalls that his fear of entering school was met by his family's threatening that without schooling he would become a lowly porter. As a result he began to identify with this humble profession until he entered school and realized it wasn't as bad as he had feared.[16]

In time the ulema would be turned into figures of ridicule. The hoca, or local member of the ulema, occupies a particular niche in the later literature of the period, becoming something of a stock figure representing the negative aspects of the old ways. This was not a new trope – the stock character of the mean teacher pre-existed the modern era – but it acquired an important new ideological and political edge in the modern period. Almost universally reviled as strict, corrupt, cruel, frequently overweight and sometimes even barely literate, he is associated with the backward, unhealthy and outmoded pedagogy from which the young were meant to be rescued by the new dispensation of state education.[17] What is interesting is that this vilification should have begun prior to the founding of the secular republic and the radical rejection of organized Islam in many areas of life, including perhaps most prominently in the field of education. We can find signs of this shift as early as the World War I years. One example comes in the Ömer Seyfettin's story *"Falaka"* (The bastinado), named after the device used to hold the feet in place while the soles were beaten. A member of the group of young nationalist writers heavily influenced by the Libyan and Balkan wars, Ömer Seyfettin (1888–1920) was one of the main movers behind the journal *Genç Kalemler* (The Young Pens) which, as we have seen in the previous chapter, was instrumental in injecting a stridently nationalist tone into the literature of the very late Ottoman period. This story, published in *Yeni Mecmua* (The New Journal) in 1917, was probably not intended for young readers but it is important both because it purports to be autobiographical and because it sets the tone for the treatment of the hoca that would play such an instrumental role in the children's fiction of the early Republican period.

Ömer Seyfettin's *"Falaka"* presents the hoca as tyrannical and archaic. The story introduces him first through his donkey whose presence served to announce to the narrator and his school mates that Hoca Efendi was present, then through his *rahle*, or low, folding reading stand, and finally through the dreaded bastinado of the title. This device hung menacingly on the wall.[18] The hoca himself is described as tall and having a white beard, with sleeves rolled up and his lower legs exposed, and not wearing a robe in either winter or summer. This bumpkin-like appearance serves to enhance the contrast with the local civil official, described as clean-shaven and wearing striped trousers. This heroic figure, fully representative of modernity, eventually intervenes to put an end to the beatings, and to the hoca's career, after the narrator tricks the teacher into beating his donkey with the bastinado in full view of the civil official and his retinue.

Corporal punishment would continue to dominate the image of the old-school hoca, especially in those publications intended for young readers during the early years of the Turkish Republic. An arresting example is found in Ahmed Rasım's 1926 reader entitled *Doğru usul-i kıraat* (The true principles of reading). The entry entitled "Physical punishment in the old schools" (*Eski mekteplerde dayak*) provides a graphic example of the depictions of violence allegedly perpetrated against children in the religious schools.[19] The story is accompanied by an illustration of a turbaned hoca about to beat the soles of a student who is held down by another similarly dressed hoca as two boys peer meekly from behind a crumbling wall.

The story turns on the adventure of a boy who is fond of truancy, reveling in his independence by playing all day long. One day he is caught and slapped on the back of his neck by the school monitor (*kalfa*), causing the boy to fall flat on his face. The main action focuses on the physicality of this confrontation that causes his face to flow with blood. Interestingly the story avoids describing the subsequent bastinado treatment he receives at the hands of the *kalfa* back at the school, leaving it to the reader's imagination, but the reader is treated to a graphic description of the protagonist's bruised and bloody feet. The story ends with the boy's mother in tears and the boy vowing never to return to that school. Interestingly the text never seems to blame the child for having skipped school, perhaps considering this justifiable in the face of the central physical horror meted out in such institutions.

The same author's fictional *Falaka* (The bastinado) of 1927 describes itself as an attempt to help "today's youth" understand these olden times.[20] But it really served to present them with an image of the old-style education as deeply frightening. The fear of the hoca (*hoca korkusu*), however tinged with a modicum of grudging respect, is the overwhelming message this tale imparts. This is a time of bogeys, peris and jinns but it is the hoca's stick that seems calculated to hold the young reader's attention.

An equally grim description of the old educational methods appears in a story by the well-known writer Ömer Seyfettin. Included in Sadrettin Celal's 1928 *Sevimli Kıraat*, this story is called *"Eski mektepler kan kardeşi"* (The old schools: the blood brother). The only unusual feature is the fact that the head teacher is a woman and the assistant is her simpleton son. This nepotistic arrangement is in keeping with the characterization of the religious schooling as backward, corrupt and generally unhealthy. But the most prominent feature of this story, particularly in the eyes of the imagined child reader, is the emphasis on corporal punishment. As if warned by the graphic descriptions of and the effects caused by the beating given to the protagonist in *"Eski mekteplerde dayak"* (Physical punishment in the old schools) in Ahmed Rasım's reader, it is the fear of the teacher's physical beatings around which the action turns.

In the dimly lit room of un-whitewashed walls, amid incessant noise of children repeating their lessons in this story, one fear pervades: "At school there was only one punishment: the beating."[21] For major offenses, the punishment was the bastinado; "There was no one who did not fear or quake because of it." Lesser offenses were dealt with arbitrarily, either by the heavy blows of the assistant or those of the "head teacher's long stick, sure to cause swelling on whichever head it fell."

The narrator of this story was, he says, spared these blows but fell victim, unjustly of course, to being falsely accused of lying and having his ear pulled so hard that it still hurt the next day.[22] The rest of the story concerns the two children's pact to come to each other's aid in the face of the tyrannical and arbitrary teacher's blows.

Corporal punishment was just one facet of the physicality of traditional communal education that was presented as something to disdain as well as to fear. Crowded, dimly lit and airless, the old schools were characterized as primitive, even barbaric. What learning took place here, these depictions suggest, did so in spite of the worryingly sensual rocking back and forth of the children in their crowded classes and the incessant din of the children shouting, or according to one representation, screaming their lessons. The *kuttab*, or Qur'an school, is generally associated with dimness, both that of the hoca himself and of the physical interior of the schoolroom. The fact that these schools were frequently situated in or adjacent to a mosque naturally did not lend to their positive treatment in the radical laicism of the early republic. In this respect the Kemalist pedagogues shared a similar impulse with the British authorities in Egypt who were attempting to reform a similar educational scene.[23] Both groups looked at traditional style of education as retrograde, crooked, overly sensual – too much rocking back and forth, chanting and physical contact – and essentially non-modern. What they wanted instead was schooling that consisted of an orderly and quiet process that would take place in a purpose-built environment quite distinct from that of organized religion. Ironically, as we shall see in Chapter 4 when we discuss reading techniques, many of the problems associated with the old-style schoolroom continued to haunt the new education in spite of the authorities' best efforts at a modernizing transformation.

In the competition between the old-style schools and the new that was taking place in the pages of children's reading materials, the winner was hardly in doubt. The modern school had the advantage of state initiative and state finance, which would operate as constants throughout the period from the mid-1880s onwards. It therefore also controlled the discussion and could portray the old schooling as outmoded and moribund in the reading materials disseminated to the students. The old schools of course were unable to compete by responding in kind. The state school, representing itself as novel, ordered, structured and "modern," therefore found it useful to produce and disseminate its own almost universally pejorative depictions of religious education which it labeled as "old" (e.g., "*Eski mektepte dayak*") even though the "old" schools continued to exist side by side with the newer state schools. Since in essence it controlled the means of constructing the discourse, it generated positive images of itself, and put out some fairly gratuitous attempts to ingratiate its style of schooling with students, as we have already seen. (This control was never total, however. In Chapter 4 we shall see how the expanding publishing field allowed occasional space for satirical treatment of state education.)

The representation of the traditional Islamic school and the domineering hoca served as a negative example to the children of the early Republican period. This almost overwhelmingly pejorative and fear-inducing depiction of the old-style education seems calculated to make the young readers appreciate the new dispensation. Like many of the other contrasting sets of images presented to child readers, the difference between the old school and the new was blissfully unambiguous. That this contrasting presentation itself differed from the way the transition from old to new was remembered in the autobiographical literature, where a considerably more nuanced assessment can be seen,[24] is further testament to the strength of the desire to distinguish the new Republican education from the Ottoman.

By contrast the depiction of the new state schools and their teachers was overwhelmingly, sometimes ludicrously, positive. Consider the treatment given to a fictional schoolteacher in a Republican school reader published in 1928. Published just after the alphabet change, the new book reflects certain problems of adjustment. There are difficulties with new alphabet, liberal use of curiously placed hyphens, misspellings, instances of odd orthography here and there, even on the title page, and a slew of other inconsistencies. The lead item in this textbook, entitled An Enjoyable Reader for Republican Children, is called "The New Teacher" (*Yeni Muâllim*).[25] The story is preceded by an illustration clearly taken from a Western publication – it is signed by someone named Carsly – that depicts the protagonist as resembling a movie star sent straight from central casting. He is clean-shaven, short-haired, sporting a double-breasted suit and a dark tie. His fedora, icon of the Kemalist re-branding of Turkey as western, rests on the corner of his desk next to a globe. His pose, with one hand in his pocket and the other extending to make a point with his index finger, exudes confidence and, above all, modernity.

In contrast to the physical punishment and cruelty of the turbaned hoca in the mekteb, the New Teacher relies on the gravitas of his good will, his love for his students and his newly anointed role. Unlike the feared figure of the hoca, his modern replacement strives to win the

Figure 2.1   The new-style teacher

children's respect by appealing to their affections. Indeed, in this example, he wants to be accepted as a surrogate father. He tells his pupils
that, having recently lost his mother and having no other family, "I
want you to be my children ... I don't want to punish anyone. (*İstiyor-um*
(sic) *ki siz benim evlatlarım olasınız ... Ben kimseye cezâ vermek istemem*).[26]
On one level this characterization represents perhaps the authorities'
ultimate wish for the development of the relationship between family
and school, a subject to which I return in the next chapter. Not only
have the children been drawn away from the family, always somewhat
suspect in the mind of the educational authorities, whether Ottoman
or Republican, and inculcated with the values of the state schooling
system, but they have also been presented in the form of the modern
teacher with a seemingly perfect representation of modern pedagogy
who doubles as an eminently suitable father figure. In this vision, the
replacement of the family by the state is treated as natural, almost
effortless, in spite of its worrying, perhaps even Oedipal, implications.

If texts such as these presented the teacher as idealized and seemingly perfect, they were nevertheless put in the shade by the dazzling oratory lavished on praising the school itself, a trend that emerged rather robustly in the late Ottoman era. Consider the first verse of the poem entitled simply "The School," which appeared in a children's magazine in the 1890s:

> Wellspring of prosperity and giving is the school
> Manifestation of the light of enjoyment is the school
> An obvious light descended from the heavens
> A migrant to the eye of the heart is the school
> Giving light to the horizons of progress
> A gift of radiant sun is the school.[27]

Attempts to forge links between school and nation did not suddenly appear with the founding of the Turkish Republic. In the late Ottoman period we find examples of attempts to project identification between the school and the "nation," the students and the citizenry, and again, the recurring tension between parents and the educational authorities. Consider an entry from Ahmed Rasım's *İbtidaî kıraat* (Primary reader), called simply "The school." Accompanied by a simple sketch of schoolboys entering a school in uniform and with their books, the selection is divided into four sections:

1. The school is a very small nation (*vatan*). At school there are very small friends. These are the nation's siblings. The one who loves the nation, both loves his home and his nation.
2. The good school friend is like a sibling (literally, *ana, baba bir kardeş demek dir*). How many siblings does he/she gain, the one who gets along with his/her friends at school!
3. The teacher is more beloved than the mother or the father. This is because he works for your wellbeing. He who loves his teacher both loves him and grows to love his nation.
4. The mountains, seas, regions, plains, houses, buildings, barracks, orchards, gardens, lakes all belong to the nation. Like you they are the property of those who love and serve the nation.[28]

Although less specific and less deterministic than the Republican efforts at nation building, the Ottoman attempts nevertheless constituted a clear precursor. The projection of loving feelings onto the school was, if possible, intensified still further during the Republican period through the use of more concrete and specific images of schools populated with fictional teachers and students. Sandwiched between two entries depicting idealized schools, following the story of The New Teacher discussed above and preceding an entry describing the funeral of a much loved, female teacher who sacrificed so much for her students,[29] comes a poem called *"Mahallebim ve Mektebim"* (My pudding and my school) by no less a figure than the celebrated Turkish author Tevfik Fikret.[30] The entry is preceded by a simple shaded illustration of a young girl with bobbed hair and wearing a collared school uniform. The girl is pictured sitting in a chair at a table on which rest a pile of books and a vase of flowers, and appears to be concentrating intently on the open book she holds in her hands. The simple poem begins with a few lines of dialogue between a girl named Şermin and her grandmother, related by the girl in the first person singular.

> My grandmother asked: – Şermin whom do
> Love very much? – Her, my grandmother!
> – Who else? – My father without doubt
> – Besides? – If you let me,
> I'll list them: my milk pudding (*mahallebi*)
> My rice pudding (*sütlaç*), my candy,
> All of my sweets.
> I also like ring-shaped rolls (*gevrek*) a little...
> But most of all I love my school,
> My school I love very much
> Beautiful building!
> What things it teaches me.[31]

The child goes on to list the various things she has already learned in her mere one week of attending this marvelous institution. The list is comprised mainly of fairly predictable geographical material: the continents, the old world and the new, the seas and so on. But the poem also points to three important facets of the school-based pedagogy being lionized. First, is the importance of the textbook – Şermin explicitly mentions having her own copy – in imparting the lessons. Secondly, the poem depicts the teacher in the role of working in tandem with the textbook, reinforcing and elaborating on its contents. Şermin says that she examined and learned the names of the continents in her own textbook (*kendim kitabım*) and that her teacher had discussed several of the oceans that day in class and that she could list them from memory (*ezberimden*). Thus, thirdly, we see the great importance attached to memorization by heart. "Today I learn the lesson, in the evening I'll prepare it. Tomorrow at school, listen. If I don't know them all perfectly, you can have my pudding. My school will suffice for me." Overlooking the extreme unlikelihood of a child's forgoing sweets for the sake of school, no matter how well liked, this example typifies the projection of optimistic pedagogical ideals into the minds of the young. This ventriloquism attempted to affect a light touch but the seriousness of the intent is difficult to escape.

Equally cloying is a fairly typical item found in a Republican reader from the early 1940s. It is written in the form of a letter devoted to the school that the child will be missing terribly over his summer vacation![32] "Dear School," it begins, "We are parting. There are tears in our eyes and a strange feeling of sorrow in our hearts ..."

The new school was built up to be the unquestioned repository of learning and authority, but it was also, like the New Teacher, idealized as something to be loved instead of feared. Further on we will encounter various means used to induce this sort of loving response among children, some of which were also adopted by the publishing industry, but it bears stating here, at the risk of repetition, that the school was at the center of the overwhelming majority of representational strategies depicting reading or learning to read in some way during this period. The almost complete lack of alternatives to school-based literacy is remarkable, and perhaps best explained by the attention lavished on educational expansion in both the late Ottoman and early Republican periods.

Children's magazines paid considerable attention to the modern school – usually in a supportive role but not always – largely because school was increasingly the one common denominator that almost all reading children shared. Indeed some children's magazines justified their existence in terms of being able to assist with and augment the learning that was taking place at school. The first issue of *Çocuklara Kıraat* (The Children's Reader), founded in 1883, states that the suggestion for the founding of the magazine itself came from "one of your teachers," and promised to keep children busy during their holidays with "puzzles and questions written for the lessons in your curriculum."[33] Even the entertainments provided by the newly emergent children's periodical literature allied themselves with the schooling endeavor.

Textbooks and magazines

So far this chapter has discussed the range of contexts in which reading was represented. Whether in the milieu of the family, the private tutor or of formal schooling, either traditional or modern, the emphasis was firmly on getting children to read. The rest of this chapter is devoted to an overview of the types of text were they being encouraged to read, and the different modes of reading that were being modeled for young readers. As is clear from the preceding discussion, it is difficult if not impossible to escape the realm of the school, and by extension the apparatus of the centralizing state that conceived and supported it, so central was that institution to the world of reading. Even when we consider the use of satire, as we shall see later, the school is front and center. And yet it is just possible to discern other worlds and other modes of reading that remained aloof from the world of officially organized efforts at promoting reading and literacy.

Reading as represented in the literature produced for children in the late Ottoman and early Turkish Republican periods emphasized, as we have seen, the formal educational context. The school, whether the old-style domain of the Qur'an, hoca and mosque complex or the newly sanctioned preserve of the civil official, the centralized curriculum and the purpose-built space, was at the center of efforts to model the correct environment for learning to read. In particular, children were encouraged to think of formal educational instruction as necessary and superior to what could be achieved at home. While the energies of the state authorities were thus marshaled to funnel children's reading efforts from a domestic to an institutional context, there was nevertheless, as we shall see below, a world of reading that persisted outside of and in some senses contrary to the officially sanctioned context.

If the school was the engine of literacy growth, then the textbook can be said to have provided the fuel. The textbook was a fitting symbol of the state educational impetus. Written to conform to a particular course sanctioned by the Education Ministry, subject to the approval of the censors, the textbook accorded with the state's wish to create a unified – and unifying – educational dispensation. Much like the perhaps apocryphal story of the French minister proudly reporting to Napoleon that at a certain hour he could be sure that all the pupils of the nation would be studying the same lesson, both late Ottoman and early Republican educationalists showed a keen desire to implement a thoroughly integrated and synchronized school system. Thus the textbook, paradoxically individualized yet conformist, stands for both the rigid organizational control of state schooling as well as its emphasis on the participation of students as individuals and not as a group that memorized and repeated its lessons in unison.

The textbooks cover a wide variety of topics, ranging from those which taught the alphabet to those that instruct the reader on the intricacies of the correct form of address to be used when corresponding with a wide range of government officials and other necessary information for future bureaucrats to such subjects as morality, history and mathematics that would be useful to any member of the educated public. The range and number of the textbooks produced in the late Ottoman and early Republican period provide a fair indication of the ability of the new state educational system to generate a market for reading materials. This market linked together both the consumers of the new reading matter and those who produced it. As we shall see in Chapter 6, the new growth area in publishing that they represented also can be seen to have affected the career trajectories – as well as the bank balances – of more than a few authors.

More significant than their textbooks' variety, their numbers, or even the extent to which they helped to create a market for young readers, was their capacity to push certain agendas deemed necessary to the creation of a modern society, first Ottoman and then Turkish Republican. As we shall see in more detail in Chapter 3, through the ways in which they addressed their readers, depicted the model child, family and teacher, illustrated them with respect to dress, hairstyle and physical posture, and most obviously in the cultural and political referents deployed in the lessons and readings they contained, the textbooks of this period were freighted with enormous political and cultural moment.[34]

While the magazines intended for children diverged from the much more predictable textbooks in a number of ways, to which we shall return shortly, it has to be said that there were also considerable areas of overlap. Both genres seem to have been hungry for copy and there are similarities to be found in terms of content – the didactically minded story featuring a clear-cut contrast between good and bad was a continual feature of both – with respect to the pool of authors from whom contributions were chosen, and in the way that the young readers were frequently addressed.

But beyond those basic similarities, the magazines departed from the much more predictable schoolroom fare in a number of important ways. If the textbooks were systematically branching out into new fields, it was the children's journals that demonstrated much more emphatically the liveliness and eclecticism of children's reading in this period. Beyond the school there lay another world, peopled by an array of new publications and bristling with energy, varied agendas and, frankly speaking, the profit motive. Beginning in the late Ottoman period there was a flood of new publications. Most of these were intended for adult audiences but those that were aimed at the emerging market for children's publication were nevertheless impressive in both number and range of activity. The first children's magazine in Ottoman Turkish appeared in 1869. The numbers increased dramatically first during the 1880s in response to the burst of school expansion during the Hamidian period and then again with the lifting of press restrictions after the Young Turk revolution of 1908. Between 1869 and the language law of 1928, no less than fifty Turkish-language periodicals for children appeared in the Ottoman Empire.[35] The rapid growth of a children's periodical press was underpinned by a confluence of factors, including the cumulative effects of the expansion of primary education, which produced unprecedented numbers of new readers as well as a growing list of educators-cum-authors who were eager to write for this market, the technological advances that made publishing low-priced and increasingly well-illustrated copy not only feasible but financially attractive, and the spread of the idea that childhood was a distinct phase of human life that warranted a dedicated attention as distinct from that of adulthood.

The overall trend in the publishing industry in this period is one of simultaneous expansion and specialization. New publications appeared to cater to an increasingly diverse readership. Publications for women, children, nationalists, the religiously oriented, professional groups and so on began to appear, quickly transforming the world of periodical publication from one centered around politics and finance to one that was increasingly varied.

Alongside the textbook, the children's magazine served as the other workhorse for children's literacy. Some periodicals were linked with officialdom, that is to say, with the patronage of important officials or even the sultan or president himself, with pedagogical initiatives emanating from the top of the pyramid of the educational hierarchy. But others exhibit an independent spirit from the very beginning. As we shall see in Chapter 5, the official line on education and the "goody goody" image relentlessly modeled in the pages of textbooks and many periodicals alike proved irresistible for the satirically minded authors and editors of some children's works. The resulting parodies were distinctly, even jarringly, at odds with the official script.

There were other things to read of course, and we cannot assume that children were content to read what was published expressly as "children's literature." Halide Edip was not be the only child of the period to have wanted to read "grown-up" literature. The fact that such collections as the History of the Prophets (*Kisas-ı enbiya*) were perennially in print suggests that it would be a mistake to try to categorize certain types of stories as pertaining only to a particular subset of readers.

Indeed, the most popular writer of the late Ottoman period, the wildly prolific Ahmed Midhat Efendi, was known for his extremely accessible prose. As his subject matter frequently included children and his writing was known for its uncomplicated style, it is not unreasonable to surmise that his readers would have included both children and adults. Indeed the author of one of the most important reading primers addresses his text to children "from the age of seven or eight to fifteen and perhaps even twenty years of age," reflecting perhaps both the fluid state of literacy in the late Ottoman Empire and the mix of childish and grownup material his book contained. Where the barrier lies in literary terms is almost impossible to say. We need think only of the success of the Harry Potter books and other crossover phenomena in our own day to see the inherent blurriness of such a distinction.

But the linguistic and stylistic simplification that such blurring entailed were only one part of the broader trend toward increasing access to reading in this period. The new avenues affected both the supply and consumption of popular reading material. The expansion of the publishing industry and the profusion of new types of reading material that it generated meant that there were things to read to suit more and more abilities, tastes and budgets. Magazines as a group were one of the most important expressions of this popularizing trend and we shall return to them shortly. For the moment we should also consider the other genres, such as the novel, the short story, popular tales with religious and folkloric origins, the pamphlet, poetry, etc. Simply put, the range of reading materials was rapidly expanding, and the publishing houses that produced this growing stream of printed material were booming. Equally important was the fact that the range of materials on offer increasingly targeted not only the edification and improvement of the reader but also his (and increasingly her) entertainment.

Not surprisingly the physical and social arenas in which reading could take place were conspicuously expanding. From roughly the middle of the nineteenth century the Ottoman lands produced a profusion of new associations and locales dedicated to reading. Just as had happened somewhat earlier in Western Europe, a network of libraries, clubs, associations, circles, cafés and reading rooms sprouted up across the provinces of the empire.[36] The possibilities for reading were opening up on an unprecedented scale. Having been initiated by the state but quickly surpassing what even the rapidly aggrandizing state could sustain, the expansion of reading was developing a life of its own. The spread of public education, the publishing industry, the appearance of new physical spaces intended for reading and the varied modes of access to printed texts together produced an interlinked web of institutions, associations and arrangements dedicated to the act of reading an increasingly diverse array of materials.

This new dispensation is clearly reflected in the eclecticism of the privately produced periodical literature produced for young readers in this period. The varied nature of the magazine offerings stands in direct contrast to the much more predictable textbooks associated with the state. If we were to select almost any late Ottoman children's journal and note the references made to the provenance of stories, poems, history lessons and news items featured in its pages, we would soon have a long and varied list. To take an example from the late Ottoman period first, we might choose the standard-bearer children's journal, the *Çocuklara Mahsus Gazete* (The children's own gazette). Published between 1896 and 1908, it appears, like its sister publication *Hanımlara Mahsus Gazete* (The ladies' own gazette) to have enjoyed imperial patronage. Expensively published, certainly by comparison with some of the more usual, inexpensively produced contemporaries, it set a certain standard for other publications of this ilk.

Consider some of the referents to be found on only the first page of a particular issue.[37] The lead story seems to take place in an undefined period of early Islamic history, judging by the name of the protagonist, a certain Malik ibn Dinar whose encounter with a small child seems to have merited its inclusion. Then there is a reference to the Prophet Muhammad's advice to greet all, whether large or small. Next there is an illustration of children in Germany fording a river in a horse-drawn cart. News from Brussels and Japan occupies a nearby column. An illustration of an orphanage in San Francisco appears on the same page, as do instructions for eating at table in the *alafranga*, or Western, mode. And all of this occurs alongside the more conventional fare, for example, lessons on correct moral behavior, the necessity of hard work, the importance of the family and so on. In short, what we have is an extremely eclectic mixture of referents, conjuring up places and time periods both near and far. What this mélange suggests is that the publishers considered it both appropriate and necessary to expose their young readers to the wider world. But the persistence of local or indigenous referents (as well as the inclusion of material from East Asia) and a historically informed sense of propriety insured that these horizons were not being expanded simply to promote foreign, and especially Western, tastes or fashion.

An example from a slightly later period reveals a similar array of referents. *Çocuk Dünyası* (The child's world) appeared from 1913 to 1926 and thus spanned the Young Turk and early Republican periods. A glance at some of the material it presented to its young readers conveys a similar eclecticism to that offered by *Çocuklara Mahsus Gazete*. References to the Old Testament, the Abbasid Caliph Harun al-Rashid, the *Thousand and One Nights* stand alongside pieces covering the legend of the Japanese warrior Oeyama, references to Goethe, Tolstoy, William Tell, the Wright brothers and first airplane. But Ottoman referents are not forgotten. Here are Ahmed Midhat Efendi, Ziya Gökalp and Mehmed Emin. "National stories" (*millî masal*) appear, as does correspondence from readers in Baku, Kazan and Bulgaria. The main difference to note here is the nationalist turn that we encountered in our discussion of the Ottoman-to-Republican transition in Chapter 1. The inclusion of some of the more nationalist writers, Gökalp, Mehmed Emin, alongside the more distinctly Ottoman voices such as Ahmed Midhat Efendi, and the appearance of some more national and even pan-Turkist references in the form of letters from Azerbaijan, Kazan and Bulgaria indicate a growing concern with Turkishness.

What stands out in these magazines, and we could easily draw on a wide number of other examples, is the mixture of references. Whether in terms of chronology, geography, genre or degree of politicization and seriousness, the variety is quite extraordinary. The overall message that these journals were imparting was that reading represented the broadening of horizons. They addressed many of the same topics that the school texts did, to be sure, but they went much further, sometimes even taking up extremely risky political subjects. For example, readers of *Resimli Mecmua* (The illustrated journal) presented its readers with a sketch of Şeyh Said in the dock while on trial for his role in the single most explosive anti-Kemalist movement of the young Republic, the Şeyh Said rebellion of 1925.[38] In a way that the staid and relatively timid textbooks could never attempt, the periodical literature presented itself – and increasingly sold itself – as a window to the wider world. Reading in general, and reading this journal in particular, they seem to say to their prospective young readers, is your ticket to participation, perhaps membership, in a world that is far wider than the confines of your family, town and schoolroom.

Reinforcing the notion that reading meant entrée into and engagement with the wider world, many of the publications for children offered features intended to draw their readers in and to encourage their active participation. Dispensing with the top-down authoritarianism and relentless didacticism found in the textbooks, the publications featured puzzles, "post-box" sections encouraging submission of letters from their readers, and illustrations, including cartoons. Many journals encouraged their readers to send in photographs and frequently published pictures of groups of children as a result. We shall return to the dynamics – and the economics – of reader participation in Chapter 5, but it is fitting to mention the efforts to encourage children's active engagement here in the context of the ways in which reading was being represented to current and potential readers. Unlike the textbooks, the children's magazines used a visual liveliness to convey the sense that entering into the world of reading was informative, yes, but also dynamic and, entertaining.

In fact, the new children's periodical literature presented a considerable contrast to what was available in the textbooks. In both periods these tend to be heavily controlled, much less eclectic, more focused on certain key thematic goals, usually centering on the school, the importance of learning, patriotism, industriousness, morality and so on. The textbooks devoted much less attention to entertainment. Rather the goal was to instruct, impart and inveigh. While both Ottoman and Republican periods employed some well-known authors (e.g., Ahmed Rasım, Orhan Seyfi, Halid Ziya, Mehmed Âkif, Samih Rifat, Sadrettin Celal, Hamdullah Subhi, Mehmed Fuad Köprülü and Rıza Nur) the periodical literature was comparatively unburdened with a meliorative agenda, although that is certainly apparent across the genres and across the periodization covered here.

Modeling reading

Having seen many of the ways in which reading was represented and acquired a sense of the types of materials being offered to children in this period, we can now turn to the different modes of reading that were modeled for young readers. As Robert DeMaria's work on Samuel Johnson has shown, reading has many varieties.[39] Dr. Johnson himself liked to distinguish between these modes in describing his own varied approach to deciphering text. Not having a young Ottoman or Turkish Johnson to guide us through the modes of reading experienced in this period, we can nevertheless identify some important distinctions among the different representations of reading being offered to young readers in this period. First we can note the portrayal of reading as a physical activity. Numerous drawings, photographs and literary descriptions of the act of reading give us a clear sense of the varied physicality of reading. Chapter 4 will allow for a more detailed interpretation of these images, but for the time being they are useful in generating a taxonomy for the different forms that reading took. In school texts, reading is unsurprisingly presented as a task performed in a seated yet erect posture. Students are depicted as reading while seated in the ranked rows of schoolroom benches that came to supplant the more traditional position of sitting on the floor before the teacher. The physical requirement of the modern, or *alafranga*, lifestyle required that reading be lifted up off the floor and performed at desks and tables. Occasionally we see pictures of students standing up among, or sometimes besides, the desks to read aloud before the teacher and his class.[40]

A more relaxed stance was also presented in the form of children reading alone and for pleasure. Several of the children's magazines from

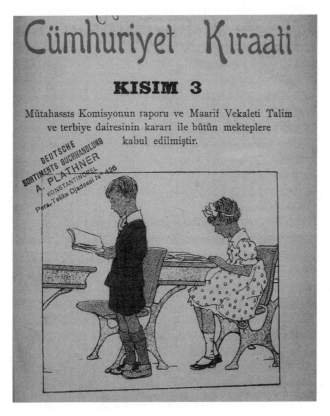

Figure 2.2   Standing to recite

this period featured prominent illustrations of children adopting a less upright, more comfortable position as they read. For example, the cover of the heavily illustrated *Haftalık Resimli Gazetemiz* (Our weekly illustrated gazette) from 1924 presented images of a boy and a girl each absorbed in reading (a magazine, naturally enough) in the upper left- and right-hand corners, on either side of the title. The boy is wearing a fez and a school uniform with a stiff-collared jacket and shorts while the girl has ribbons in her hair and is wearing a long-sleeved dress. Each is seated, apparently comfortably, in a reading chair with curved arms. The image given off is thus one of reading for pleasure, and the rest of the cover is given over to a central portrait of a child surrounded by ten medallions depicting scenes from around the world, e.g., the pyramids of Egypt, a Chinese junk under sail, elephants, a Pacific atoll, etc., so as to reinforce the message that reading was a ticket to the wider world.

Even more pleasure-filled are the descriptions of reading that take place in private, away from the schoolhouse, the seemingly endless proddings toward improvement, moral and otherwise, and the suggestion of the profit-motive of the magazine. Halide Edip's memoir provides us with what is perhaps the purest expression of a young child experiencing reading for sheer pleasure. Having told her readers that she "only lived when Ahmed Agha was reading stories" of the folk-heroic type to her as a young girl, Halide Edip subsequently describes her progress through various types of reading materials, each with its own attractions, difficulties and referents. Beginning with the Qur'an, she went on to read from her aunt's book of African travels, and then to encounter a variety of material, including a macabre story in a manuscript titled "The Adventures of Death."[41] Relatives and attendants read to her aloud from books and told her a variety of stories, indigenous as well as foreign. Each left its own imprint on the young Halide Edip.

Another Halide, Halide Nusret [Zorlutuna], whom we encountered briefly earlier in this chapter, describes the unalloyed pleasure she drew from reading. Like Halide Edip, Halide Nusret's initiation into the world of reading was her encounter with the Qur'an. She soon moved on to other, more secular-minded texts and eventually developed the same "addiction to reading" (*okuma tiryakisi*) that had taken hold of her mother.[42] Her mother encouraged her to read and memorize poetry – she mentions Namık Kemâl and Ziya Paşa in particular – but also says that one of her most pleasant childhood memories was reading the newspaper together with her mother.[43] We shall return to examine Halide Nusret's world of reading and writing in the final chapter but here it is important to stress her love, indeed her passion, for reading. One day after she had been sent to school and had imbibed the family's reading habit she describes returning home to find an unforgettable surprise. Her father had placed a book on each step of the staircase in the upper portion of their house. At the time she was surprised that her father, of whom she was rather awed, would have made such a remarkable gesture, but reflecting on it later she realized that for a child such as she who was crazed with her love of reading, there could not have been a better present.[44] This "crazy passion for reading" was a defining characteristic of her life and of her self-image.

The two Halides' experiences represent perhaps the epitome of private reading for reading's sake. But some texts, typically magazines, tried to bridge the gap between the regimented world of the school and the less structured world of children allowed to read on their own time. One such attempt was made by the children's journal *Yeni Yol* (The new path). It combined both concepts in one issue, featuring as story depicting children at school who were instructed to select some texts and read then for half an hour of individual effort. *Yeni Yol* modeled a half-way station between reading as a communal, classroom activity and reading as a home-based, private practice. The protagonists Orhan and Türkan are presented as each being able to choose a book that interests them (*kendilerini alakadar edecek birer kitap*) and then retiring to a corner to read on their own for half an hour.[45] The story that one of the boys chooses concerns space travel, a Jules Verne-like depiction of travel to the moon, and the discovery of a new celestial body.

This was a very different sort of reading from that normally practiced in the more disciplined environment of the school. It is distinguished by several factors that set it apart. It occurred in a separate physical space, often eliciting a different bodily stance. It was generally silent (but if aloud, for example in working out the sounds, it was performed alone, unattested by peers or figures of authority), and it tended to be self-directed. So we find reading represented as taking place away from the public eye: in the upstairs room of an aunt, over the breakfast table, in a nook of the house or under a tree. The retreat to a separate physical space was accompanied by a more relaxed and unrestrained physical posture. Stretching out with a book on the floor of a living room, reclining in a comfortable chair and, perhaps the ultimate voluptuary experience, reading in bed – all can be found in representations of reading in this period. Similarly we find reading increasingly represented as something children can do of their own volition and not out of duty. This reading is done silently, in one's own mind instead of being performed out loud in order to be judged by a teacher (whether the hoca of the kuttab or the state-supplied teacher of the new schools), one's fellow students or a parent. Thus reading is depicted very differently, at once something done in public spaces such as at school, in a stiff posture and from pre-selected texts. Equally apparent however is reading one one's own time, in a private space, relaxed and focused on a text of one's own choosing.

In other words, reading as an individual, and not a communal task, alone with one's book (or magazine, or novel) and one's thoughts, is juxtaposed alongside and in contrast to the collective, voluble and scrutinized type of reading called for in the schooling sector. Both forms of reading were important to the development of a modern society as we have come to know it but it is important to remember that they represent very different impulses. Individualized reading was critical to the development of modern, read individualistic, atomized society whereas collective reading was instrumental in forging the modern nation.

The individualized impulse should be seen both as an unusual, perhaps even paradoxical, response to the nineteenth-century version of globalization and the seemingly relentless eclecticism of new stimuli supplied by an ever diverse body of reading materials and as a natural reaction dictated by this very diversity. The response was at once both inward in orientation and individualized in attainment and directed outward in terms of its subject matter and the forging of links with the wider world, as expressed by Halide Edip's yearning to read about far-away Africa. This is the period, globally speaking, of a variety of self-reliance movements. We have the *Self Help* impetus of the influential Samuel Smiles,[46] the self-strengthening movement in China, and numerous other movements aimed at both individual and communal or national revivification. Ostensibly projecting a back-to-basics impulse, these movements were nevertheless inherently modern in the way that they responded to the phenomena of their time, in their organization and in the way that they utilized new technologies for the dissemination of their ideas and communication among their followers. Despite vast differences in geography, culture and economic conditions, peoples around the world were responding to the rapidly quickening pace of life, new inflows of information, products and influences, imperialist or otherwise, by attempting to regroup and marshal their existing resources in order to effect self-improvement, on the national, religious, societal and individual levels.

Naturally enough, there is a new preoccupation with the individual self at the center of this new world of reading. The state and to a lesser extent the publishing industry would try to impose their authority on this atomized readership, urging them into collectives, none greater than the nation, but the pull of readership as internalized and independent would pose a constant and perhaps ultimately indomitable force.

This chapter has described the various ways in which children's reading was represented in late Ottoman and early Turkish Republican society. It has tried to show that reading was presented as a varied phenomenon, projected differently in different contexts and for different purposes. The taxonomy of the ways in which reading was represented has been useful in order to underscore the various faces of reading being offered to potential readers and those already initiated into the growing ranks of the literate. But more important than a mere catalogue of the guises of reading is what they tell us about the various agendas with which the practice of reading was invested in this period. For it is clear that reading always meant more than the mere deciphering of letters and words. Children's reading was freighted with tremendous import, reflecting hopes – and fears – concerning the educational, religious, social, economic, political and cultural shape of that society. Indeed nothing less than the future direction of society was held to be at stake.

The attempts to influence young readers were sometimes overt and sometimes inchoate. In spite of the intentions of state officials, textbook writers and magazine publishers and in spite of the sharpening political agenda in the late Ottoman and early republican period, no single overriding agenda dominated in this reading material. From the child's perspective, the cumulative effect of this varied, indeed eclectic mélange of ideas, lessons, stories and images must have frequently appeared baffling. Puzzlement derived not just from the disparate provenance and content of the material confronting young readers in the aggregate, but also from the tensions inherent in society that were making themselves felt in the individual books and magazines themselves. The tensions lurking behind the modeling and representation of reading were many. Reading was presented as both a physical activity and a mental one, as both an individualistic pursuit and as a collective enterprise, as a sacred task (whether in the name of religion or the newly emerging nation) and as an unabashedly profane endeavor. To read was something done both at school and at home, in public and in private. It was an activity was remarkable commercial ramifications, but also one that was portrayed as able to transport the reader beyond the mundane considerations of money and career. Literacy was thrust on the young as a ticket both to self-improvement and the melioration of society and country and to a world of diversion and entertainment, as both extremely (sometimes deadly) serious and as frivolously fun. The voice confronting the nascent readers alternated between the authoritative, delivering a nearly constant flow of didactic information and exhortation, to the nearly conspiratorial, luring the readers cum customers into a shared sense of belonging.

3
Context and Content

Pushing further in the direction of reading content and the messages that sustained the drive for literacy in the late Ottoman and early Republican periods, this chapter identifies four thematic tensions facing young readers. Each of these pairings – the religious and the secular; the family and the nation state; the new and the old and the global and the local – affords the opportunity to highlight the contrasts that played such a major role in establishing the didactic certainty prevalent in the children's literature of this period. At the same time these pairings also reveal the ambiguities that undermined these seemingly clearcut binaries against the background of the changes affecting the late Ottoman and early Republican periods. The chapter shows not only the range of genre, politicization, humor and geographical references on display in this rapidly expanding literature but also the extent to which readers' choices were beginning to be dictated as much by the market as by the pedagogical imperatives of officialdom, whether Ottoman or Republican. The shifting context surrounding the publication of reading materials intended for the young comes through clearly as the chapter examines each of these thematic categories in turn.

As with the types of reading encountered in the previous chapter, these categories are not airtight or mutually exclusive. Indeed there is often considerable overlap between them. For example, the tension between religion and laicism spills over into the discussions of the relationship between the family and the state and the new and the old. The purpose here is not to draw fixed lines of demarcation but rather to suggest the broad patterns of thematic continuity and disjuncture, unity and confusion that confronted the young readers of the Ottoman-to-Turkish transition. Nor are these categories meant to imply the sort of binary, either/or relationship that has formed such a strong part of the problematic modernization paradigm. These categories should be seen as spectrums along which various texts and the attitudes that underpin them can be placed. The examples taken from the materials presented here frequently adopt stances that confound and blur the binary view, revealing the complexities and contradictions inherent in learning to read in this period alongside the rather more obvious contrasts.

Late Ottoman and early Turkish Republican authors created an abundance of reading materials. The most common forms were the readers (*kıraat*), usually but not always produced for the state school system, and the children's periodicals offered up to the market by the private sector. The large numbers in which this literature was produced indicate the increasing supply of and demand for reading material in this period. Overall, most publications were intended for the adult market, which was thriving, especially in the Tanzimat years and afterwards. But a rapidly increasing number were written specifically for children, a relatively new development. Cüneyd Okay has identified over fifty children's periodicals produced in the old script alone.[1] A further index of the attention being lavished on this new genre is the active participation of a long list of many of the top literary and political figures of the period. Children's materials contained the writings of such figures as Ziya Gökalp, Mehmed Fuad Köprülü, Mehmed Emin, Ömer Seyfettin, Tevfik Fikret and Kâzım Karabekir, to name only a few. But the sheer size of this literature means that it has been necessary to be selective in this study. What makes this body of materials particular useful here is the broad time span they cover and the fact that many authors produced similar titles across one, two or even three decades. For example, Selim Sabit published texts for children over a period stretching from 1870–1913,[2] while Ahmed Cevad [Emre]'s publishing life reflects a remarkable shift from Ottoman Islam to Republican nationalism that took him from publishing late Ottoman texts intended to teach the reading of the Qur'an to writing republican texts that dovetailed with the Kemalist program. Almost all of these texts were locally written and published. Some of the readers contained selections appropriated from foreign sources from time to time – illustrations were borrowed more liberally, as we shall see in the next chapter – but outright translations from foreign books were relatively rare, marking a crucial difference between children's literature and that intended for adults where translations were commonplace.[3] These materials thus offer the opportunity both to witness the emergence of a Turkish children's literature and to appreciate the evolution of the political, social, economic and cultural forces affecting learning to read in this crucial and rapidly changing period. It also reveals the changes that were taking place in such related areas as the publishing industry, illustrations, dress, architecture, the language itself (not only alphabet change but also vocabulary and style), attitudes towards children, gender roles and an almost unending variety of similar topics.

The religious and the secular

The association of the Republic of Turkey with secularism and with reading is well ingrained. Thanks in large part to its attention to symbolic gestures, the Turkish Republic convinced both domestic and foreign audiences to accept that the new state was modern, non-religious and supportive of, if not directly responsible for, a range of social and economic trends that emphatically included literacy. Like many new regimes in the region, the young Turkish Republic promoted and indeed identified itself by denigrating the *ancien régime*. The resulting dichotomy pitted an outmoded, Islamically defined, fundamentally backward and illiterate Ottoman past against a new, secular, modernizing and literate Republican present. Despite, or rather because of its simplistic presentation, this characterization of the rather more complicated relationship between empire and republic proved exceedingly durable. It might be expected therefore that a study on learning to read that stretches across the Ottoman/Republican divide would be devoted in part to chronicling the ways in which the Republic ushered in the new era of secularism and literacy. Either sadly or happily, depending on your position, the record cannot support such an assumption. Although the Republic certainly did devote considerable energy and resources to expanding the ranks of the literate, it is also true that in doing so it benefited greatly from pre-existing Ottoman efforts in the same direction. These were less carefully scripted and in some senses not especially targeted efforts; as such they did not receive the attention and attract the association with the same sort of iconic images as the Kemalist program. Our understanding of the Ottoman period has been heavily conditioned by Republican desiderata. Nevertheless, when we look closely at the sorts of effort, the types of publications, and the role of both the state and private sectors, we cannot fail to detect remarkable similarities in both the late Ottoman and early Turkish Republican literacy campaigns. The question of continuity and change hangs over the issue of secularism and literacy.

The discussion of the religious and the secular with respect to both context and content must begin with a simple but frequently overlooked point: the late nineteenth and early twentieth centuries witnessed a series of remarkable changes affecting the process of learning to read and reading. To begin with, education was itself undergoing tremendous change. Indeed, the very point of education was practically being turned on its head. At least this is the traditional view, one that inevitably serves to accentuate the Westernizing, "modernizing" aspects of the transformation that would reconfigure the old empire into the new republic. As the previous chapters have shown, however, this story is rather incomplete and on occasion frankly misleading. Certainly many aspects of Ottoman society were changing, and education and the culture of reading was one of them; more and more state schools were being opened and the lessons taught in them came to resemble the mix of subjects familiar to students around the globe; teachers were increasingly drawn not from the ranks of the ulema but from new cadres of state officials trained for the express purpose of teaching in the new educational apparatus. Schooling was being made to prepare students for concerns in this world such as entry into the state bureaucracy or business and not, as had more nearly been the case in the past, to prepare their souls for salvation in the next.

And yet for all of the changes, there was also much continuity. The new state schooling broke from traditional education in a number of significant ways, but like similar modernizing efforts around the globe it also retained a prominent role for religion and a heavily religious version of morality. The purpose of building so many state schools was frequently conceived and expressed in explicitly religious language. This in part reflected the need to respond to religiously motivated educational challenges that took the form of foreign missionary activity, the proselytizing of neighboring states or the work of the empire's own minority groups. The institutions created by the late Ottoman state employed men from the pre-existing educational dispensation as ministry officials, teachers, attendants and, important for our story here, authors. Many of these were members of the ulema who were products of and frequently continued to work for the religiously organized educational institutions while they were engaged by the new, and supposedly radically different, system. What's more, the commissions appointed by the Sultan to oversee the detail of such critical decision-making as redrafting the curricula for the new state schools were frequently chaired by the highest ranking religious dignitary, the Şeyhülislam, and staffed by an equal number of religious and civil officials. Furthermore, the technology of print could as easily be used to generate "religious" titles as it could "secular" ones. Late Ottoman titles such as Guide to prayers, or the Question-and-answer catechism,[4] or The new alphabet: I'm reading the Qur'an,[5] reflect the adaptability of the new educational regime to suit either a religiously or a secularly minded educational dispensation. In other words, the "modern" education of the late Ottoman Empire was often far from "secular" in its conception, staffing, curriculum, publications and oversight. Conversely, the "secular" education of the Republic eventually came to dispense lesson content that was overtly Islamic in several key aspects. But these blurred edges have tended to be overlooked in the rush to discern the trend toward modernization, westernization and secularization. While the mixture of secular and religious influences in organized education remained an area of contestation – and remains so to this day in Turkey – there were other factors affecting reading and the environment in which it occurred that must be taken into account.

Language is one such factor. The Ottoman state system of education emphasized Turkish, logically enough considering that its primary motivation was to educate competent bureaucrats. But it also taught Arabic and Persian as well as French and a number of minority languages depending on the composition of the local population. This meant that quite apart from their experiences at home, children were learning to read in a variety of tongues and alphabets; the impact of such variety naturally differed according to individual taste, teachers and familial influence. Early experiences with reading different languages were often remembered in different ways as well, conditioned by the break up of the empire and the politicization of the question of language as a whole. But for most of the late Ottoman period, the primacy of Turkish among this linguistic variety – and therefore in this study – was a natural and altogether unremarkable feature of the Ottoman system. It was only when nationalist agitation converted the language question into a national one that the linguistic topography was radically altered. This was a process gradually gathering force behind the scenes in the Tanzimat and Hamidian periods, and then given particular energy in time of the Italian invasion of Libya, the Balkan Wars and especially World War I – decrees governing signs and foreign language reached nearly ludicrous proportions during wartime[6] – and culminating in the radical linguistic engineering project of the early Republican period.

The early Republic effected drastic linguistic change. The best-known example is the alphabet change inaugurated in 1928 and the larger "language revolution," as the Turkish phrase has it, which continued throughout the Kemalist period and afterwards.[7] But for many the most shocking innovation would have been the reading of a Turkish translation of the Qur'an for first time in 1932,[8] and the change in the call to prayer (*ezan*) from Arabic to Turkish that same year, however short-lived that switch ultimately proved to be before reverting back to Arabic. The extent to which these changes were profound or superficial is open to debate. Certainly diminution of the primacy of Arabic carried tremendous symbolic resonance, as did the separation of the younger generation from the literature of their forebears. On the other hand, a tendency to overestimate the effect of the "Turkish transformation" has also been noted.[9] Interestingly enough, the impetus for abandoning or at least curtailing the prominence of Arabic was given voice by those with a religious orientation *before* the Kemalist policies were put into effect. For example, the periodical *İslam Dünyası*, which addressed itself to students in the mektebs and the medreses, had already asserted the necessity of preaching in the vernacular in the late Ottoman period. Following the pragmatic example of the Russian Muslims, it called for abandoning the "useless reliance on Arabic" and found it pleasing that some mosques in Istanbul had recently begun preaching in both Arabic and Turkish.[10] Arguments based on the efficacy of language were clearly not limited to those advocating a secular or nationalist agenda.

Another factor affecting learning to read and reading was that of the physical environment. Frédéric Hitzel has made the important distinction between religious and secular places for reading.[11] The mosque complex, along with its Christian and Jewish counterparts, was clearly the epicenter of the religiously imbued reading environment, but religiously inflected reading was of course not limited to such officially sanctioned and public settings. Reading at home often began and continued in a religious vein. For Muslims the Qur'an naturally took pride of place in early reading. Religious stories in the vernacular language soon followed. Nevertheless, with the passage of time the possibilities for reading in the secular mode clearly increased. To the more or less standard secular options which included the libraries founded by Sultans, their wives, daughters and any number of high-ranking officials, would soon be added other public reading establishments, such as the reading rooms (*kıraathane*) where reading was not required to remain in a religious mode. Furthermore, cafés can be seen to have blurred the boundaries between religious and secular in the context of reading. Dr Rıza Nur (1879–1943) recalls the reading of semi-religious texts (e.g., Muhammadiye, Battal Gazi, etc.) in a clearly non-religious context but in "religious silence," in the cafés of Sinop on the Black Sea coast.[12] We shall return to discuss the role of such innovations as the reading room and the public library when we take up the thematic pairing of Old and New later in this chapter.

But for most children, learning to read and reading took place at home and at school. The religious or secular aspect of either setting varied widely, depending naturally enough on the individuals, institutions and traditions involved. The material children encountered when learning to read was naturally as varied as the educational offerings available. When approached in the broad sense the educational situation that obtained in the late nineteenth century Ottoman Empire can be viewed as something of a palimpsest. The oldest marks were those inscribed by the "traditional" institutions of learning provided by the various religious denominations. For the Muslim population this meant the Qur'an schools, or *mektebs*, generally attached to the local mosque, and then a range of higher institutions called *medreses* (*madrasahs* in Arabic) devoted to the Islamic sciences, and situated in the larger towns and cities. For the non-Muslim populations, there were parallel institutions, ranging from the simple to the advanced, all devoted to providing an ecclesiastically – or rabbinically – organized education. Beginning in the late eighteenth century a few new markings began to be laid down as the agenda of western-inspired modernization, dictated at first mainly by military concerns, appeared in the empire. This was followed by many more and much bolder markings in the nineteenth as the new educational competitors began to challenge these longstanding institutions. The new entrants appeared mainly in two forms, one foreign and the other domestic. The foreign schools were mainly those of the missionaries, inspired by millenarian zeal and the impetus to convert. While these had important repercussions across the Ottoman lands, their main effects were seen among the non-Muslim populations, some of whom experienced deep fissures as a result.

But it was the changes adopted by the Ottoman state that produced the more significant and long-term effects. The state had previously entered the field of education only insofar as it needed to train the small number of scribes who ran the affairs of state, estimated at about 2000 at the beginning of the nineteenth century. Following the expansion of the military and the adoption of Western military practices, a number of major – and expensive – changes followed, such as the need to expand tax revenues, to feed, clothe, house and educate the growing number of soldiers, the expansion of state authority into the provinces and so on. All of this required a massive increase in the size and versatility of the state bureaucracy. A conservative estimate of the number of men employed by the burgeoning central government by 1900 is

35,000, a massive jump in the course of a century.[13] A supply of well-qualified bureaucrats was now one of the Ottoman state's main needs, and schooling organized along Western European, especially French, lines was seen as the main vehicle for training them. The Qur'an schools and medreses were simply not considered up to the task. The remarkable expansion of public education that resulted in the Ottoman Empire meant that as the century progressed more and more children – or realistically speaking their parents – were faced with new schooling options. This was particularly apparent in the larger urban areas where traditional, modern and a variety of foreign-run schools existed in close proximity to one another. What's more, the state school curriculum was subject to frequent change, both as a result of officialdom's seemingly incessant desire to tinker and adjust course content and due to the shifting political agendas that accompanied the changes from the early nineteenth century to the Tanzimat, Hamidian, Young Turk and Republican periods.

All of this change made for considerable range and variety in the experience of early schooling and learning to read, and in the choice of texts in particular. The range of voices, attitudes and, generally speaking, the entire ambience associated with acquiring literacy was remarkably varied. As in the West, learning to read from Holy Scripture was common practice in the Ottoman Empire in the nineteenth century.[14] For all but the empire's native speakers of Arabic among the Muslim inhabitants this meant that the first efforts at learning to read took place in a language other than the mother tongue.[15] What is interesting about this bilingual practice is that it seems to have gone unquestioned for centuries. It was only with the advent of nationalist linguistic notions that demanded a one-to-one correlation between people and language and, naturally, the spread of secular and utilitarian thought, that sending a Turkish-speaking child to a school to read the Qur'an in the original Arabic – translations of the sacred text are frowned upon in Islam – began to be considered problematic. Even so, young Ottoman readers were soon provided with a variety of material in the vernacular languages. A good many of these can be labeled "secular" but many others, perhaps even the majority in the nineteenth century, were essentially religious or semi-religious in their inspiration and affinity. Just as French children were moving beyond Biblical reading to encounter such works as the *Fables* of La Fontaine, so too did young Ottoman readers move past the Qur'an to such fare as the Stories of the Prophets or more secular works, often tinged with a strong ethnic flavor, such as the Köroğlu destanı. Then again, new reading primers intended for the new schools and the new genre of children's magazines made available a wholly different range of material, much of it centered not on the mythical and religious past but on the present and even the future. In short, it is the variety of material that stands out in this period.

When we turn to the kinds of material being read at school, the contrast between the curricula and various texts employed in both the traditional Qur'an schools on the one hand and new public educational systems on the other is clear enough, although we must also remember that the new educational dispensation was continually being altered to reflect the shifts in contemporary thinking. Thus the Tanzimat-era school program that was drawn up with substantial input from French educationalists was substantially altered during the period of Abdülhamid II (1876–1909). The main result of these periodic and thorough vettings was to make late Ottoman state education more Ottoman and more Islamic in character. Western subjects were de-emphasized and a considerable amount of classically Islamic content such as Qur'an, Hadith and jurisprudence were introduced into an otherwise largely secular lesson plan.[16] Beginning in the Young Turk Period and gathering pace in the early Republic the pendulum swung back in the other direction. Much but not all of the religious content was stripped away as the secularist agenda of the state won out. But as the subsequent and ongoing history of curricular struggles in the Republic shows, these battles are rarely decisive.

In the Hamidian period, so critical for establishing the tone of children's reading matter and when official attention focused on a heavily Islamic sense of morality, religious messages were unsurprisingly both prominent and widespread in children's readers. Indeed, reading and religion were frequently presented as inseparable. Authors selected religious material for conspicuous placement in children's texts. Consider, for example, Kitapçı Arakel's popular reading primer, *Talim-i kıraat* (Teaching Reading) of 1887. It is filled with references to religiosity, including the importance of fearing God, the necessity of consulting religious books for proper advide and the blessings of God's providence and wisdom. From time to time these lessons are imparted in catechistic, question-and-response format.[17] Or take another of the texts written by Ahmed Rasım, for example. In his *Kıraat kitabı* of 1314 (1896–1897), a book published with the oversight of the Ottoman Education Ministry and intended for elementary school students who had finished learning their ABCs, the first text is devoted to morals (*ahlâk*) and is called simply "God" (Allah):

> Children!
>
> When you get home from school in the evenings you say to your mother, I'm hungry! I'm cold! I'm tired! She fills you up and sits you down by the fire she has lit. She does things that make your tiredness disappear. Would you not say how good it is to have a mother to...
>
> Children!
>
> There is someone even more merciful and good than your mother. That one is God who gave you your good mother, who created the world, who created out of nothing the sun and moon that we see. God is one. He sees everything. He listens, he hears, he knows the good and the bad that you do. He loves those who do good, but not those who do bad. Let us try hard. Let's be God's beloved servants who do good.
>
> [The next lesson is entitled: "The Earth, Geography..."][18]

Ten years later Ali İrfan [Eğribozu] urged a similarly moralizing message to ensure that Islamic manners and Ottoman customs be maintained.[19] Lamenting the destruction of "our material and spiritual power" due to the failure to embrace the *sharia*, the author of *Vatanı seven okusun* (Let he who loves the nation read, or perhaps more idiomatically, If you love your country, read!) urged a program of revival: "Let us strive to preserve our constitution, to look after the preservation of and swearing allegiance to our constitutional administration, to rectify our morals (*tashih-i ahlâk*), to guard our Islamic manners and Ottoman customs..." and so on with a long list of economic, educational and cultural optatives. The common theme is the necessity of effort and striving, rooted in the Qur'anic verse *"Laysa lil-insan 'illa ma sa`i"* (A man shall have to his account only as he has labored, to use Arberry's interpretation) (53: 39), cited in the original Arabic. Ali İrfan's seems to have been an individually inspired and self-funded effort; the title page of this booklet states that it was to be distributed gratis. But it was not out of step with the officially sanctioned efforts of the late Ottoman era generally and the Hamidian period in particular. The Qur'anic citation employed by Ali İrfan is in keeping with the infusion of state education with a much more robustly Islamic emphasis during the period of Sultan Abdülhamid II.[20]

But it would be mistaken to equate all or perhaps even most of the children's literature in this period with an Islamically infused morality.

Naturally enough, many of the texts created for the benefit of children were concerned with straightforwardly secular issues. Even the dominating figure of Ahmed Midhat Efendi, the so-called school master of late Ottoman literature who frequently adopted a heavily moralizing tone, was more apt to be concerned with the material, and not the spiritual or even the sectarian, concerns of young children. His 1887 *Terbiyeli Çocuk* (The well-mannered child) offered an uncomplicatedly pedestrian example of correct child behavior.[21] The author sets the well-mannered child's idealized activities off against those of his didactically useful evil twin, the ill-mannered child. From explaining when the well-mannered child should wake up – rather optimistically defined, from a parental point of view, as neither before nor after the rest of the household – to detailing how to dress, wash himself, eat breakfast, behave in the street, work at school and conduct himself during playtime, Ahmed Midhat's narrative covers a full day in the life of this model child. Conspicuous by its absence is any mention of organized religion. Indeed, although the language of religion is frequently invoked – the terms *abdest* and *günah* appear with some regularity – they are never the less employed in the service of the most mundane of behaviors. For example, while abdest/aptes can mean the ritual washing of face, hands and feet prior to Muslim prayer, there is in this instance no mention of prayer or prayer times in the otherwise detailed activities of the well-mannered child. The fact that he is immediately afterwards given such extra-canonical instructions as to how and with which towel he is to dry his face and how to comb his hair makes it clear that his morning toilette carries no religious connotation. Similarly, the term "sin" (*günah*) occurs not in conjunction with any moral transgression but rather in the context of eating breakfast. The well-mannered child, the reader is instructed, does not eat his breakfast while standing up. To eat while on foot, he or she is told, is quite a disgrace. "Bread crumbs will fall here and there. On the one hand they will become scattered. On the other they will be trod upon and this is a sin."[22] Clearly the attention of the passage, as with so much else in this volume, is with the necessity of adhering to culturally conditioned customs, and not religious commandments. Compare this to the same author's nearly contemporary booklet devoted to explaining the details of Muslim prayer. This takes the form of a matter-of-fact but generally imploring explanation of the fundamentals of ritual cleaning and prayer. The first sentence establishes that the text will be written from a clearly Muslim perspective. "All people belong to a particular religion. Each religion has its own form of worship. We, God be praised, are Muslims. And we have many forms of worship as well. The greatest of them is prayer (namaz)..."[23]

Ahmed Midhat Efendi's work is practically obsessed with middle-class concerns. Physical cleanliness, following rules, honoring one's elders, avoiding trouble, volunteering answers to the teacher's questions, etc.; these are the manifestations of proper social standing and upbringing.[24] In the ample time afforded after the child returns home from school he is meant to serve his parents. If they have no chores for him to do then he may go out into the garden and play. But he is absolutely forbidden to go out into the street and play with the neighborhood children.[25] The author's assumptions concerning both the existence of a garden behind the family home and the desire to separate the child from his contemporaries in the street – presumably those without gardens of their own – is symptomatic of the class consciousness that formed part of expectations surrounding literacy – and the audience for which he was writing – in this period. These expectations would change as more and more schools were opened, taking in more and more of these neighborhood children as time went on.

But a great many of the reading primers produced in the late Ottoman period did carry an overtly Islamic message. This was natural given the extent to which a revival of Islam and Islamic traditions were identified with imperial revivification. It was as if all of the many textbook writers, despite coming from a variety of backgrounds and geographical areas, found it natural to emphasize Islamic morality alongside such themes as cleanliness, obedience, hard work and, of course, literacy. But religiously inflected content was a clear starting point for many. M. Safvet's 1308 (1890–1891) reader, called simply The Reader (*Kıraat*), is a general compendium of stories and entries on such subjects as the Ottoman Empire, the ignorance of ancient tribes, civilization in general, natural geography and so on. It begins with a section on religious principles (*Akaid-i diniye*), a staple of the morality courses taught in the state schools.[26] Faik Reşad's identically titled work, published five years later, presents a similar mixture of the secular and the religious.[27] Passages on such subjects as cats and parents are interspersed with those on more religiously tinged subjects such as effort, contentment and obedience. Such religiously coded messages were frequently mixed together with the imperative to read. For example, Ahmed Rasım's *Kızlara mahsus kıraat kitabı* (The girls' reader) plunges its young audience into the religious content from the very beginning with texts on the Prophet Muhammad and Abu Bakr, the first Caliph in Islam. It then localizes the text by presenting a long and illustrated description of Istanbul before moving on to a general discussion of geography and the continents. A section devoted to "Books" (*Kitaplar*) continues the simplistic and condescending style. "My girl, you have books and paper for writing. What great things these are! Although these books are widespread and inexpensive today, they were once so valuable that only the rich were able to own them."[28] Historical time, at once valorized and collapsed to emphasize a connection with the glories of the Islamic past, is also presented as the source of material progress, in this case making possible the great treasure of reading and writing. Just how grateful the young readers were to be told of their good luck they were and how much they shouldn't take their books for granted is of course impossible to discern.

The link between reading and correct behavior, at times given a secular at others a religious emphasis, is nearly omnipresent in these texts, reinforcing the message that learning to read was more than merely deciphering letters and words. Taken together these texts link literacy with a cluster of concepts that include progress, morality and material gain. The sense of moving forward, whether individually or communally, is particularly strong. This notion of progress starts with learning to read. Arakel's reader has the child narrator of one of its passages explain the importance of patience and hard work: "At the moment I cannot read very well. But if I work carefully I will soon begin to read very well. And if I learn to read well, how happy I will be!"[29] Another example of this pervasive, melioristic tendency is the textbook written by Ali İrfan entitled *Malumat-i diniye* (Religious information). It describes itself as having been written to conform to the latest curriculum of the Ministry of Education and composed in an open and plain language in order to teach the youth of the nation (*nevrestegan-i vatan*) about their religious life.[30] Even though this is a work of religious duties with a Qur'anic section at the back, the book nevertheless is fully focused on the present day. It begins, "We all know that our age is the age of progress. In particular, our time is very valuable."

Away from the officially produced texts, it is the eclecticism and seemingly haphazard juxtapositions of the children's literature that stand out. As was mentioned in the previous chapter, the fare proffered by periodicals such as *Çocuk Dünyası*, was so mixed in terms of the religious-to-secular spectrum, as to defy placement upon it. The eclecticism and exuberance of the late Ottoman period begins to diminish, logically enough, during wartime. The increasingly martial tone evident in the period after 1911 was noted in the previous chapter. In this period of "national economics" (*millî iktisad*) and heightened patriotic agitation, matters of national importance made their way into the children's magazines themselves, both in their content and in the growing competition between publishers. This rivalry could be tinged with an ethnic flavor, as the boycott of non-Muslim businesses during the Balkan Wars extended to the Armenian-owned periodical *Çocuk Duygusu*, which adapted by presenting content of a Turkist and militarist nature in response.[31] Although in some publications, e.g., *Bizim Mecmua* of 1922, the war seems very far away indeed, in others, such as the stridently nationalist *Çocuk Dünyası*, the effects of the period were clearly felt: a smaller sized edition, fewer illustrations, and a generally cheaper look prevailed, reflecting wartime economic hardship perhaps as much as the changing political outlook of this period. Whatever the ownership of the magazines, the world represented in their pages seems to shrink during wartime; there are fewer references to life beyond the empire's contracting borders, and an increase in imaginary material, some of it quite surreal, as well as a retreat into the safer realm of the "national tales" (*millî masallar*) which draw on a largely undefined and ahistorical past during the reigns of sultans unspecified. The losses and general insecurity of this period seem to have produced a psychological need in the inchoate Turkish nation for a Turanian fantasy.[32]

In the early Republic young readers encountered a more uniform and more ideologically targeted range of readings. Loyalty to and defense of the new nation were paramount themes, supported by attention to physical strength, military training, political score-settling and historical revisionism.[33] Political events came back into the frame from time to time, but they were always carefully monitored and controlled. For example, *Resimli Mecmua* included an illustration of Şeyh Sait trembling before the court that would sentence him to death for leading the eponymous revolution against the Kemalist state in 1925. But such coverage was rare. More typical was the range of material that included references to building the new nation on the domestic front and such subjects as American actresses appearing in Istanbul, the fakirs of India, and Turkish battleships in the international field. Increased vigilance and control meant that the publications of the early Republican period tended to be far less eclectic. Instead, shaped by a concerted effort on the part of Kemalist ideologues, they were inclined toward a greater unanimity of voice and a more tightly focused coherence in terms of materials selected.

The changes effected by the early Republic are clearly reflected in the altering of illustrations in reading primers for school use. One example suffices to depict the direction and intent of the Republican transformation. It shows a remarkably clear shift in emphasis from religious to civil imagery. Seracettin Bey's *Kolay kıraat* (The easy reader) reveals the way in which the Kemalist period altered the presentation of the Muslim holiday (*bayram*) to young readers.[34] The 1925 edition of this reader presents an illustration of a drummer wearing a turban while another turbaned man holds a staff reminiscent of those used by the Janissary band. In the revised 1927 edition the same text is accompanied by an illustration showing that the two adult figures have been re-clothed in Western military attire: the drummer now wears a peaked cap with a visor and the children are now sporting more clearly western-style clothes, as symbolized by the boy's sailor suit. Bayram has been nationalized, republicanized.[35] Such a remaking of public ceremony was hardly left to accident. This was a time in which the young Kemalist state was paying special attention to vetting printed materials, those designed for educational purposes in particular, in order to bring material into line with republican expectations. For example, according to a 1926 report, only 10 out of 68 primary school textbooks were approved. Forty-one were accepted on the condition that changes insisted upon by the commission be made.[36] Although the parameters had clearly changed, those responsible for vetting school texts in the days of the late Ottoman Empire could only have applauded the thoroughness and zeal of their Republican successors.

As we have seen, learning to read and reading were often linked with a religious purpose or milieu. A religious invocation was a frequent point of departure for those writing texts for young children to read, and reading passages often reflected the religious spirit. But this was not always the case – indeed, it was becoming less and less so with the passage of time. With the outbreak of the wars that marked the last years of the Ottoman Empire and occasioned the birth of the Republic of Turkey, the rather varied experience of reading and religion began to change. With the establishment of even stricter mechanisms of control and censorship than even the late Ottoman state could muster and the seemingly unstoppable sweep of secularist and nationalist fervor, texts produced for young children were radically altered during the early years of the Turkish Republic. There was an irony here in that the de-linking of the religious, in this case the Islamic, from the national was occurring even though Islam had only recently played such a decisive role in rallying the country together during the Turkish independence war. Although the Islamic emphasis was quickly being discarded in the service of harnessing reading to the national movement, it would resurface before too long in a way that imprinted the religious on the very nationalist enterprise that was trying to get rid of it. In retrospect it

could be said that the single-mindedness of the early republican impetus to monopolize textbook content eventually backfired with respect
to the religious/secular divide. With the end of single party rule in
1950 the tenor of Turkish politics shifted to reflect the more conservative basis of the country and set in motion a process that ultimately
made state education – and its textbooks – the bearers of conspicuously
Islamic content once again.

The family and the nation/state

Learning to read and reading were invested with a number of weighty
tasks, none perhaps as momentous as the wish to cement the link
between the young readers and the nation. In both the late Ottoman
and early Republican periods the same underlying desire to forge the
bonds of nationhood is readily apparent even if the emphases and
details of this projected identification changed over time in response
to events and changes in political leadership. Given the youth of the
targeted audience and the relative novelty of both state-sponsored education and widespread literacy, attracting the loyalty of their new readership meant that authors and publishers had to breach the barricades
of the main focus of identification, the family. Children's literature
from this period exhibits a number of approaches aimed at accomplish-
ing this task. Sometimes subtle and sympathetic, sometimes brutally
direct in their approaches, the authors frequently tried to model children's behavior and thought with the intention of drawing their young
audience away from the orbit of the family, portrayed as representing
the outmoded elders and into the arms of the nation as represented by
the state, attempting to create a "veritable cult of youth."[37]

Here there was a potential problem, for the rhetoric of the nation
itself depended heavily on the family. The solution was to appear to
validate the role of the family while at the same time undermining it. It
is perhaps helpful to think of the resulting tug of emotions being played
out in the children's literature as a contest between the family and the
state, frequently represented by the school or other forms of officialdom, for the right to provide the child with the correct upbringing.
Some authors presented this dual relationship as a seamless partnership; as we have seen, well-intentioned parents were depicted as providing their children with the proper upbringing as far as they were able
but then having the wisdom to see that their offspring's future lay with
the world of organized schooling and literacy that only the state could
properly provide. Other writers would present a more emphatic case,

insisting on a sharp contrast between home and school, often in a way that cast aspersions on the family's ability to dispense national feeling and the spirit of progress. An early example is that of the late Ottoman educator Mehmed Ziya's *Çocuklara kıraat*. This short-lived fortnightly journal was emphatic on the need to break the family's hold on education. "Can the education that a child receives from his father and mother suffice? No chance! Actually, is it not the case that the stories that are considered education in our homes consist of baseless, shocking words and mere illusions?" He goes on to insist that reading books in school is the only way forward.[38]

Some writers showed more faith in the family to inculcate the proper national values. Not coincidentally these tended to be authors who wrote for private consumption. Doubtless aware of the economics of the situation, they would have remembered that it was usually the parents who were, after all, paying for the books and magazines for which they wrote. An example of the positive approach toward the family's role in the service of the nation can be found in Ali İrfan's *Birinci kıraat* (First reader). This book generally adopts a strong tone of Ottoman patriotism. It features portraits of both the reigning Sultan and Osman Gazi, the eponymous late thirteenth-/early fourteenth-century founder of the imperial line, as well as illustrations of contemporary late Ottoman children in military dress, with flags and playing soldier games. In a preface addressed to both the teachers and the parents of the book's young audience, the author underscores the need to provide reading texts suitable to the educational and moral development of young Ottoman children.[39] Referring to the fact that in Europe thousands of new primary-level reading materials are produced each year, Ali İrfan urges a similar effort in the Ottoman lands. Among the most important and useful of the "worldly and otherworldly social and moral matters" that he singles out for inclusion, both in the preface and on the title page, are: "love of the nation (hub-i vatan), education, agriculture, trade, industry, sound belief, obedience, and acts of piety." The first lesson makes the author's view of the family quite clear. After mentioning the Ottoman capital of Istanbul, again a way to provide some local setting, the text goes on to say:

> Like everyone we too love our nation (vatanımız). Because from the time that we are born of our mothers the first air that we breathe is the air of the nation. Thereafter we grow up drinking the nation's water and eating the nation's bread. Our comfort and happiness and that of our mothers and fathers and all of our ancestors who have come and gone are due to our nation.

Our nation resembles our house. Just as we pass the time comfortably at home, so also do we live comfortably in our nation. Those who go away from the nation become very sorrowful. Because just as a man far from his home becomes homesick, so also does he who goes away from his nation become equally homesick.[40]

The family analogy continues, with siblings likened to the citizens (*vatandaş*) of the nation. Then, raising the prospect of strangers entering the house/nation, the text declares that,

Naturally none of us wants a stranger to enter our house/nation or for anything in our house to be diminished. In this way we are obliged, by religion, by reason, and by order, to guard all of our nation's rights and to preserve all of its contents. Those who would act as enemies of our nation are like those who would venture to rob our homes.

Thereafter the refrain is one of rousing the readers *cum* citizens to work hard – literally day and night – in order to prevent these unspecified enemies from perpetrating their ill will on "our sacred nation."[41]

The lesson concludes with a clear attempt to cement the relationship between the citizen reader and the nation. Interestingly, the text changes font here and the following section is rendered in a new script resembling a handwritten text, probably to emphasize the need for the personal involvement of the individual readers.

Therefore: Let the words, 'Ottomanness forever, Long live our beloved nation, Let's sacrifice ourselves for the nation' (daim olsun Osmanlılık, yaşasın sevgili vatanımız, feda olsun vatana canımız) be always on our tongues, in our hearts, and in our thoughts and let us serve our beloved nation with heart and soul until we die.[42]

As if to reinforce the connection with the Ottoman nation, a map of the empire appears on the facing page. This is followed by a rather clumsy but didactically unambiguous poem:

Vatandır valide-i millet vatandır
Vatandır hame-i ümmet vatandır
Vatandır layık-i hürmet vatandır

(It is the nation, mother of the people, the nation
It is the nation, head of the community[of Muslims], the nation
It is the nation, worthy of honor, the nation)

In a very short time this reader has managed to bring together a powerful mixture of religious, political and geographical images, and to make them appear to merge into a harmonious whole. In reality, the terms employed, much less the concepts they embodied, were fraught with nuance, overlap and ambiguity. Subject to considerable scholarly attention, particularly in light of the growth of the power of nationalism, the terms used here can nevertheless be difficult to translate. "*Vatan*," which I have been rendering as "nation" in the sense of the French "patrie," was increasingly used, as in the West, to connote the geographical and socio-political sense of a people united by land, language and history. It could also be translated as "motherland" or "fatherland." It was the subject of the invented *hadith "Hubb al-watan min al-iman,"* (Love of the nation is part of belief) perhaps in order to provide it with the historical depth it lacked. The terms *"millet"* and *"ümmet,"* by contrast have a clearer pedigree. Millet is used to signify the greater religious community, Muslim or non-Muslim, and also as a synonym for nation and nationality. *Ümmet* (Arabic ummah) is the most unambiguous of these terms, referring to the Islamic community of believers.

Thus while the author began this children's reader with the notion of the nuclear family, centered naturally enough on the dynamic between mother and child, he quickly dispenses with this more familiar familial milieu in order to hammer home his main point concerning the need for a concerted Ottoman effort. This movement from the familiar specifics of the domestic family to the image of the family as an extended and ultimately abstract notion combining both religious and national referents is fairly typical of the wish of children's authors to pull their young readers into the world of adult concerns. In particular, these authors wanted to emphasize the possibility that the extended family of the nation could supersede the localism and parochialism of the nuclear family. They deployed several means to bring this about, including both negative associations such as fear, as represented in the previous example, and victimization, which began in the Ottoman period and, as Navaro-Yashin has noted, continued to play an important role in informing Turkishness in the Republican era,[43] as well as positive ones such as invoking progress and the benefits of education. Such manipulation aided the process of politicizing the children's literature of the period.[44]

One has to wonder just what child readers made of the undefined foreign bogeymen of Ali İrfan's text, but the mixture of national and religious import makes a strong statement about the nature of the perceived threat. In the aftermath of World War I children's texts would specify the nation's enemies, namely, the invading Greeks and their supporters among the Western powers and invoke religious solidarity to encourage national action. Before the Republic turned away from the overt use of Islam, it was seen as a natural common denominator, even in a period of increasingly strong Turkish nationalism. For example, the children's periodical *Yeni Yol* included a regular feature devoted to student correspondence. In one issue this column is written by a certain Mehmed Şücaüddin on the subject of "Our religious duties."[45] The way it approaches this subject is worth noting, given the importance of religious feelings in a story later remembered almost entirely as a national, secular way. This entry begins with the statement that, "Muslims are each others' friends," and then cites the Qur'anic passage in the original Arabic. Providing the historical example of assistance offered to the early community of Muslims by the Helpers (*Ansar*) of Medina in the seventh century C.E. serves as a prelude to arguing for the Muslim duty to "our coreligionists who escaped from the tyrannical acts of the Greeks in Rumelia and the [Aegean] islands." He urges his readers to help by sending aid and by founding societies to assist them. "They were like us but now have lost everything, even their families."[46] Far more concrete than the metaphor of the nation as extended family or even the invocation of the first generation of Islam, this periodical's direct approach and contemporary subject matter must surely have caught the attention of the young readers in the way that the generic material in the textbooks could not.

Parenthetically, it is important to emphasize that the political imperative so prevalent in much of the children's reading material from latter years of the Ottoman Empire and the earliest years of the Turkish republic prefigures by several years the official attention lavished upon the young later in the decade. Mustafa Kemal's famous address to the nation's youth, part of the six-day speech he delivered to the Second Republican People's Party Congress in October 1927, left no doubt as to the seriousness of the mission he was assigning to them: "O Turkish youth! Your first duty is to maintain and protect Turkish independence and the Turkish Republic for ever." Raising the specter of the possible reoccupation of the homeland and the potential treachery of its possible future leadership, Kemal implored the youth of the nation to come to its rescue, finding the necessary strength to do so in the "noble blood which flows in your veins."[47]

Children's material did not usually focus on such daunting and weighty tasks but it did frequently feel the need to assert the superiority of their teachers over their parents. Even a publication as prone to taking a satirical line such as *Yeni Yol* engaged in bald pronouncements concerning the comparative debts children owe to their teachers as opposed to their parents. In a Morals column entitled "The students' duties towards the teachers" the subject is broached this way:

> If you think about it adequately, you will confirm that you are many more times obliged to honor and love your teachers than your parents; because they are the ones who are always working to give you life within life.
>
> Your parents open your eyes to the light of day, but the teachers serve to enlighten your thoughts with knowledge. This is to say that you make your parents happy and that it is the teachers who make you happy.
>
> Who is it that provides you with elevated thoughts of this world of humanity? Who is it that tears away the screen of ignorance that is in your thoughts, who explains the greatness of capacity and existence and, opening your capacity to learn, urges your soul forward onto a broad path known as virtue?
>
> Is it not your teachers?
>
> My dears! ...
>
> Think a little what great rights the hocas have over you. Mother and father leave you at a young age on the path to education, and it is the teachers who support you through instruction and upbringing (tahsil ve terbiye). They bring out the capacity to learn in each one of you by giving fortune and happiness. Do you not know what they require in return for this considerable work and service?
>
> Pay a little attention to their words, respect the lessons they give and show them a little love.[48]

The passage goes on to emphasize the role of the school as the place where all these wonderful things happen, the place where "bounty and perfection are acquired. This place is the school." The school is the locale where a person begins in earnest to understand his life, his world and his existence. "A human being comes into the world ignorant but capable. The school drives the ignorance away."[49] The parents' role is devalued completely, associated by default with the ignorance attributed to the child's arrival into the world. Luckily the school and its teachers, as representatives of the new nation, are there to redeem him.

In these texts the school is usually presented as a generic but unquestioned reality, a beneficial feature of modern life. Interestingly enough, children's memoirs frequently present similarly unproblematic descriptions of their entering school. No doubt because their parents took care of the relevant details such as admissions, fees, and red tape, their accounts often mirror the blithely simplistic approach to how they found themselves at school.[50] In fact, of course, there was frequently an important decision to be made about which of many schools to attend, especially in the urban areas. There were schools run by the various religious establishments and those operated by the state, and these came in military and civil varieties; there were a number of foreign, usually missionary, options; and there were boarding and day schools to choose from. Anecdotal evidence reveals the family discussions – and arguments – that these choices provoked. In this, late Ottoman and early Republican families were little different from their Western European counterparts. As Ariès noted, these typically "nineteenth century" concerns frequently reflect the increasing role of maternal concern for and influence in her children's educational and social progress and therefore in decision-making over school choice, an intrusion into "a province which had so far been exclusively paternal."[51] The familial territory into which the state was bent on interfering was itself changing.

With the expansion of educational options, school choice was becoming steadily more difficult, while the increased importance attached to education and literacy rendered them ever more momentous. Frequently children's educational pathways incorporated the different types of schooling on offer with the result that their young *vitae* personified the variety now inherent in the educational system at large.[52] Faced with the plethora of educational options, families often hedged their bets.

In the meantime officials grew increasingly bold in pursuing a strategy intent on winning children to the side of the state. In the late Ottoman context, the burden of opening some distance between children and their families was shared between the religious and civil bureaucracies. As I have demonstrated elsewhere, the hoca was a constant and central figure in the expanding network of Ottoman state schools. He was crucial to the state's ability to act *in loco parentis*. Involved in most aspects of education, from curricular planning to teaching and overseeing the pupils' moral development, the hoca played a vital if underappreciated role in the new educational dispensation, particularly in the early stages when demand for state-trained teachers exceeded supply. In the Republican period he would be turned into a source of ridicule and replaced by the state-supplied teacher, a member of the civil bureaucracy, and often a woman. Whoever its protagonists, we can trace a clear policy aimed at removing the family from the process of education. Beginning in the late Ottoman period when it was shared by the ulema and civil officialdom, it intensified during the early Republic when the decisiveness of Kemalist policy settled the argument in favor of the seemingly all-conquering state.

Naturally enough many authors downplayed the potential conflict between the home and the state and presented the family as correctly encouraging their children to partake of state education. The elevation of the teacher as the proper authority figure was sometimes accomplished without showing disrespect to the parents or the family milieu. Other authors were more brutal in handling this potentially sensitive topic. Either way, with time the link between child and nation, as mediated through the school and the new teacher, assumed greater and greater significance. With the family pushed to the background, the field was open for a more direct relationship between child and state, a relationship effected largely through the medium of reading.

Reading made possible the presentation of a cluster of traits and constructs linking correct children's behavior with the progress of the modern state. By emphasizing sacrifice, hard work, obedience, cleanliness, respect for authority, the promise of the modern and of course, literacy, the late Ottoman and early Turkish republican states were simply modeling the sort of ideal child that was becoming familiar across the world in this period.

In many if not most of the texts available for young readers there is a clear expression of the imperial, and then national, imperative for progress through reading. Sometimes, especially and during periods of crisis, this point is made explicitly, as we saw from some examples drawn from the immediate aftermath of the Greek invasion in Chapter 1. More often the message is implicit. A good example is Ali Nazima's 1320 (1904) *Oku yahud yeni risale-i ahlâk ve vezaif-i etfal* (Read, or the new treatise on morals and children's duties), a title which accurately expresses the connection the book makes between reading and the moral and material progress of the body politic. Utilizing a variant of the good child, bad child technique, in this case further refined as a distinction between the child who can read and the one who cannot, Ali Nazima's reader proceeds in a manner that seems calculated to attract the attention of his young readers. Cevher is emphatically introduced as the literate child – "Cevher knows how to read!" (*Cevher okuma bilir!*).[53] He is described as a satisfied, contented child because he attends school regularly and has listened attentively to what his teacher has had to say. Now he is reading a book filled with very beautiful stories. In the evenings this dutiful child helps his parents with the housework and then reads out loud to them from this book. He thereby shows his parents the progress he is making and they are sufficiently pleased that they give him a material reward. This takes the form of money with which to buy another book, and his paternal uncle joins in to make him a gift of a two-volume book containing beautiful illustrations. At the end of this section the readers are then addressed directly, "Dear children! Do as he does; strive to read well."

A section devoted to the story of Nesib, the negative example, follows this passage.[54] Nesib is described as less fortunate than Cevher. In spite of being older in years, he still does not know how to read. He gets to school late because he stops to play with his friends along the way. He thus arrives after the reading lesson is over. Once there he is lazy, chatty and disruptive. Ignoring the teacher's lessons, he fails to learn anything. Turning again to the young readers, the text asks, "Do you suppose that he is fortunate? Not at all." The description continues, emphasizing the negative consequences of Nesib's behavior. These include being punished by this teacher and being scolded and locked in a closet by his mother. But the most painful aspect of Nesib's illiteracy is the humiliation he suffers in front of his fellow children. Despite the fact that Nesib is ten years old, the reader is told that he is in the same class with children who are as young as five and six. What is worse, these little ones make fun of him because he can neither read nor write. Much of the rest of the text is dedicated to a series of similar pairings, each emphasizing a different quality that the idealized child should exhibit. There is also a section on school memories, which includes a segment devoted to showing replicas of school mark sheets, a not-so-subtle reminder, perhaps, of the need to work hard in school. But what stands out is the sense of shame that is the chief result of the failure to learn to read, a failure that is clearly linked in an inverse relationship to the national impetus for progress and advancement.

Ultimately, the state attempted to assume some of the family's traditional roles. The 1926–1927 Republican curriculum stated that civics courses ought to teach that Turkey is a family- and work-oriented country, and that children should be made to adopt a view of the family, state and nation working together as one.[55] The 1929 regulations governing primary schools treat the school as a social microcosm. "The school must establish a veritable small society for the students." This was part of the republican educational strategy aimed at strengthening the children's "national feelings." As the 1929 regulation phrased it, "It is necessary to constitute Turkishness and the Turkish nation as the basic axis in education."[56]

A particularly fascinating Republican take on the familial/national dynamic is on display in Ahmed Cevad's 1929 reader which contains the skit of Osman and Turhan analysed in Chapter 1. Tellingly entitled The Turkish Reader for Republican Children, this volume presents an evolution in microcosm of the role of the nation and the family across its pages. It begins, traditionally enough, with an entry on a mother and her child.[57] This first lesson concentrates on the role of lullabies. Apart from the title of the book, the fact that it is intended for use in primary schools, and that it conforms to the 1928 regulations of the Education Ministry's National Instruction and Educational section's directive, the state and the nation are nowhere apparent. After a few short pieces devoted to some anodyne stories about fish comes a poem entitled *"Hamdiye Abla"* (Big sister Hamdiye). Perhaps reflecting the demographic impact of the continual warfare that afflicted the Ottoman Empire from 1911 to 1922, this poem quickly reveals that Hamdiye and her younger brother Hamdi are orphans. Their mother's death – no mention is made of the father – means that the poor girl is left to manage for both of the children. Hamdiye Abla sews their clothes. "Needle and thread do not leave her hand from morning until evening."[58] But there is no mention of complaint or self-pity. On the contrary, they are both presented as "good" children, but special attention is lavished on the older sister:

> The hard-working girl
> She rises early in the morning
> She washes her hands and face
> She threads her needle
> If there is a tear, she mends it
> If she has lessons, she reads and writes...[59]

Alone in the world (apart from her younger brother who perhaps because of his sex is deemed to be free from domestic duties), Hamdiye perseveres through hard work, self-reliance and, crucially, reading and study. Though subtly linked, the emphasis on education and self-help are clear. Still there is no overt reference to the political, but that will come soon. While the milieu presented for the girl is one of housework and study, for the boys there is the military. A short skit called "Military

Service" (*Askerlik*) shortly follows. The marshal tone is clear from the first few lines:

Aydemir: I am a soldier. I have a rifle. See how I march (he marches): One, two, left, right.

Ferit: I have a drum. Hear how I beat the drum (he beats): Dum, dum, dum!

Aydemir: Forward march! (They march.) ... [60]

Another layer of meaning is added a few pages later with a poem entitled "The Flag." Lending specificity to the so-far fairly generic scene, this piece describes the flag of the Turkish Republic:

How beautiful is our flag.
Red is my favorite color.
Our flag's color is red.
The crescent and star are on our flag.
What could be more beautiful than the moon and the star?
I love our crescent and star flag more than anything.
Every Turkish child loves his flag thus. [61]

As the young readers advance through the pages of this volume, they are confronted with more and more images intended to forge an identification between them and the official line. Having introduced the child readers to fictional children in a number of different settings, becoming steadily more politically identifiable, the readers are now introduced to the school, the institution intended to cement further the bond between individual reader and nation. The poem entitled "Our School" (*Mektebimiz*) is a fairly straightforward expression of loyalty and appreciation that we have come to expect from this sort of material. It describes the school, explains what takes place within its rooms and presents the teacher as a beloved figure, worthy of deep respect. With the school thus happily if rather generically depicted, the text moves on to "The first letter" (*İlk mektup*), a poem describing a child's writing to an absent father:

Yıldız's father is a soldier.
It has been a year since Yıldız has seen him.
In that year Yıldız has learned to read and write.
Now Yıldız has sat down to write her father a letter.
This is the first letter that Yıldız has written.
How happy will Yıldız's father be when he receives it! [62]

Recalling and perhaps compensating for the missing father in "Hamdiye Abla," this entry emphasizes the link between family, nation and education. The implication is that the school, introduced in the previous poem, has enabled Yıldız to be able to read and write. It is not surprising, given the martial tone established in the last decade of the empire and amplified in the early years of the Republic, to find the first practical manifestation of that education to be a letter to a father who is absent for reasons of military service. This situation is reinforced in the following section, a passage for dictation which neatly expresses both the practical side of reading typical of a primer intended for use in the schools and the ulterior motives of the state. The first section of this entry provides questions intended to be answered orally by the pupils. Leading questions all, their concerns are overwhelmingly martial:

Are any of your relatives soldiers?
Do you want to be a soldier?
Do you love the soldiers?
Why do you love them?

There then follows a section for written dictation, which takes the form of a girl's letter to her soldier father. The lines of the letter are in keeping with the letter that Yıldız was writing to her father in the previous entry:

My Dear father, my solider father,

It has been a year since you went away. I am going to school. I am learning to read and write. I am even able to write you this letter.

Your loving daughter Yıldız.[63]

Reading and writing are inextricably linked with patriotism and sacrifice for the good of the nation, as the triangle between child, family and state, established during the late Ottoman period, was being pulled sharply in the direction of the state in the Republican era. Once the family has been effaced, the task of national identification becomes easier. Now the nation can be depicted as being represented in microcosm by the school or even the classroom.

In fact, the early Republic likened the nation to one large classroom. As İsmet Paşa explained during a speech in 1928, the country was a classroom and Gazi Mustafa Kemal its headmaster.[64] Of course, Mustafa

Kemal enjoyed multiple roles – and sported almost as many outfits – in posing as father, teacher, cultural guide and political (formerly military) leader. The strong personal lead he took in implementing the alphabet change and the "language revolution" left their traces not only in the radical impact on what and how citizens of the republic read but also on the nearly indelible and ubiquitous images of him as educator-in-chief. The appropriation of reading and literacy is significant in light of the movement from family as nuclear social unit to family as national union. Given the heavily engineered composition of the new Turkey's identity and its very public search for authenticity, these images were crucial in forging links between the individuals and the abstract concepts inherent in political allegiance.[65] And that is precisely where reading, in the broadest sense of the term, played such an important role. Communication through a series of linked texts and images was vital to the efficacy of the top-down political, social and cultural project of the Kemalist state.

At the same time it is crucial to note that the Kemalist project built on the expansion of reading carried out during the late Ottoman period. For example, with respect to children's literature, Paul Dumont sees little change between the nationalism of the war years (1911–1918) and what followed in the early years of the Republic. The series of texts written by such figures of the regime as Ziya Gökalp, Mehmed Emin, Ömer Seyfettin and others were an attempt to inculcate the youth with patriotic fervor at a time when the young Republic was still fragile.[66] A children's literature devoid of the patriotic didacticism so familiar, despite its minor variations, during the Hamidian, Young Turk, and early Republican eras would have to wait until the late 1930s and the 1940s and then only timidly would a corpus of children's books less systematically devoted the spreading of patriotic themes emerge.[67] Even then, as Ersanlı Behar and Yael Navaro-Yashin have demonstrated, the textbooks in use in the state schools of the Republic were critical in imposing a certain historical and geographical sense of Turkishness that relied heavily on victimization and blame.[68] As we have seen, most clearly in the children's offerings written by Mehmed Fuad Köprülü, much of this blame was directed toward the *ancien régime*.

In this respect the early Republican period appears as just one phase, albeit the most radical and for some, most important, one in a continual evolution of Ottoman to Turkish identity. From late 1940s onward another shift occurred, that from "secular Anatolian culture to what is called 'Turkish-Islamic synthesis'." It could only go so far at that time, but later, after 1980 military coup and the presence of a center–right government under Turgut Özal with strong links to Islamic circles, it extended its reach under the guise of army secularism, thereby reinforcing the notion of continuity despite change.[69]

Let us now return to the process that was working to supplant the family with the nation and pick up the thread of the same textbook that gave us young Yıldız writing a letter to her father away at the front. After a few humorous pieces, one concerning a lamb that goes to school, another comparing children's learning to read and write with young ducks learning to swim, which seem incongruous alongside the pieces devoted to national and military themes, the more normal attention to the modern republic returns. Military concerns, including more letters to distant soldiers, and signs of modern technology in the form of the telephone and the train now predominate. A late entry called "Playing Army" (*Askerlik oyunu*) reveals the degree to which the family has been written out of the state's projection onto children's lives. This reading revolves around three children pretending to be soldiers. One beats a drum while the other two march around the room with rifles on their shoulders. While they are marching – "one, two, left, right" – the door opens and a bear walks into their game.[70] Seemingly unfazed, the children incorporate the bear into their play. But when the children's mother enters the scene, she is badly frightened (*ödü koptu*) and grows terribly pale. Eventually the bear's owner comes and leads the intruding animal away. What remains is the inescapable impression that the family, represented here by the hapless mother, has become marginalized. Whereas at the beginning of this children's reader the mother was front and center, by its end she is, like the family in general, reduced to a minor, inadequate role. While separation from the family, and the mother in particular, is a part of the process of growing up, it is nevertheless clear that in this reader we have another dynamic at work as well. It is as if the process of national acculturation and indoctrination is far too important to be left to the family.

As Tiregöl puts it, "Much of the national education program involved transposing family loyalty and love to nation." This process intensified in the 1930s. Textbooks that appeared in the early years of the decade urged children to memorize the motto "I love my fatherland more than myself, even more I love my mother."[71] Pointedly, the state was moving further into the domestic domain. "A new course was introduced in the 1936 curriculum called 'family knowledge'...to ensure that children would become good mothers and fathers." In other words the state was arrogating to itself the right to define "good" in both national and familial terms.[72] But as we shall see, non-official publications could undermine the official stance.

The attention of children's authors to the subject of the nation and the family clearly predates the founding of the Republic. They expound similar themes across the Ottoman-to-Republican boundary. In some cases the same authors publish essentially the same texts in both periods, only making superficial changes to keep them up to date with their readership and the new demands of the national curriculum. In other respects the Republican program only represented an intensification of a pattern of symbolic identification that had been visible in the Ottoman era. The Republican period placed greater emphasis on such symbols of the nation as the flag, the role of the military in society and the Turkish language than the Ottomans had done but this was largely a change in intensity and not a radical departure from what had gone on before 1923.

Geography was another useful dimension in effecting identification between student and state and also provides more evidence of unacknowledged continuity from the Ottoman period. This national sense of reading also extended to "reading" the nation in a geographical sense, reading – and identifying with – the imperial or later national map. In his section entitled "*Osmanlı*" (Ottoman) included in his 1914 Beginning Reader (*İbtidaî Kıraat*), Ahmed Rasım offers a simple lesson on what the term "Ottoman" means, in terms of dynasty and state, emphasizing the empire's territory on three continents, enumerated by region and described as inseparable portions of the nation (*ayrılmaz vatan parçaları*). The treatment ends with the author's addressing his young readers in the following terms: "Children. Our greatest duty is to prevent others from seizing the nation and being given a portion of it territory,"[73] words that would not appear out of place in later, republican texts. The text is presented alongside a map showing all Ottoman territory. The very next item is on duty (*vazife*). The same author composed a story titled, The National Map (*Vatan haritası*) in another reader. This is a story of "Turkish" Ottoman prisoners of war during World War I in Egypt. When their British captors deny their repeated requests for a map of their beloved Turkish homeland, they draw one from memory,[74] thus reinforcing the importance of inscribing national notions of geography.[75]

With the consolidation of the link between state and nation it became possible for the official line to associate the nation with familiar and indeed familial roles with which children were accustomed. Perhaps the ultimate demonstration of the desired fusion of the bond between state and individual appeared in the story where a male teacher "adopts" his schoolchildren as his "family." A sort of adult counterpart, perhaps, to the orphaned Hamidiye Abla is the New Teacher presented to readers in a story by the same name in Sadrettin Celal's 1928 reader entitled *Cümhuriyet* [sic] *Çocuklarına Sevimli Kıraat.*[76] In this story, accompanied by an illustration of a handsome young man dressed in a double-breasted suit and necktie, the new teacher presents himself to the class as a caring and conscientious instructor. Striking a contrast with the stories of the old-style teachers and the bastinado, this pedagogical paragon announces that he doesn't want to punish anyone. What's more, he tells the children that, having lost his mother the previous year, he is all alone in the world. "I have no family, now your are my family... I want that you should be children." He urges his charges to work hard and to prove themselves through their behavior, showing them to be the conscientious, dutiful children he suspects them to be. "In that case, your school will become a large family, and I will find my consolation in you."[77] (*İşte o zaman mektebiniz büyük bir âile haline gelecek, ben de sizin-le müteselli olaca-ım* (sic).) With this suggestive image we can perhaps say that the desire to enclose the state school and young readers in a familial embrace reaches its fullest expression.

The new and the old

In the preceding sections of this chapter we encountered numerous contrasts between new and old and the global and the local so we will only touch on a few selected features of these sets of contrasts here. These binaries are found throughout the children's literature produced in both the late Ottoman and early Republican periods. At times they appear as clearly defined contrasts; at others there is a greater degree of ambiguity. The didactic certainty we have often seen sometimes gives way to blurred distinctions or outright contradictions or paradoxes.

In her work on the cartoon imagery that appears in the wake of the "Young Turk" Revolution of 1908, Palmira Brummett identifies the contrast between old and new as one of the main themes of that era.[78] Literature produced for young readers clearly shows that the juxtaposition of the new and the old was a preoccupation shared with the previous period. Children's literature from the Hamidian era is replete with references to the modern but also exhibits considerable interest in "traditional" subjects. In fact when examined more broadly, late Ottoman childhood encountered novelty in many forms – reading material was just the start. Children were presented with a range of new experiences in this period. They were confronted with new products, including toys and games as well as books and journals. They learned about many of these new possibilities through the novel medium of direct advertisement. They were increasingly expected to wear new types of clothes – sailor suits were a prominent costume[79] – and to have their appearance recorded for posterity through yet another new medium, the photographic portrait.[80] New expectations about healthcare, education, morality and, indeed, childhood itself were transforming young children's lives well before the empire came to an end.

Reading itself provided a vehicle for a variety of attitudes toward the old and the new. Reading the same texts as one's forbearers allows for the feeling of continuity and connection with the past. Hence the importance of a canon, a corpus of "classical" literature that has both stood the test of time and also stands to validate the predilections of the current generation. Reading can also serve the attempt to sever the present from the past; the Kemalist language revolution was clearly prosecuted with this aim, among others, in mind. New modes of reading, new genres, new readership, and new subjects all generate – and celebrate – the sensation of breaking with the past. But reading can never be either entirely novel or completely beholden to the past; it is rather a means of linking the old and the new. The very fact that readers see themselves as following in a tradition may in fact reflect an unprecedentedly modern consciousness. In other words the link with the past may exist in terms of the material being read but the similarity in identification with previous generations may only exist in the imagination. The changed context will inevitably alter the meaning of what is read under new circumstances. Both Ottoman and Republican reading materials emphasized the newness of reading, foregrounding it as a vehicle for access to new horizons and only rarely as a means of connecting with the past.

The fact that reading is simultaneously both new and old has often escaped those who wanted it to act only as a vector for change. The revolutionary claims of the reading initiatives, whether Ottoman or Turkish republican, are interesting as much for what they claim as that which they try to conceal. In fact, even "new" reading material requires the existence of "old" predecessors if only to provide them the contrasting sheen of novelty. We have seen above the prevalence of older texts, some going back to the fourteenth century. The field of Turkish literature demonstrates that this period contains a remarkable combination of new and old. For example, story cycles going back to the first half of the seventeenth century and the reign of Murat IV (1611–1640) remained important well into the nineteenth century, and may well have been more popular than the "popular histories" and stories that were written in the modernizing era.[81]

The persistence of old stories amid the dizzyingly modern array of texts and images is a remarkable feature of the late Ottoman and early Republican periods.[82] The enduring popularity of works like the Stories of the Prophets (*Kisas-i enbiya*) seems to have acted as an Ottoman analogue to Fontaine's *Fables* during the first half of the nineteenth century in France in the sense of linking a new readership with older content.[83] As elsewhere the phenomenon of the chapbook aided the popularization of reading in Turkey; from the middle of the nineteenth century and especially from the 1880s onwards, the old stories were committed to print in the form of affordable and accessible printed copies, thereby increasing the range of material available to young readers.[84] Fatma Aliye (1864–1936), the first modern Ottoman woman writer of import and daughter of the notable Ottoman historian Ahmed Cevdet, learned to read in the traditional way, beginning with the Qur'an which she is said to have committed to memory by the age of five.[85] To this she added an Islamic catechism (*ilm-i hal*) and a fifteenth-century poem in Ottoman Turkish devoted to the birth of the prophet Muhammad. When she was seven years old her reading took in the popular epic poems set in the long-ago, such as those of Battal Gazi and a selection from the Köroğlu destanı, and other works including the *Thousand and One Nights*.[86] Eventually she moved on to texts of more recent authorship, both French and Ottoman Turkish. But here still Fatma Aliye would encounter traditional fare, such as Yusuf Kâmil Paşa's translation of Fénélon's *Télémaque*, a variety of grammar books, and less painfully perhaps, Ahmed Midhat's *Letayif-i Rivayat* (Amusing Stories).[87]

The Republic, for all of its insistence on modernity, did not abandon these old stories entirely. Early Republican children's publications continued to include several of the traditional stories, such as the love story of Leyla and Mecnun, which seems to have been first compiled in written form by the Ottoman poet Fuzuli in the sixteenth century but turns up in the pages of the children's magazine *Çıtı Pıtı* during the early years of the Republic.[88]

Another way that early Republican's children's magazines attempted to bridge the gap between new and old was to employ an Eastern version of the Rip Van Winkle story. Our Illustrated Weekly Gazette published a story entitled "The Pharaoh Who Awoke After Eight Thousand Years" which describes the adventures of a frustratedly out-of-place Pharaoh who returns to modern-day Egypt but can neither speak the language nor regain any semblance of his former status. Eventually he mounts a camel, one of the few things familiar to him, and rides into the city. There he is astonished by everything he sees: "very tall buildings...enormous streets...tramways...automobiles." After giving up trying to shine shoes, he eventually retreats to his resting place and goes back to sleep.[89] This story emphasizes the contrast between modernity and the premodern past. The modern world has produced so much in the way of change, symbolized by the technological developments so favored by children's reading material, that the poor Pharaoh is unable to adapt.

In spite of so many references linking reading with the past – or perhaps because of them – there is an unmistakable preoccupation with novelty in the material prepared for children. The word "new" (*yeni*) appears with remarkable regularity among titles for young readers. The fascination with and prominence of innovation, especially of the technological kind, is a recurring theme in periodical literature of this era, a visible sign of the less visible but no less insistent belief in the progress of modernity. Identifying a book as "new" in its title was also symptomatic of and reinforced the commodification of reading, a topic to which we shall return in Chapter 5. A book could be sold, in part, on the basis of its newness, implying that its competitors were out of date, tactics used equally to sell brands of toothpaste or razor blades. In the Republican period it was as if proclaiming that a book or reader was "new" in its title was enough to make it so. In many cases this probably had more to do with concealing the otherwise more obvious connections with the book's late Ottoman counterparts than with actually identifying any novelty involved. Many books continued to appear with only minor, superficial changes to their titles and illustrations after the Republic was announced or, again, after the hat law made some of their illustrations appear out of date.

The burgeoning use of illustrations in children's publications was crucial to displaying the new. Children's publications seemed to fall over themselves in showcasing the artifacts of the modern period, both real and imagined. Like their elders who increasingly had access to illustrated periodicals such as *Resimli Kitab* (The illustrated book), child readers found themselves faced with such iconic examples of modernity as airplanes, trains, suspension bridges and the telephone.[90] Some publishers went beyond the limits of the modern reality and presented their young readers with illustrations of futuristic adventures, such as space travel. One magazine cover illustration offers a picture of a crudely drawn metal sphere with a bluntly pointed nose cone blasting across the starry heavens, with bright red and yellow flames streaming

Figure 3.1   Spaceship cover art

from its three legs.[91] Rather incongruously but in keeping with the mixed messages so common in these publications, this futuristic image is set within a larger and more typically childlike image of a girl in a bonnet with a lamb, a fairy with wings and a castle in the distance (Figure 3.1).

Reading on a vast social scale and reading in public were themselves innovations of the modern period. As Paul Dumont has noted, one of the many things that would have shocked the incomparable seventeenth-century Ottoman writer Evliya Çelebi were he to have returned in the modern period would be the effects of the printing press.[92] He would have found the manuscript culture almost vanished, replaced by the increasingly widespread dissemination of printed books and magazines, now within the economic reach of a much greater segment of the population. Slow to arrive in the Ottoman context, printing seemed bent on making up lost time in the late nineteenth and early twentieth centuries.[93] In this period it is common to come across children who possess a fairly large number of books and magazines, even to the point that many needed their own bookshelves; evidence we will consider in Chapter 6. Declining production costs and rising literacy rates had created a situation that contrasts sharply with the book-owning figures available for the late eighteenth century when owning more than a several books was a relative rarity.[94]

It is the very newness of the widespread dissemination and consumption of reading – and writing which was necessarily the other side of the coin – that is held up as something to be celebrated and appreciated by the young. Chapter 5 will address the subject of the consumption of reading material in detail but here we can pause to consider the role played by two phenomena that served to bridge the gap between the pre-modern and modern worlds of reading: reading rooms and guides to the composition of letters.

While the café has been a feature of Ottoman society and literary culture since the middle of the sixteenth century, a purely nineteenth-century innovation was the *kıraathane*, or reading room, a type of café in which reading played the main role.[95] One of these in particular, that called the Kıraathane-i osmanî, located on the central thoroughfare in Istanbul and run by the Armenian Serafim played a particularly important role in introducing generations of Turkish writers to modern literature.[96] A simultaneous development was the opening of a number of public libraries with a modern look. Replacing the *alaturka*, low-level reading desks (*rahle*) and the practice of piling books on their sides came the distinctly *alafranga* tables and chairs and the card catalogue.[97] With time these institutions seem to have lost their eponymous purpose, as reading became more and more an activity that people practiced in private, at home. The *kıraathane* is today something like a men's club, a place of noisy conviviality where various games are played but little reading actually takes place.

Another example of the way reading – and writing – served to bridge the gap between the old and the new is the book intended to demonstrate the proper forms of correspondence. Written both as a lesson book (*ders kitabı*) and as a general guide for letter-writing, Ahmed Rasım's version of this genre demonstrates the range of activities required in the changing world of reading and writing.[98] Encompassing a variety of forms and media including private and official correspondence, military reports, letters of congratulations, telegrams and so on, this handy guide provided the ritually observed opening lines required for correspondence with the various branches of officialdom (from the Sultan down to a local *kaymakam*), civil, military and religious, as well as suggested missives for holidays, birthdays and so on. It detailed styles of composition for a *carte visite* and, reflecting the attention to innovation of a technological variety, how to compose a telegram. It is difficult to imagine what young readers would have made of a telegraphic example such as the one that starkly reads: "Unfortunately your father died this evening."[99]

Although Ottoman-era texts already tended to favor the new at the expense of the old, after the establishment of the Republic the balance tipped much more sharply in favor of emphasizing and celebrating the new. In other words the choice between new and old increasingly assumed an ideological edge. Newness stood for the modern, republican way that actively discredited what it portrayed as the negative aspects of the old, Ottoman practices despite or indeed because of the many traits they held in common.

Republican-era reading material deployed a variety of strategies toward the past. As we have seen, the putative cruelty and backwardness of the old-style schools and their teachers were frequent targets. The ignorant hoca, armed with a stick or the bastinado ably served the republican impulse to vilify, mock and render ludicrous the immediate past in order to justify and glorify the modern. The Ottoman era could be further discredited by ridiculing antiquated language, as obscurantist and absurd. A letter to readers in *Yeni Yol* takes them to task for perpetuating what it considers obscurantist writing practices. The letter applauds the ideas conveyed in the subscribers' letters but deplores the "antiquated and absurd habits we would have thought had been long forgotten. Why are there still traces of the "Hazine-i Mektubat" [a reference to the guide to correspondence discussed above] in your letters? My dears, today's education speaks to you in an open, honest syntax and in no place causes you to use such expressions as Çakerlier, Da`ileri, Bendeleri [your humble servant, your well-wisher, your servant] and I don't know what else."[100] At other times the past could be ignored entirely or appropriated in a highly selective manner, as we saw in the account of the "Turkish" past in which one of the foremost republican historians of the Ottoman period pointedly avoided mentioning the Ottomans despite the action taking place on the Ottoman-Hapsburg frontier.

Another approach to the past was to use it – and especially its negative aspects – as a means to appreciate the present. Ahmed Rasım's "Vatan tarihi" (History of the nation) in his reader entitled *Doğru usûl-i kıraat* advocates reading "national" history as a means of inculcating love of nation. By avoiding the "mistakes" of the past, learning about the saviors of the nation, and loving the nation, reading history can be harnessed to the service of the nation.

Turkey (Türkiye), this blessed nation (vatan), this lovely nation (yurt), how was it before, for example, what situation was it in one hundred

years ago when your grandfathers' fathers were alive, what conditions, what experiences did they have, what conditions did it pass
through, who transformed it into its present state, who were the ones
who caused you to know your rights, who granted you liberties, who
made you owners of your lands? If you learn these, i.e., your nation's
history, its goodness and blessings will awaken feelings of love and
thanks in you. With these feelings having been awakened, you will
be better able to render beneficial services to your fellow country-
men, now and in the future.[101]

Using the Ottoman past, and in particular, its errors (as seen from a
republican perspective) was a means of garnering children's appreciation of the benefits of the contemporary republic. Another approach
was to leap back across the centuries to compare the events in the first
century of Islam with the plight of the Muslim Turks during the recent
fighting against the Greeks, as we have already seen. But the ancient
past could equally be consigned to the discredited ways of the Arabs
and Persians, as we shall see shortly.

Alternatively, the past could be reinvented. During the later years of the
empire and the early years of the republic Turkic themes came to the fore.
Emphasizing the pre-Ottoman and conveniently ahistorical origins of the
Turks in Central Asia was a useful means of sidelining the Islamic component in the heritage of the Turkish republic. Following a trend established
by the Turkish nationalist ideologue Ziya Gökalp during the years of World
War I, republican-era children's magazines began to include elements of
the Turkic myths. The Ergenekon and Bozkurt legends are evocative of this
trend. Both are the names of epic tales that depict the pre-historical life of
the Turks in Central Asia. Ergenekon is the name of the mythical valley in
the Altay mountains of Central Asia where the Turks were meant to have
gathered to escape the Mongols. Bozkurt means grey wolf, the figure that
emerged as the symbol for Turkic nationalists. (The name Ergenekon was
similarly appropriated by a shadowy nationalist group in contemporary
Turkey that are under suspicion for a number of violent attacks, including
the murder of the Turkish-Armenian journalist Hrant Dink.)

In the children's literature this material is introduced in an accessible
manner. *Çocuk Dünyası* printed the story under the title "Ergenekon –
Bozkurt" and the subheading "Events of the Turks." It is framed as story
about a girl named Sevinç. One Friday evening she returns from her
boarding school, a plot device that doubtless is meant to convey the
modern outlook of her parents. Sevinç is addicted to reading books and
takes up a volume called *Kave* by Şemseddin Sami from the bookshelf.

Her reading prompts her to ask her father questions. Her father begins to explain that *Kave* (Kaveh in Persian) is an Iranian tale but her mother interrupts to demand that Sevinç read Turkish and not Iranian legends, giving her forceful intervention a gendered dimension:

> You men always do this. You are always explaining the legends of the ancient Greeks or the Persians. You know nothing of the tales, legends and stories that we have either heard from our mothers or read in Turkish histories. You talk about Venus but you never think of our outstanding beauty the Fallow Deer. You know Hercules but you haven't even heard the name of Veli the Wrestler. You teach your children about Kave but you never say a word about Gray Wolf, the savior of the Turkish nation. You know about the Promised Land of the Jews and the Slavs' Tsargrad (Constantinople) but you don't even know about the Red Apple (Kızılelma, the union of all the Turks) which is known by all the Turkic peoples.[102]

Thereafter Sevinç's mother proceeds to teach her the Ergenekon legend and other Turkic tales and initiating her into the practices of the Turks, including the iconic display of the head of the grey wolf and pre-Islamic new year's rituals.

In the company of stories and poems devoted to fostering national identification among the young, the Turkish myths play an important role. By dispensing with the historical past and replacing it with one of fantasy and legend, these publications were effectively drawing a line under the Ottoman and Islamic past. The poetry and prose of Gökalp was enlisted to set the stage for this national imaginary and people it with heroes. That these figures were almost exclusively military leaders allowed these publications to link them in their young readers minds to the current agenda of the young republic. For example, Gökalp's "Türk'ün Tufanı" (The Turkish Flood), one of several rhymed works he composed with the intention of inculcating patriotism in children,[103] appears in *Çocuk Dünyası*. This poem emphasizes the need for national leadership, stressing the role of leaders such as the legendary Oğuz Khan, before underscoring the need for Turks to have strong leadership in every period for their continued existence, raising the fear of those who would wish to tyrannize them.[104] Gökalp's poem "The Fallow Deer" again emphasizes the need for the Turks to have strong leadership while the story "For My Reawakening Mother(land)" (Hayat Bulan Validem İçin) takes up the subject of the Greek occupation of Izmir, comparing the invaded nation to his sick mother.

Reading children were thus confronted with a variety of perspectives on the subject of old and new. Reading itself was a venerable tradition and something now being done in new ways, with new types of text and new content. Some of this content was itself old, going back many centuries in some cases, but the new context required that it be read and understood in unanticipated ways. Like many of the goods and practices displayed on the pages of their textbooks and magazines, such as new outfits, new habits and roles, new products of many kinds, reading these newly produced reading materials necessitated novel approaches and a fair amount of flexibility on the part of their readership.

Tensions abound in this material and this lack of fixity could only have furthered the processes by which the much more established premodern practices associated with learning to read and reading were being complicated and unsettled by the emerging textual dispensation. How this was received by young readers is naturally difficult to fathom but we can safely assume that the new mix of texts, content and roles added a degree of stimulation and excitement to the process that must place great attention to the new, including the ways in which the old was repackaged in novel ways.

The global and the local

The new was frequently associated with the global, with what was considered up to date around the world. Literature created for children, the magazines in particular, were instrumental in creating a sense of internationalism. Children were now being exposed to a much wider range of geographical referents than ever before. It was considered modern for them to be so informed, and one of the many benefits that reading could claim to bestow. The wider horizons were selectively constructed; there were far more references to Paris and San Francisco than, say, to Addis Ababa or Delhi but there was a strong emphasis on emphasizing the wider world. Consider, for example, the cover illustration of *Haftalık Resimli Gazetemiz* (Our Weekly Illustrated Gazette) which shows a boy and a girl each seated in the upper corners while underneath them a series of medallions depicting scenes from all the four corners of the earth are displayed, as if to reinforce the ways that reading would transport them around the world (Figure 3.2).

This globalized – and globalizing – approach sat in tension with the simultaneous impetus for reading to serve as an agent of identification between child and country. On the one hand authors and publishers were keen to demonstrate that reading is a gateway to the wider world, an

Figure 3.2   Reading's wide horizons

activity that opened new horizons. Literacy, they seem to say, provides entrée into a civilized and international world as represented by recognizable images taken from the four corners of the earth, shared appearances, as evidenced by sailor suits for boys and hair ribbons for girls, and a shared interest in a "modern" lifestyle with respect to education, family relations, moral development and economic advancement.

On the other hand, a countervailing tendency is readily apparent, one that persistently focuses on the indigenous. Local styles, whether architectural, sartorial or cultural, predominate in this trend and do so in both the late Ottoman and early Republican periods. The local emphasis certainly did not mean a retreat from modernity. Numerous illustrations show modern inventions and conveniences in recognizably domestic scenes. For example, the polite child whom we encountered greeting the elderly man in Ahmed Cevad's *Çocuklara sarf ve nahv dersleri: Türkçe öğreniyorum* does so under a prominently placed gas streetlamp and the airplanes that adorn the cover of *Çocuk Dünyası* fly against the minarets of the Istanbul skyline. Some authors forcefully opposed a globalized literature for children. Consider, for example, the approach taken by *Yeni Yol*: "We don't want an imitation or a translation of the magazines of Europe. We want to publish a journal that is consonant with the spirit, level and knowledge of our own world and that which is different from that of the western world."[105]

Children's reading material from this period displays a tension between two tendencies, the international or cosmopolitan, with its attention to the worldwide spread of modernity and a fairly generic approach to childhood, and the local or national tendency, focused on indigenous concerns, morality, holidays, dress and so on. Children's publications seem to vacillate between these two positions, often giving evidence of both on the same page. This is apparent both in textual content and illustration. Through their explanations and references, children's reading materials translated international or abstract phenomena into the local idiom. For example, when explaining the dual movement of the earth, spinning on its axis while revolving around the sun, Arakel's reader likens it to a Mevlevi dervish, twirling on one foot while moving about the lodge (*semahane*).[106] Images conveyed the world in more direct fashion. When illustrations were not appropriated from foreign publications, they inevitably reflected local realities. Whether in dress, architecture or specific objects, the illustrators of children's reading materials managed to convey a local ambiance. As we might expect, the tendency to promote local and, indeed, national images increased during the periods of war and national stress associated with Balkan Wars, World War I, the Turkish war of independence and the nation-building project. Let us now consider some particular evidence of the trend toward localization.

A good example of the simple, locally produced – and illustrated – reading primer is Ahmed Cevad's 1908–1909 Grammar and syntax lessons for children: I am reading Turkish. The book's first lesson contains only small illustrations of simple items, each with its name in Ottoman Turkish underneath, e.g., rose, cat and book. It is readily apparent that the illustrations have not been appropriated from a foreign source. The picture of the man (*insan*) shows a man with a moustache and beard, wearing a fez and a high-collared shirt under a jacket. The woman (*kadın*) wears a headscarf pushed back to show some of her hair. After the 12 objects there are two sketches of urban landscapes each recognizable as and labeled Istanbul and Salonica.[107] Several pages later, after imparting the rudiments of grammar, the book provides some texts for reading, dictation and writing. These themes are mostly local as well:

> The city of Istanbul is an extremely beautiful and large city on both sides of the Black Sea straits. It is the capital of the Ottomans.
>
> The first Ottoman ruler was Sultan Osman. The name of our beloved current ruler is Sultan Mehmed V.
>
> The book is man's most faithful friend. I love my books. All of my books have beautiful illustrations inside.
>
> The pen doesn't write; there is no ink left in my inkstand. The point of my pencil has broken.
>
> Paris is the capital of France. France is in Europe. Brazil is in America. Much coffee is grown in Brazil. Yemen is our province. Yemen is in Asia. The world's best coffee comes from Yemen.[108]

The overseas world has not been forgotten entirely here but it is clearly secondary in importance to the Ottoman lands.

This localism is most apparent in the illustrations that accompany texts. We have just referred to Ahmed Cevad's text whose story entitled "The Polite Child" (*Nazik çocuk*) shows a child with his book bag under one arm respectfully saluting an elderly Ottoman gentleman who wears a frockcoat and fez and walks with a cane. The dome of a mosque and its minaret are clearly visible on the horizon. Equally indigenous is the series of smaller images that illustrate such subsequent texts as The Return from School or During the Afternoon Recess. These sketches are extremely simple and their scale is very small (measuring approximately 1.5 square inches) yet manage to convey a clearly local flavor. They show a uniformed Ottoman schoolboy, identified as Behçet in the accompanying text, returning home from school, kissing his mother on the cheek, asking how she is and then telling her excitedly about his successful day at school. ("If you only knew what a lovely story we read.") She praises him and gets him to promise that he will always be hardworking. Later his sister arrives home from her school and the two siblings sit down to do their homework together. The second passage is accompanied by three simple drawings showing the schoolboys in their uniforms and fezzes at recess (some of them play leapfrog), sitting at their desks in orderly rows for lessons and leaving school at the end of the day. These are simple but effective demonstrations of how children should behave at home and at school, hovering somewhere between the realistic and the ideal but always effecting a clearly indigenous setting.

The following year the publisher Tüccarzâde İbrahim Hilmi brought out The golden book: The first children's reader. This volume presents its readers with a similar cast of indigenous characters, such as the fez-wearing student, a carpenter, Ottoman soldiers, but does so in a much more overtly political context.[109] Here are the national heroes Midhat Paşa and Namık Kemal; there is a picture of a village labeled "The Ottoman nation" (*Osmanlı vatanı*), a scene depicting a modern Ottoman family at table, entitled Family Affection (*aile muhabbeti*); teacher in classroom; a reading on Sultan Osman and Ottomanism (*Osmanlılık*), including an illustration of marchers with a banner of the 1908 revolution which reads "Freedom, Brotherhood, Equality" (*Hürriyet, uhuvvet, müsavviyet*), identifiably Ottoman coinage with the sultanic emblem (*tuğra*) conspicuously visibile and so on. There are a few images drawn from European artists but they are in a small minority and thus serve to emphasize the indigenous context of this reader.

But as the empire gave way to the republic, the tendency toward localism could veer into a much more limited, even chauvinistic agenda. This was particularly apparent in the pages of the periodicals that began their publishing lives with the founding of the Republic. Consider the approach of *Yeni Yol*, the longest lived of the new children's publications during the 1923–1928 period.[110] It exhorted its young readers to supply the initiative, determination and enterprise necessary to become the inventors, machinists and technical people, and company heads that the young nation required. Such initiative and bravery was nothing less than a holy (*mukaddes*) guiding principle for the nation.[111] Whereas the Ottoman-era periodicals displayed an inclusive approach, this soon gave way to one which pursued an aggressively nationalist line. In a signed article entitled "Love Turkishness" (*Türklüğü sev*) the editor Nedim Tuğrul ordered his readers to "Love your nation!" and indicated that this was intended on a less than inclusive basis by incorporating strong Anti-Persian and anti-Arab sentiment.[112] Several of its stories feature examples of fearless Turkish children who gave up their lives in the defense of the nation against the invading Greeks. One story in its pages was entitled "Greek Savagery and the Atrocities in the village of Taşhöyük, Eskişehir." Where the magazine was somewhat inclusive was in its appeal to a pan-Turkist sense of belonging by emphasizing the modern Turks' shared heritage with the likes of Cengiz and Atilâ. Invoking these world conquerors was accompanied by equally martial and violent imagery.

Don't forget that you are the children of your forefathers who caused the earth to shake and turned the world upside down. You are the blood descendents of Hulagu and Timur Leng [Tamerlane] who personified the tales of the Arabs and Persians and demonstrated their sovereignty with blood and killing.

Waxing increasingly violent, Tuğrul instructed his readers to,

Reject the slanders cast upon your ancestors by the foreign countries...Break the hands that touch your grandfathers, break into pieces the mouths that slander them, take out the eyes that look with contempt upon them and crush the heads of those who think evil of them.

These narrower, more urgent and more violent appeals stand in stark relief to the more integrationist, modern message of assimilation and integration into the contemporary world – and with the images of a benign kiddieland that suffuse many pages of the same magazine.

Geographical literacy helped to inform the new reading public. Whether in the form of maps, verbal descriptions or illustrations, awareness of and emphasis on the wider world was an important aspect of learning to read. Beginning in the late Ottoman period and continuing into the Republican era, children's reading material encouraged interest in the wider world. In its simplest form this meant maps and texts devoted to geographical literacy.[113] For example, Ahmed Rasım's reader featured a geographical lesson as its second text – the first was devoted to morality by way of likening God's beneficence to a supra-maternal role for mankind – and approached it in an equally simplistic way. "Do you know the shape and form of the world on which we live? Our world is round like a cannonball or a melon. Look at the drawings in your book. They show you the halves of the earth, round like cannon balls."[114] On the facing page are two simple illustrations showing the eastern and western hemispheres. Different texts provided different approaches and levels of detail but the common intention was to increase their readers' knowledge of the wider geographical field. Illustrations were a natural ally in stimulating the curiosity of the young. Often the pictures were deployed in order to illustrate a particular story or news item. At other times their inclusion could be somewhat random, as was the case with *Çocuklara Mahsus Gazete* where images from cities around the world appeared as if in a series running across its various issues. Places depicted included both the local, such as Moda (a neighborhood on the Asian side of Istanbul), Jerusalem and Suez in Egypt, and such faraway cities as Budapest, Paris and Havana. Perhaps the most emphatic example was the journal called Our Weekly Illustrated Gazette (*Haftalık Resimli Gazetimiz*) whose cover, illustrated above, featured a series of circular medallions each depicting a different ethnographical scene from around the world. In each of the upper corners of the cover was a picture of a boy and a girl in a chair reading the magazine.

Creating geographical identification was an important element in children's reading. The Ottoman period, as we have already seen, witnessed the beginnings of modern geographical identification between children and their territory. Map education would eventually become the most important tool in this process but it built upon an earlier method aimed at encouraging the bond between young readers and the Ottoman lands. As we saw in Ali İrfan's reader, this method relied on identification with the political leadership as personified in Osman Gazi and the reigning sultan Mehmed Reşad. The territorial link was more inchoate. The term *"vatan"* (motherland) was invoked and employed as the title of the first text in this reader. But the geographical definition of the motherland was left vague, perhaps creatively so given the shrinking borders of the late Ottoman state. The Ottoman lands were defined as being "wherever we Ottomans are born and raised and wherever the writ of our glorious Padishah and our beloved government extends."[115]

Children's publications were not always consistent in their depictions. As we have seen, they generated a number of mixed messages with their illustrations and their sometimes clumsy attempts to instill patriotism and correct behavior. Still some trends are clear to see. The pages of Our Journal (*Bizim Mecmua*) trace a shift from a generic, almost Disney-like world of stylized animals and fluffy content to a localized, Turkified presentation. With issue number 7 in 1922 the journal abandons the kiddie-like tone and illustrations in favor of pictures depicting a clearly local Ottoman boy beating drum in front of a mosque. The illustration shows the lights strung between the mosque's minarets as is the custom at the time of Ramazan. Other images depict Turkish boys and girls, often the flag visible in the background. Issue 21 sees a return of foreign artwork on the journal's cover but thereafter the artwork is locally produced.

Yeni Yol presents an interesting mélange of national imperative and childlike entertainment. The early issues are infused with a strong national message, as might be expected from a magazine founded almost in step with the appearance of the Republic. As noted above, issue 15 contained the strident command to Love your nation and some strongly exclusive national language. By issue 34 Mustafa Kemal arrives to fill the blank spaces that appeared on the covers of preceding issues.

But there is also a fair degree of slapstick humor and generic entertainment alongside the image of the leader of the nation. The mixed messages continue in the next issue which features a foreign illustration of two dogs pulling apart some embroidered linen while a girl with a bow in her hair cries out, a comic strip about a boy who tries to get his cat to retrieve his sunken toy boat, some holiday (*bayram*) congratulation notices and several earnest group photographs of school children and scout groups.

This haphazard admixture continues when *Yeni Yol*'s colored covers arrive with issue 41. These convey an exuberant sense of buffoonery but are clearly locally produced, given the appearance of a fez. Also visible are a fairy with wings, a girl in a very un-Turkish bonnet with a lamb. The rear cover shows a picture of school mayhem, with dogs depicted as the teacher and pupils. Inside there are more scouting group photographs; one installment of a series of photo essays on Turkish cities (in this issue Ayvalık) and an article on tiger hunting. An interesting shift occurs in 1926 (issues 103 and 104) with the fanciful cover illustrations of generic children being replaced by specific, named Turkish boys and girls. Inside, the main article is devoted to İsmet Paşa's visit to Silifke. Then come articles on how animals carry their young and a series on Houses in the Civilized World, with images of New York and Chicago. These are complemented by more Photos of Our Hardworking Youngsters (*çalışkan yavrularımızın resimleri*). Some of the boys sport caps with visors and peaks, some girls wear bows in their hair. One girl appears in a necktie and a cap, others are wearing cloche-style hats; another girl has chosen to dress in a sailor suit. All of the children have Muslim names. The back cover of issue 108 displays 36 photographs of individual school children, each identified by locale, school name and given name. Most come from Istanbul and its environs but there are a few exceptions, such as Uzunköprü, Söğüt, Adana, showing that the networks of nationally oriented reading are extending into the provinces.

Faik Sabri's 1926 textbook entitled "First Geography Readings for Children" effects an interesting mix of the international and the national as it transports the reader from the general to the specific. Its first text is entitled "The Child Who Doesn't Like Geography" and takes the form of a conversation between two brothers. Reşid, the older sibling, explains that geography is really about all the things that interest Ferid, the younger brother.[116] It contains references to "people unlike us" (black-, red- and yellow-skinned people); fierce and exotic animals in forests and on the open seas and so on. The second text, "What is Geography?," continues the dialogue between the brothers. Lessons on the sun and the moon follow. By lesson 14 Ferid's introduction to the wonders of geography has reached the subject of The Five Continents. This is a familiar subject, with semicircular projections of the earth, a focus on the landmasses and the seas, and a globe, but all is explained via the ongoing frame story of the fraternal dialogue.

By lesson 42 they have reached The Map of Turkey. Ferid's older brother draws him a map of Turkey and labels the lands and seas. After those two lines of text there appears a map of Turkey over which is superimposed an image of a schoolboy with outstretched arms. Dotted lines extend beyond the frame of this inset image both horizontally to the east and west and vertically to the north and south. The caption explains that when you face the map your right side is the east and so on. This simple image thus conveys both the practical act of cartographic orientation and a sort of physical identification with and enframing within the political map of Turkey. Subsequent chapters are devoted to "Ankara and Istanbul" and European Turkey (*Paşa Eli*). When the brothers' discussion turns to Edirne, Ferid notes that "two or three years ago the Greeks took Edirne from us. Later we took it back from them." The Çatalca lines are mentioned as the point of the furthest advance of the Bulgarians in the Balkan Wars. "They wanted to enter Istanbul; but our brave soldiers drove them back." The brothers make similar references to the Gallipoli campaign of World War I. National concerns are very much at the fore and continue in the next chapter, "Anatolia." The chapter on The Countries of Europe presents tableaux of some of the main attractions of Europe: London Bridge, Stockholm, the Italian lakes, Paris and so on, while Asia and Africa are depicted as fairly exotic with pictures of a Rajah's palace with decorated elephant. Asia is "localized" only insofar as a matter-of-fact statement to the effect that, "The biggest part of our country is in Asia. The Turkish Republic covers the southwest of Europe," thus laying claim to a geographical identity at once both Asian and European. These early Republican texts reflect a clear departure from the preceding norm.

Most children's publications observe no such arbitrary geographical boundaries. Their illustrations display a global outlook. Ottoman and Turkish places are presented in a blend that includes, as in the pages of *Çocuklara Mahsus Gazete*, Suez, Moda Burnu, Port Said, the imagined lighthouse of Alexandria, Tangiers, Budapest, Paris, Havana and Jerusalem. In this global, inclusive view, what was new was presented as similar, whether one was in Paris, London or Istanbul. Hot air balloons, airplanes steamship navigation were, in this presentation, all equally likely, wherever one was reading.

This last technological innovation provides the frame for a chapter in a 1909 textbook that neatly bridges the emerging local concerns with global awareness and aspirations. With a story entitled "The first company/partnership" (*İlk şirket*), the author Tüccarzâde İbrahim Hilmi attracts his readers' attention with a model steamship. This is accomplished both textually and visually. The story employs a direct style to set the scene and draw in his audience, "The lesson had begun. The children were sitting in their places, waiting for their teacher. A large wooden box was resting on top of the table..."[117] Meanwhile the young readers' eyes will have no doubt taken in the illustration set in the middle of the passage several lines below. There they see a large-scale model of a steamship, now out of its box, with its details (funnel, masts, etc.) being commented upon by their teacher. The boys, all wearing the fez like their teacher, sit in rapt attention as he explains that he is going to impart a story with a moral. The story concerns a group of students of the same school from 15 years ago who formed a partnership, pooled their pocket money by abstaining from diversions and snacks, and contrived to present their school with this yard-long model of a steamship. But this was not the full extent of their partnership. After leaving school the young men continued their joint enterprise in the adult world. Following their teacher's advice regarding the value of a steamship, they contrived to raise funds for the purchase of the real thing and used it to ply the waters of the high seas. The teacher concluded the story, "According to what I have heard their business has done so well that today they operate large steamships and earn quite a lot of money. Now you too should form a partnership like theirs. The work that a single man can do is nothing. Can it equal that of five or ten people coming together for a common purpose? Partnership. Always partnership!"[118] This tale begins in the local context of the late Ottoman schoolroom but soon extends, like reading itself, beyond the immediate setting to the wider world, a world of endeavor, profit and internationalization.

Like a camera lens that can expand and narrow its focus depending on what the photographer wishes to emphasize, these publications used the new technology at their disposal to depict both a local and an international vision. Photographs of Paris and San Francisco vied with the image of the Turkish schoolboy enframed by the map of his newly created nation. The ways in which young readers were encouraged to conceive of their country depended on these sometimes complementary and sometimes contradictory approaches. Printed material allowed for a variety of visions to be presented, ranging from the global to the

very local level. Photographs of school groups and even individual readers shared space on the printed page with faraway images. The blend of
approach naturally reflected the mindset of individual authors, illustrators, publishers and censors. As a result children's material could
appear both pictorially alluring and confusing. The messages were as
mixed as the geographical referents, reflecting the various competing
tendencies: toward wider world (global citizenship, modernity, etc.) and
toward narrower belonging (national, even, at times, chauvinistically
so). These different and seemingly antithetical strands provide a telling example of the varied impulses with which reading was freighted
in this period of transition. There was frequently no universal trend or
pattern to be discerned; antithetical views were often on display in the
same publication, even on the same page: strange and familiar, frivo-
lous and serious, secular and religious, inclusive and exclusive, new and
old, international and domestic.

Children's reading material was striving for what we would today call
identity formation via reading. It drew children into the world of adults,
sometimes by a rather matter-of-fact approach, and sometimes disarm-
ingly, and therefore more seductively, through creating a shared culture
of reading and belonging that encouraged feelings of connectedness
and mutuality. I would argue that the competing tendencies explored
in this chapter actually encouraged the process of identity formation,
although perhaps in unintended ways. The messages that reading
imparted were diverse and, as we have seen, sometimes even frankly
contradictory. In spite of the impulse emanating from officialdom to
impart a like-minded consciousness in the minds of young readers, the
material produced in this period of change was irrepressibly varied. Its
shear liveliness and diversity ensured that no single message could carry
the day, even though this became less and less true in the early years of
the Turkish Republic when the pressures for uniformity and the means
of ensuring it increased.

4
Mechanics: Text and Image

After more than 2000 years of trying we still do not have a satisfactory understanding of how we read.[1] Scholars have noted the importance of interactive links in the evolution of the history of reading, aware that various processes interact with each other in complex ways. Yet we remain largely ignorant of what actually happens to us mentally, physically and emotionally as we cross the liminal border which separates the realms of illiteracy and literacy. Marcel Proust termed reading a "fruitful miracle." More recently students of reading have focused on its physiological aspects, such as the optical, neurological and cognitive pathways that allow reading to take place.[2] We know that the ability to interpret and in turn to produce a written form of communication is largely dependent upon and inextricably linked with speech. As Steven Pinker expresses it, "children are wired for sound but print is an optical accessory that must be bolted on."[3] The primacy of the oral/aural ensured that pre-modern societies privileged the spoken as opposed to the written word. "For most of written history, reading was speaking...Reading has always been different from writing. Writing prioritizes sound...Reading, however, prioritizes meaning."[4]

For Muslims the seminal reading is the Qur'an, which literally means "recitation." As the single most important text of a world religion, the Qur'an is of course atypical. Indeed, Islamic learning valorizes the inimitability *(i'jaz)* of the Qur'an to a very high degree. Yet the holy book is in a way also typical of any pre-modern text in that it was committed to writing merely to preserve the oral and aural aspects of the original, pre-textual communication that emanated, in the view of Muslims, from God.

This study is situated in order to observe the transition from pre-modern to modern modes of reading. The assumption here is that the changes that take place in the definition and practice of reading together with the elements of continuity provide us with important information about the arrival of the modern. The late Ottoman and early Turkish Republican context affords the opportunity to see the many ways in which the practice of reading both responded and contributed to the changes of the modern period.

This chapter addresses the mechanics of learning to read. Frequently overlooked by historians and social scientists eager to assess the broader impact of literacy, the particular details involved in acquiring and developing literacy can tell us a great deal about the emergence of modern society in first the late Ottoman Empire and then the Turkish Republic. By examining such facets of literacy as the ways in which children were taught the alphabet, the changing pedagogical approach to reading, and the ways in which illustrations both bolstered and occasionally undermined the official version of learning to read, this chapter attempts to get at the specific activities – the nitty-gritty – involved in learning to read. It starts, appropriately enough, with the so-called "traditional" approach.

Halide Nusret Zorlutuna (1901–1984) has left a vivid description of the way in which she, like many others, learned to read. The first chapter of her autobiography *Bir Devrin Romanı* (A time's tale) begins simply enough with her first "reading" experience.[5] Typically, this "First Lesson" involved the repetition of Arabic passages from the Qur'an. The words are at once both familiar and strange to those whose mother tongue was a language other than Arabic.[6] She thus begins her book in a rather striking manner, simply presenting her readers with the Qur'anic lines she first heard and then was meant to repeat:

> *Eûzu billâhi mine'ş-şeytani'r-racim*
> *– Eûzu billâhi mine'ş-şeytani'r-racim.*
> *– Bismillâhi'r-rahmani'rahîm*
> *– Bismillâhi'r-rahmani'rahîm, etc.*[7]

After this exchange, which takes up most of the book's first page but offers little in the way of setting or explanation, [Zorlutuna] provides a few bits of identifying information. She sets the scene by describing its characters: a young woman with a white head covering and a young girl, also with her head covered, sitting across a low table from one another. The girl is looking directly in the young woman's eyes and repeating what she says "like a parrot."[8] While this helps the reader to place the recitation in context, an air of mystery nevertheless surrounds the scene. Over the page further details emerge, but new mysteries also appear. "This young woman is my mother," described as the suffering daughter, orphaned when forty days old, of a young officer killed in war with Russia, and now the husband of a man sentenced to hard labor in Sinop prison, described as a "holy ordeal." The setting thus takes on an aura of sorrow, patriotism and religiosity; the number 40 has important connotations in the Islamic context.

"The small girl across from this young woman and carefully repeating what she said – as you will have guessed – was me. According to the unsurprising tradition of that time, I had begun to read at the age of four years, four months, and four days."[9] But just how was she learning to read, and what did reading mean in this context, and at this time, estimated by the author to have been 1905?

The mechanics were simple: Like children the world round,[10] her initial efforts were physical; her mother traced her finger over the letters in the book in front of them.

> – Elif![11] she said
> – Elif! I said.
> My beautiful, straight, simple Elif!..
> Then a second letter.
> – B.
> – B.
> And thus it was that I – like all my contemporaries – had my first lesson at the age of four years, four months, and four days.[12]

This scene combines many of the main characteristics of what is usually referred to as the "traditional" or "old" mode of learning to read. It is repeated in a number of tellings that transcend differences in geography, social class, gender, native language and so forth.[13] In such scenes the details may change – the teacher can stand in for the parent or another relative, for example – but the essential elements of this often-repeated pattern are nearly constant. These include: the presence of a, or more usually "the," religious text (in this case the Qur'an); the inclusion of aural/oral repetition or recitation; the accompaniment and instruction being given by a family member or perhaps a member of the religious classes; the presence of a religious and in some cases also a national context (both are present in Halide Nusret's example); and a degree of ritual – a rite of passage – in the methods and/or the timing of the transformational event itself.

As Zorlutuna's example shows, the actual practice of learning to read inevitably begins with the problem of deciphering text. The choice of text is clearly important, involving cultural and linguistic inflections that are central to locating the importance of reading within a range of broader contexts, and we shall return to these issues below. For the time being, however, let us concentrate on the problem facing the young Halide Nusret and all those attempting to learn to read in this period. The first issue with which they were confronted – the texts in question having almost invariably been chosen by the adults involved – was that of deciphering script. In the first instance this meant learning the letters of the alphabet.

These first movements, repetitive and largely divorced of meaning, of fingers tracing over letters, of pen put to paper, prefigure the larger but frequently internal migrations that will be freighted with import. But before meaning could be derived, the process of learning to read concentrated necessarily on deciphering first the alphabet and then on the ability to recognize words, phrases and eventually sentences. In other words, reading was in essence a two-part process. The first was rather more mechanical; today we would call it neurological. It involved making out the shapes of letters and words and recognizing a correspondence between these linear markings and their aural referents. Once this correspondence was achieved, the neophyte reader was able to engage with the task of understanding the ideas that lay behind the signs. As the publisher and writer Sabiha Sertel (1895–1968) put it in her 1928 *Yeni Kıraat* (The new reader), "Reading has two aspects: 1) recognizing the written or printed words and sentences and 2) the ideas generated from these recognitions."[14] By arguing for subsuming the physical aspect of reading to the mental Sertel typified the radical new pedagogical methods. Instead of "parroting" she wanted children to understand what they read. To this end she wanted them to practice reading sufficiently often so as to be able to recognize words at first sight. Recognizing the root sounds of each word would enable young readers to associate meaning with words. Crucially she also advocated that children be kept from moving their lips while reading, from reading out loud and from marking their place on the page with a finger or a pen. (This last practice, like reading out loud, was tolerated in the early years but was to be eliminated by the final year of primary school.) Reading should be silent and still, a victory for the mental aspect of reading over the physical.[15]

Such a preoccupation with suppressing the physical in favor of the cerebral aspect of reading reflected the natural progression inherent in learning to read. The movement from reading as an external practice, concerned with the deciphering of letters on paper, scripts and the parsing of simple words and phrases, to an internal one centered on the absorption of meaning mimicked the growth in proficiency of a beginning reader. Both aspects were necessary, of course; the mental aspects were only possible once the physical dimensions, involving eyes, ears and mouth, had been mastered.

This cumulative quality inherent in learning to read, in which basic and essentially mechanical skills served as the building blocks for the development of internalized mental stimulation, meant that learning to read was inherently transferable. In other words, learning the alphabet provided the ability to move beyond the confines of the initial text to other genres, other cultural affiliations. This transportable quality of reading is one of its greatest assets; it gave the initiated the ability to apply their newly acquired skills to a potentially unlimited range of materials, contexts and genres, initially, at least, restricted only by the confines of the reader's alphabetic and linguistic range. But this tranferability has historically provoked periodic bouts of apprehension and attempts to control what was read. We need only think of the alarm registered over the popularity of the "penny dreadfuls" in English-language countries or the dismay registered by the educated classes toward the growth of popular reading material in Russia to appreciate the universality of this problem.[16] The practice of reading is historically linked, as we have seen, with notions of morality and social control.

But we must begin with the attempt to impart and control the physical elements necessary in the process of learning to read. For Turkish-speaking children of the Ottoman Empire and until 1928 the Republic of Turkey this meant learning the Arabic alphabet. Since Ottoman Turkish was written in the Arabic, or properly speaking the Arabic-derived, script its readers had to come to terms with the issue of pronunciation or vocalization. They confronted the problem of the ambiguity of the Arabic script in which almost all texts appear without vocalization marks, i.e., the vowel markings necessary to know the reading of a particular word are not normally supplied in the various languages which make use of the largely consonantal Arabic script. This became one of the reasons put forward in early Republican times to justify its replacement with the Latin script in 1928. This problem had already been recognized in the late Ottoman period but the issue was dealt with in considerably less dramatic fashion. In 1878 the Ottoman government created a commission to search for a solution to the problems associated with the joining and separation of letters in the Ottoman Turkish script, compound words and especially the lack of almost all vocalization. The discussions seem to have ranged far and wide and included the views of those in favor of accepting Latin letters. But the prevailing view was that it was not possible to change the alphabet that had after all been used by the various Muslim peoples for many centuries. The alphabet was likened to a house and it was thought better to remain in the same abode but to carry out renovations in order to avoid the drastic step of moving houses altogether.[17] It was only with the radical program of the early Republic that the drastic "house-moving" inherent in the shift to the Latin script was so dramatically effected.

In 1881 the Primary Schools Directorate of the Ottoman Ministry of Education issued a communication regarding the necessity of looking into the problems linked with the mispronunciation of words in Ottoman Turkish. Particularly worrying was the possibility that mispronouncing certain words could lead to the sin (*günah*) deriving from misreading the Holy Qur'an.[18] But this was more easily remedied considering it was mainly the hocas who were then doing most of the teaching of Turkish-speaking children. The ulema would presumably know a sin when they heard it. Still it was thought necessary to train them to be on guard against this problem and to impose that frequent stopgap: inspection. Other remedies suggested included opening a teachers' training school, generalizing the Ottoman Turkish alphabet, and applying the principles of phonics (*usûl-i savtiye*) to the growing educational sector.[19] Of these, only the inspection and opening of the teacher training college seem to have been consistently applied, but it is interesting to note that the mention of these "modern" pedagogical notions appeared well before the birth of the Republic.

In the realm of textbooks, change was readily apparent. A comparatively early work such as Kayserili Doktor Rüşdü's 1857 ABC entitled *Nuhbet ül-etfâl* (The children's choice) and the more widely employed *Elifbâ-yi Osmanî* (The Ottoman ABC) by the prolific and influential Selim Sabit Efendi produced what the Republican educationalist Aziz Berker referred to as a revolution in the instruction of reading and writing and the creation of a progressive professional mentality.[20]

But although the trend was moving from a situation in which few if any allowances were made to making material accessible to the young in terms of language or content to a nascent understanding that reading, like any other subject, ought to be taught as a skill that could be developed in incremental stages, the pedagogical transition was uneven. In many cases the language of children's material remained difficult. This was noted by Aziz Berker in his 1945 study of primary education in Turkey. Taking an ornately composed passage drawn from the late Ottoman children's periodical *Çocuklara Kıraat* which was published between 1881 and 1882 as an example, Berker seemed to revel in the absurdity associated with young children being able to comprehend its elaborate sentence structure and lofty references to the imperial personage of the sultan.[21] In so doing, Berker was indulging in what would become a fairly standard but logically somewhat circular republican practice of ridiculing the old language as something incomprehensible to people reared on the radically "reformed" Turkish instilled by the state after 1928. Nevertheless, the author had a point; the extent to which late Ottoman authors of children's materials attempted to compose or select texts appropriate to the age and grade level of the child audience was extremely patchy. Indeed, the unevenness extended into the Republican period as well. The cover illustration of a children's publication entitled *Gürbüz Türk Çocuğu* (The healthy Turkish child) presents a picture of two very young children next to a chalkboard on which one of them appears to have written the following statement, "The civilizational level of every nation depends upon the attention it pays to its children," hardly the sort of language one expects from children still to lose their baby fat (Figure 4.1).[22]

Still, concern with the mechanics of reading continued to exercise the minds of those attempting to improve the pedagogy of reading in both the late Ottoman and early Republican periods. The case of Selim Sabit Efendi is instructive in this regard. A good example of a crossover figure of the late Ottoman period, Selim Sabit received both a *medrese* and a western-style education. A member of the Grand Education Council (*Meclis-i kebir-i maarif*), and director of the empire's *rüşdiye* (advanced primary) schools, he also served as chair of the important schools inspection commission (*Encümen-i teftiş ve muayene*). For our purposes it is noteworthy that he authored at least ten school textbooks, devoted to such subjects as geography, grammar, history and so on.[23] But it is his treatise intended for training primary school teachers that best illustrates the developing pedagogical spirit of the late Ottoman period. First published in 1870, his *Rehnüma-yı muallimin: Sıbyan mekteblerine mahsus usûl-i tedrisiye* (The guide for teachers: principles of instruction for primary schools) emphasized the "new method" (*usûl-i cedide*) of teaching.[24] Later adopted in the Muslim areas of Central Asia where it gave its name to the modernizers who favored it,[25] Selim Sabit's version of the "new method" included instruction in small groups who would take it in turns to work with their teacher, an emphasis on dividing students into four different groups and adopting a sequential approach

Figure 4.1   Ventriloquist tendencies

to introducing subjects. For example, his program for the Ottoman state primary schools is as follows:

1st year: ABC; Qur'an; morals (*ahlâk*); mental math; writing

2nd year: Qur'an; catechism (*ilm-i hal*); introductory information (*malumat-i ibtidaiye*); counting and enumeration; large text handwriting (*hatt-ı sülüs*)

3rd year: Qur'an, Qur'anic recitation (*tecvid*); history of the prophets; the four mathematical operations (*âmal-i erbaa*); the Qur'anic script (*hatt-i nesih*)

4th year: Qur'an; geography; Ottoman history; Turkish grammar; the rıka script.[26]

Progress was meant to be regimented and orderly, unlike the one-room school of traditional education.

When it came actually to teaching students the first item on this list, Selim Sabit Efendi offered a detailed plan. Teaching the letters of the alphabet was to be accomplished by dividing the children into groups of three to five, by writing the letters on the board (*levha*) and by point-ing out their forms and names. The teacher was meant to demonstrate the letters to the students with a narrow pointer. After the students pro-nounced each one individually the teacher was to repeat the demonstra-tion, pronouncing the letters himself. Then he was to have the students say them in unison so that they become accustomed to their pronuncia-tion.[27] The emphasis is on understanding, with the children's progress being measured by having the children answer questions intended to reveal how much of the lessons they have absorbed. Comprehension and central control are the bywords of the new pedagogical method intended to replace the emphasis on rote learning and the individual-ized authority of the old-style religiously inspired learning.

Thus in the late Ottoman period we can already make out a strong interest in controlling the pedagogical practices associated with acquir-ing literacy. While, as Zorlutuna's example demonstrates, simple rep-etition divorced of cognition, often of the Arabic Qur'an, may have continued to be the norm outside of school, pedagogues like Selim Sabit were working to ensure that the "new methods" were the way of the future. This novel pedagogy aimed at rationalizing and standard-izing what had hitherto been approached "naturally," or at least what its practitioners considered to have been handled in an unconscious or unscientific manor. The Republican period continued to develop this same approach.

ABCs

Teaching the alphabet is the logical place to assess the changes afoot in the pedagogical world of the late Ottoman Empire and the early Turkish Republic. Combining such different aspects associated with learning to read as the physical (tracing with finger on book, writing on board), the visual and the aural/oral (hearing and then reciting, either singly or in unison), the ways in which the ABCs were taught allow us to appreci-ate the trends from late Ottoman to early Republican, including after 1928 the added task of teaching a new, imported alphabet. Even the name used to refer to the ABCs in Turkish would change from *"elifbâ"* to *"alfabe,"* reflecting the shift from an Arabic and Islamic inspiration to a decidedly Western approach. This shift was accompanied by a distinct change in content, which became increasingly political and a change in appearance which grew steadily simpler, bolder and more colorful. We can also witness a change from a variety of types of fonts and hand-writing styles in the late Ottoman period to a much more conformist approach to teaching the basics of reading in the Republican era. Most important, perhaps, was the emphasis on internalizing the process of learning by doing away with rote memorization, physical movement and noise.

First, let's take some late Ottoman examples. There are many to choose from but I have first selected one produced in the early 1890s for use in the empire's primary schools. The author of this ABC text, a certain Servet Safi, is not a household name among the writers of children's educational material for this period, a sign perhaps of the expansion of the business of writing school materials, a phenomenon we return to in the final chapter. Entitled "The New Method Ottoman Alphabet" (*Nev usûl elifbâ-yi osmanî*), this book formed the thirty-second title in a series of primary school materials produced by the publisher Kasbar.[28] In the preface the author, after the obligatory testimonials to Sultan Abdülhamid's nurturing of education and progress, justifies his pride in putting out this work. "Why shouldn't I be proud since the little dears, leaving behind their repeated attacks, are able [by using this book] to read a passage easily and to write many words within three months." What is notable about this text, beyond the buoyant enthusiasm of its author, is its practical approach, the variety of scripts presented, and the pervasive Islamic surround.

Servet Safi's text approaches the task of teaching the alphabet prag-matically. It begins by presenting several different versions of the alphabet, each in a slightly different script. The opening page offers a rectangular grid. Running across the top and effectively forming a "banner headline" is the besmele (*basmallah*), the Arabic invocation, "In the name of the God, the Merciful and the Compassionate."[29] The grid below contains 7 rows of 5 squares; each of the squares is filled with a different letter and the 2 squares in the bottom corners are left blank to accommodate the 33 letters of the Ottoman syllabary. Each square is dominated by a large version – something larger than the equivalent of a 48 pica font – of each letter in its stand-alone form. Below it in a smaller font are the variant forms used when connecting the letter to others, initial, medial and final. On the facing page two more depic-tions of the alphabet are rendered in smaller font. Again the besmele presides over the page, looking down from the top. The two versions of the alphabet differ mainly in the fact that the first is presented in alpha-betical order while the second group of letters is displayed in what is referred to as a disordered (*karışık*) sequence. The first footnote appears in order to elucidate and to provide the first of many practical suggestions. Here it recommends that children beginning to learn the alphabet will obtain extraordinary benefit from learning it by rote with the use of chalk and board or a writing slate (*taş tahta*). Physical methods are invoked to reinforce the mental activity required. What is wanted is for the children to be able to write each letter automatically.[30] The text then moves on, logically enough, to teach about vocalization of the letters, taking care to explain their purpose and to provide free-standing examples before adding further levels of complexity. The footnotes are addressed to unnamed adults, presumably the children's parents and teachers, as if the author is concerned to make sure that the proper concepts behind the lessons are fully understood. Again the notes mention the need to practice the letters over and over using a writing slate until they are committed to memory.

Soon the *rıka* style of script is introduced, clearly distinguishable from the print fonts used to this point.[31] As rıka was the most commonly used handwriting style, and the one used throughout late Ottoman civil officialdom, this is yet another sign of the ABC's practical bent. After the letters are presented in serial fashion for memorization, the author begins to gather them into clusters so that the child readers will be able to practice reading and pronouncing them as building blocks for the words that are soon to follow. But the first combinations contain no ligatures; they merely comprise two letters that cannot be joined in the script. And they are given full vocalization in the text, something quite unusual for normal printed texts in Ottoman Turkish but considered necessary here for the neophyte readers. Then, continuing on methodically, the text presents once again the combination forms of the letters: stand-alone, initial, medial and final. Then the students are ready for joined-up letters. These appear in two-letter combinations, two consonants first and then consonant–vowel pairings. Finally, the students are deemed capable of handling their first drill (*ta'lim*) involving real words, e.g., *baba* (father), *onu* (to him/her/it), *yukarıda* (above), *anası* (his/her mother), etc.[32] Other, increasingly complicated patterns are put forward until eventually the words no longer appear as individual and random islands of reading but rather as linked parts of a larger written context. At the same time the vocalization marks are dropped (to reappear only over difficult or potentially ambiguous words), a signal that the sense of the words is generated by their association with those which come before and after, in short, by their context. Short strings of commands gradually give way first to short phrases and basic sentences and then to more elaborate structures. Vocalization is given more liberally at first and then appears only when words are considered to be new or potentially ambiguous. In the longer passages that appear toward the end of the book it disappears altogether. Now the emphasis is on having the students read fluently and for content. Again, the tenor is didactic, full of encouragement for children to begin studying and of warnings for those that do not. One of the final readings has as its subject an elderly porter who struggles to carry heavy loads up steep streets. He tells a group of children skipping school that he would have avoided such an arduous, menial fate if only he had had gone to school and learned to read and write.[33] The volume provides more in the way of Qur'anic verses before ending with a final address aimed at urging the students to make progress with their reading and writing.

A similar, if cruder and shorter, version is supplied in *Elifbâ*, a text produced for provincial primary schools by the Ottoman Ministry of Education in 1317 (1899–1900).[34] Its text appears to be handwritten, in other words not typeset. The work is progressive in the sense that it proceeds with a logical pedagogical intent, demonstrating the concern with comprehension and a cumulative approach pioneered in the Ottoman context by Selim Sabit. Its first pages display letters in boxes showing each of the three possible vocalizations. Then the letters are shown arranged in various combinations but still appear in their unjoined or stand-alone state. A footnote alerts the teacher to the fact that the students should continue only once they have mastered reading each section of the book. Then two-letter words are produced with the instructions given for the teacher (here that they should be placed on the board and memorized or there that the teacher should repeat the examples twice, etc.). Each page and therefore each lesson has the reader advance a step further, taking in another orthographical element added (e.g., the doubled consonant [shadda], the long vowel forms, the intial, medial and final ligatures, etc). Building skills cumulatively marks this as a "scientific" or "modern" approach to teaching reading, as does the fact that some of the examples are artificial, not words at all but rather letters representing sounds chosen so that the young readers will learn to read through phonetic means and not merely by recognizing words as fully formed units. For example, one of the "words" in boxes is an almost unpronounceable assemblage of four "h"s given in order to demonstrate the different forms the letter takes according to its position in the word.[35] As with the previous example, the final selections for reading are Qur'anic, revealing the mix of "traditional" and "modern" elements in the late Ottoman approaches to learning to read.

Late Ottoman readers were almost invariably practical in their approach. The new pedagogy firmly embraced any technique or lesson plan deemed to produce results. Ali İrfan epitomized this workmanlike approach in his First Reader (*Birinci kıraat*) which likened the business of reading and writing to any other task. "Every job has its tools," his text pronounced and went on to declare that book-reading was a modern activity, linked with the rise of the modern school and that it was a tool of education just as the blacksmith or the farmer had their own tools for their trades.[36] (This industrious approach to reading contrasted with the emphasis on reading as a special treat or as essentially a fun activity that pervaded much of the extra-official approach to reading, as we shall see in more detail in the final chapter.) The reading primers emphasized progression from stage to stage, for example, from letters to words to phrases to longer passages. Once the letters had been mastered it was time to move on to words. Ahmed Cevad's *Resimli Osmanlı Lisanı* (The illustrated Ottoman Language) opens with a passage devoted to "The idea of the word" (*kelime fikri*) which consists of a line of text followed by hypothetical dialogue between a teacher and his students:

The book is useful. The student who reads learns many things.

After having his students read this line, the teacher asks one of them:

In the passage you were made to read, is there one word or many words?

Sir, there are many words.

Do these words have a meaning or not?

They do, sir.

When you answer, what are you doing?

Sir, when I answer I am using a certain number of words.

So, my sons, in order for us to explain what we mean, the meaningful utterances that we use are called words (kelime). Meaningless utterances can also come out of our mouths but we do not call them words (kelime) but at the very most utterances (lafz).[37]

The textbook then draws a line under the dialogue, changes the typeface and offers a précis of the lesson, providing some pedagogical prompts in the way of questions that teachers can pose and drills to be carried out on the classroom blackboard and as homework. Maintaining the progressive approach, the text's next lesson is on the idea of the sentence (*cümle fikri*). Again the lesson proceeds logically, starting out by with a single line that reads, "Ahmed – the book – to tear," and then goes on to a clear if rather methodical description of how individual words can form a sentence.

But not all lessons were so baldly pedantic. Later in the same text late Ottoman readers would encounter a lesson intended for "reading and dictation" called "How the lesson is to be memorized." Instead of merely explaining how to commit a text to memory, the reader provides a more compelling narrative intended to convey the same message:

> The schoolmaster (hoca efendi) had given the class a story to be memorized. This was ten lines long and took up half a page.
>
> After returning home little Necib went to his room. He closed the door and opened his book. He read the first sentence and then read it again and then again. He read it exactly ten times. Later he put his finger in the book to keep his place and read the same sentence from memory: he knew it...He read it again and again. Now he had had learned the first sentence beautifully. Then he started on the second...[38]

A simple illustration of a boy wearing a fez sitting alone at a table and holding a book in front of him accompanies the text. We shall return to the interplay between text and image later in this chapter but for the moment we can simply note another example of pragmatic didacticism in the way that reading was being modeled for its young practioners.

Some late Ottoman primers show interesting signs of linguistic innovation. Remarkably ahead of its time when it appeared in 1320 (1902–1903) was Yanyalı Ali Rıza's *Okuma yazma* (Reading and writing) which advertised itself as "a book written in pure Turkish (*som Türkçe yazılmış bir bitikdir*), thus going out of its way to establish its solid proto-national credentials. *"Bitik"* is an old Turkish word for "book," quite rare in comparison with the more common *"kitab"* which seems to have been avoided due to its Arabic origins. This lithographed book, priced inexpensively at 2 kuruş, 2 para, incorporated some rather odd orthography, and used footnotes to gloss the equally unusual insistence on "pure" Turkish vocabulary. This attempt thus anticipates the Republican "language revolution" by about a quarter of a century.

Vocabulary was not the only subject of experimentation. Another interesting variant in the development of the ABCs comes with the 1333 (1914–1915) publication by the *Encümen-i ilmî* (the scientific council) of *Yeni harflarla elifbâ* (The new letters ABC).[39] While the book begins like any other, with the invocation of God (*besmele*) in Arabic at the start of the first page, it is immediately apparent that the book represents nothing

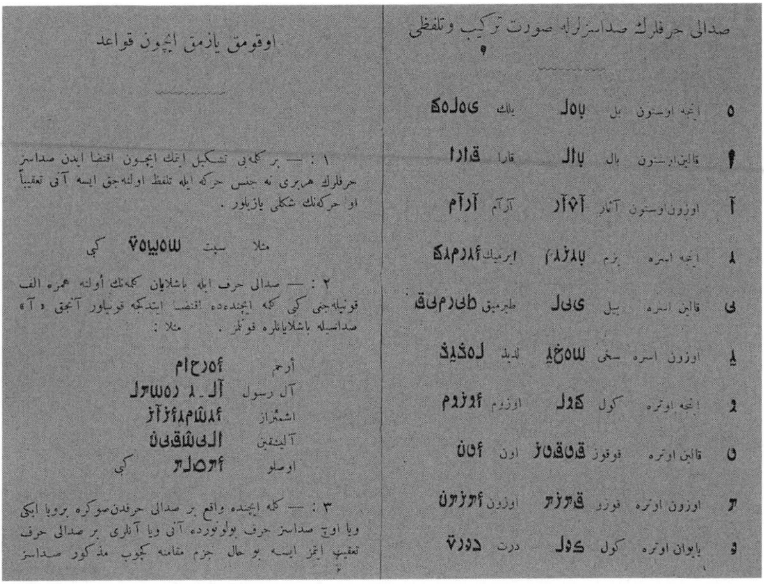
اوقومق یازمق ایچون قواعد

صدالی حرفلرك صداسزلرله صورت ترکیب وتلفظی

Figure 4.2 Alphabet experimentation

less than a radical attempt to refashion the alphabet. As can be seen from the accompanying reproduction of the first few pages (Figure 4.2), the text puts forward an adapted version of the Ottoman script. The chief impetus behind the effort seems to have been to render the alphabet regular and permanently vocalized. In other words, it was an attempt to do away with the potential for ambiguity in the Ottoman syllabary. In this new version of the alphabet, there was no joining together of letters; it ceased to be a script in the proper sense of the word. Likewise, according to this new plan, each vowel sounds was always to be explicitly represented by a specific letter. The proposed alphabet created variations on the three main vowels in order to indicate whether they represented short or long. For example, the "u" sound, represented in its long form by the letter "*vaw*" in the traditional Ottoman Turkish script was now to be further elaborated by three variants. The stand-alone vaw was to represent a "thick" or velar "u" sound, while curlicues before and after a more vertically aligned vaw were to represent, respectively, the "long" (*uzun*) and "broad" (*yayvan*) versions of the vowel. While this text was infused with the same sort of pedagogical enthusiasm that marked the other late Ottoman examples we have witnessed – the new letters are all carefully defined; examples are given, moving from the simple to the complex, and even a French version of the new dispensation is provided for those readers previously unfamiliar with the Ottoman script – the net effect of the new alphabet, apart from its visual oddity, was its bulky inefficiency. As its examples readily demonstrated, using this new alphabet required a writer or typesetter to expend almost twice as much effort and ink in order to produce the same word in the old script. In other words, what was gained in certainty and reversibility seemed clearly offset by the loss in efficiency and fluidity. Still the text marks an interesting and visually arresting – the reworked script has a passing resemblance to Armenian – late Ottoman effort to rework the script, and should perhaps be seen as a milestone on the road to the eventual although by no means inevitable replacement of the script with a modified Latin alphabet by the Republic in 1928. There were thus attempts from individuals and from the Ottoman government to wrestle with the question of the script well before the advent of the Republic and its famous linguistic radicalism.

Other late Ottoman ABCs continue the trend toward a modern pedagogical approach. A raft of new features were deployed to facilitate the task of learning the Ottoman Turkish alphabet in order to expand the ranks of the literate. Increasing attention to emphasizing the practice of learning to read from a linguistic and scientific perspective manifested itself in the form of lengthy introductory and explanatory prefaces to the ABCs, the growing use of footnotes, and the emerging recourse to illustration. For example, Ali İrfan's *Son elifbâ-yı osmanî* (The latest Ottoman ABC), published between 1328 (1910) and 1330 (1912), advised teachers to read both his Introduction and his prefatory section on pedagogical method (*usûl-i tedris*).[40] Here he derided the existing techniques for teaching children to read, claiming them to be slow, boring and based on parrot-like repetition. Reprising Servet Safi's theme, Ali İrfan claimed that what was normally accomplished in the primary schools by way of teaching the alphabet over a two-year period could easily be learned in a single month with the use of his new text. The solution lay in leading the children to understand what they were learning and not continuing on to the next lesson until they had fully understood their lessons. There followed explicit instructions to the primary school teachers on how to integrate the book in their teaching.

Text as image

The text itself reflects an interest in pedagogical transparency and a striking visual clarity. As in other ABCs from this period, Ali İrfan's text begins with a grid whose boxes are devoted to the individual letters. But unlike some previous versions here the boxes are less cluttered, showing the letter only in two versions of the same form, one printed and the other handwritten. Below the customary invocation of God, now drawn in an elaborate version of the Kufic script, the facing page contains information pertaining only to four letters. Each is shown in a very large font, again in both printed and handwritten forms. Corresponding to each letter, a clearly drawn illustration is depicted across the page and labeled with the corresponding word. Thus across from the letter *"elif"* is a drawing of a hand and the caption *"el,"* meaning hand. Between the two is the image of pointing hand, intended to lead the eye from the letter on the right to the picture on the left side of the page. After sufficient lessons have been mastered, the illustrations disappear but the text continues to move at a fairly slow pace. Words are given individually, sometimes in printed and sometimes in handwritten letters presumably so that the young readers can grow accustomed to seeing the letters and words appear in alternate forms. The pace of progress is kept fairly slow. By page 59 the students are still meant to be reading individual words. Sentences and paragraphs come later. The emphasis on clarity and a slow progression reflects the growing pedagogical interest in inducing complete comprehension on the part of the child.

The Republican ABCs carry on the pedagogical bent established in the late Ottoman period. Many of the same techniques are applied, both before and after the adoption of the modified Latin script in 1928. The imperative of teaching a new alphabet to children – and because of the alphabet shift to adults as well – who were perhaps not entirely familiar with the old one presented a new challenge. For the most part this task seems to have been finessed by treating the old script as a sort of linguistic back-up. In the ABCs which begin to appear in 1928 in order to teach the new Latinized script, the old Arabo-Persian script is deployed as a reference point born of practical necessity. Emphasis is given to the new script but it is understood that the meaning would necessarily be ensured only with reference to the old. Thus in the *Yeni Dil Encümeni Alfabesi* (The new Language Council's ABC) the Latinized script takes pride of place but the Ottoman script is nearly as prevalent in the initial pages of the text. For example, the title page gives a one-to-one correspondence between the Latinized and Ottoman versions of such details as the book's title and the statement of official permission, and the first page likewise devotes equal time to the Latin and Ottoman renderings in its lesson on the vowels.

But change is readily apparent. First of all, the term used to identify the book as an ABC has changes from that of *"elifbâ,"* a term which incorporates the Turkish versions of the Arabic names for the first two letters of the alphabet, to *"alfabe,"* reflecting the linguistic turn to the West.[41] Then, the Latinized script is given precedence in terms of font size. Next, the Ottoman script is used to explain unfamiliar looking abbreviations, such as "v.s." (ve saire, meaning "etc."). Apart from these changes, what is interesting about this ABC is its apparent rush to get beyond the mechanics of teaching the new letters in order to use them to impart content. After only four pages devoted to explaining the mechanics of the new script, this officially produced book moves on to providing sample texts for reading. Not surprisingly, given the book's official origins, the first such passages have clear political overtones. The first is a brief statement of Mustafa Kemal's likes and dislikes, entitled *"Gazi ve insanlar"* (The Gazi and the people), which consists of a simple statement: "The thing which the Gazi most dislikes in people is hypocrisy, and the things he likes the most are cleverness and character (zekâ ve karakter)." The second is an excerpt from a speech about duty that Mustafa Kemal gave at Samsun entitled "The Individual and the Nation" (*Fertle Millet*). The following texts, some in prose and some in poetry, are taken from the writings of a solidly nationalist stable of authors that included Namık Kemal, Tevfik Fikret, Ruşen Eşref and Yakup Kadri. These patriotic passages are presented entirely in the Latinized script, with the only instance of the old Ottoman hand appearing in the form of footnote glosses. After these reading passages, the lessons reappear, elucidating various specifics of handling the new orthography, e.g., how various suffixes and grammatical particles should appear. Next there is a two-page chart of the new alphabet, both in printed and handwritten forms. Now the Arabic script is reduced to providing the titles for the various columns. Finally there are complete tables for verb conjugation in all of the various tenses and moods.

In spite of the desire for textual completeness and exactitude, however, the difficulties inherent in the rapid shift to a new alphabet made themselves apparent. In contrast to the attention to the minor details of producing the new orthography, there are a number of places where errors or a lack of consistency appear. For example, a "ğ" or "soft 'g' " is mistakenly supplied for the hard "g" in the word "gibi" in the first line of the selection from Mustafa Kemal's speech, or the word *"üzere"* is rendered as "üzre."[42] In all probability these errors reflect the typesetter's lack of familiarity with the new alphabet. Some sentences begin without upper case letters and others have a font that does not fit with the rest of the type, revealing the problems in achieving standardization during the early stages of the "language revolution."

So far we have confined our approach to largely textual matters, focusing on the ways in which those advocating literacy – and writing the texts to promote it – addressed the basics of the production and absorption of written language. But of course coming to terms with letters on paper, whatever the alphabet, was only part of the process of learning to read.

In other words, we must move from the first of Sertel's two basic aspects of reading to the second. The first is the world of apparent certitude in linguistic matters, involving the precision of forming the letter and the rules of grammar and orthography. The various charts and tables that emphasize the binary correspondence between word and image epitomize this first world. The second realm is the wider world of ideas carried by these words and symbols. Here we can almost sense the authors of children's readers straining to compel their charges to think or respond in a certain way, as if they could transfer the certitude of learning the alphabet to the wider field of thinking and ideas. We feel the shrill refrains of their didacticism and professed certainty, as if they are trying to fix the patterns of youthful imagining along certain patriotic, moralistic and even economically determined patterns. Technology provided a boon for this desire for fixity and right conduct in the form of the reproducible image. Advances in lithography and offset printing since the late Ottoman period allowed textbook authors to manipulate and depict on the written page precisely what sort of children this learning to read was meant to engender – how they were to look, dress, hold their bodies and so on. But as we shall see, the presence of images in children's reading materials would not always assist the officially derived view of youthful comportment.

Letters are a kind of image of course and we have seen some of the ways in which they were depicted in the children's literature of the period. Variations in font size, handwritten (as opposed to printed) fonts and the arrangement of letters in grids all contributed to drawing attention to the basic building blocks of literacy. But the incorporation of pictorial images opened a wide range of options, for didactic as well as other purposes. The most basic attempts at incorporating pictures in reading texts can be seen in the inclusion of visual material in a generic way, not clearly linked to text. Here the message seems to be that these are publications intended for children. These texts are signaled by images, frequently appropriating Western models, of plump-cheeked happy children at play, or better yet, engrossed in the act of reading.

Another strain integrates the images directly into the text. This is most clearly seen with the ABCs. We have already noted the striking use of visual symbols in Ali İrfan's ever practical text which reinforces the impression of certainty through a one-to-one correlation between letter and image. So we see the letter *"elif"* and the shape of a hand (*el*); "de" and the shape of a pitcher (*desti*) and so on. Here we also noted the use of the icon depicting a pointing hand, clearly intended to lead the reader's eye from the letter to the word depicted.[43] Then we have Ahmed Cevad's *Altın Alfabe* (The Golden ABC) of 1928 where images play an integral part straight from the first page of the book. *"Bu ne dir? Bu* [image of a horse] *tır."* (What is this? This is a [image of a horse]).[44] On the next page the same mixture of letters and images occurs, this time to identify another simple word beginning with the letter "a," namely "ay" or moon. It is interesting to note the foreign provenance of the images used in this text. The illustrations presented on the cover and the frontispiece, both depicting a young mother reading to her children, carry the signatures of Western artists. The illustrations present a fairly generic world of children in sailor suits and dresses, of kittens and puppies. There is very little to suggest the provenance of the artwork, but close inspection reveals its non-Turkish nature: the occasional village landscape with a church tower, the architectural style of the buildings that are occasionally depicted, and, of course, the giveaway signatures. At first the appearance of these visual borrowings seems to conform to the pattern of generic appropriation, that is to say, of images only loosely connected with the text in question. But then, as we have seen, once the teaching of the alphabet commences, we can discern the strong extent to which the images are linked to the business at hand. Indeed it would be hard to find a better example of the intense integration of image and text than in the use of images as icons for words. The semiotic correspondence between visual representation and the written word is explicit and unambiguous.

With the passage of time the ABCs of the early Republican period came to reflect the inclusion of more specifically Turkish visual material. An interesting example can be found in M. Turan's ABC produced in the mid-1930s. The title of this book, *Öz Türk Dilile Kolay Okutan Alfabe*, which might inelegantly be translated as the Easy-to-teach-to-learn-to-read ABC in pure Turkish, already suggests the influence of the drive for a more "genuine" Turkish.[45] Yet the cover illustration depicts what appears to be a pastoral scene of vaguely Western European derivation; a man is sowing seed in a field while an ox wagon and a building with a spire can be seen in the background. Inside the book, directly opposite the first page devoted to teaching the alphabet appears a full-page portrait labeled *"ATATÜRK"* which depicts the nation's leader sporting a white bow tie and dinner jacket. The emblem of the six arrows of his Republican People's Party (CHP) is instantly recognizable on his jacket's lapel.[46] Over the page, a large crescent moon (the icon of the Turkish flag), "ay" in Turkish, is used to illustrate the letter "a." Subsequent pages offer a mixture of indigenous and foreign images to teach the rest of the alphabet, interspersed with selections of nationalist poetry. One poem, called *"Ana yurt!"* (The motherland!) is illustrated with a map of Turkey, explicitly informing its young readers that the nation is their mother, while others exalt the person of Atatürk and the Turkish flag.[47] Still further in the future, color would become an important feature of the ABC. For example, Münir Hayri Egeli's *Alfabe Oyunu* (The alphabet game) would combine vivid color, large-scale images, and an active pedagogical approach; the children were meant to cut out cards, some with images and some with words and images, match them and assemble basic sentences. Eventually we find a fully Turkicized ABC. The famous image of Atatürk at the blackboard explaining the alphabet features on the cover, and inside the images that correspond with the letters are thoroughly drawn from a domestic stock. For example, "B" is represented with *"bayrak,"* while the accompanying illustration specifically depicts the Turkish flag with its distinctive crescent moon and star.[48] The letter "j" which is not native to Turkish is represented by the image of a safety razor blade and labeled *"jilet,"* evidence of the continued adoption of loan words in the Turkish language.

Visual certitude

The textbooks used to teach reading were intended to project visual certitude. Reacting perhaps to the contradictions on content and context inherent in learning to read that we encountered in the previous chapter, to the wide potential range of semantic associations that the reading brain is forced to grapple with,[49] and more generally to the increasing, sometimes bewildering, possibilities unleashed by the modern era, reading texts strove to provide fixity. Together with their counterparts produced to teach such subjects as mathematics, history and morality, they shared a yen for instilling lessons that were clear and carefully avoided ambiguity or uncertainty. The didactic impulse was everywhere apparent in the literature associated either directly or indirectly with the educational establishment, but is perhaps most strikingly observed when illustrations are involved. They are the ultimate expression of the desire to instill visual certitude. As we have already seen, clearer methods were being adopted to render letters, indicate correspondence between words and images, and to rearrange font size and the appearance of the printed page.

Now the images moved beyond merely controlling the shapes and size of letters and the identification of basic vocabulary; they were increasingly employed in the service of projecting an idealized vision of how children should read, study, interact with their peers and elders, in short, how to live. To this end they employed a range of visual symbols that could be deployed to suit various pedagogical uses. As Brummett noted in her work on cartoon imagery in the Young Turk period, such "symbols are the result of a complex cultural synthesis" in which printed texts played an important role.[50] The technology behind engraving and lithography allowed the authors of children's texts to depict explicitly their view of the life of the ideal child and to integrate these illustrations with their texts. A good example of such integration can be seen in Ahmed Cevad's *Resimli osmanlı lisanı* (The illustrated Ottoman language). Like many of the texts produced in this transitional period, this reader drew its illustrations from both imported and local sources. The first illustrations in this text are seemingly generic, including a pastoral scene and a typical array of animals. When the subject turns to the serious business of education it offers its readers the story of *"Nazik çocuk"* (The polite child). The illustrations now become recognizably Ottoman: the schoolboy greets an elderly man wearing a fez on a street with a minaret in the background. The passage delivers a typically idealistic expectation of filial piety, and begins, "Young Ahmed is a polite child. Whenever he sees people whom he knows in the street he greets them in a very well-mannered way. He always says, 'Yes, sir' or 'No, sir.'."[51]

A few pages later there is a similarly didactic piece intended for memorization concerning the proper attributes of a young girl. In a rare instance of attribution, the poem is listed as deriving from the periodical *Çocuk Dünyası* (children's world). Two small illustrations of unclear provenance show a girl washing herself at a basin in her bedroom and then busy with her homework at a table under a suspended kerosene lamp, while the text addresses the virtues of rising early, hygiene, a proper diet and hard work.[52]

Across the page is an exercise intended to encourage the young readers to describe what they see in the accompanying illustration. The simply drawn picture shows a boy in a sailor suit playing with the parts of a toy village assembled on the table before him. There are people and animals, houses and barns. One of the buildings is labeled in French as a dairy (*"Laiterie"*), revealing both its foreign derivation and the general tendency for children's material to draw on a mixture of domestic and imported sources in this period.

The utility of juxtaposing text and images is pursued still further in the pages ahead, but given an increasingly Ottoman accent due to the local production of the attendant illustrations. Accompanying a passage intended for reading and dictation (*kıraat ve imla*) entitled "How the lesson ought to be memorized" (*Ders nasıl ezberlenir*) we have a small inset illustration of a boy wearing a fez and a sailor suit and reading intently from the book he is holding with both hands on the table in front of him.[53]

Next comes a series of illustrations depicting "A day [in the life] of the good children" (*İyi çocukların bir günü*). Next to a simple sketch showing the two children and their parents around the breakfast table, the text explains:

Hüsnü and Aliye are siblings. They rise early every morning.

They wash their hands and faces with soap and plenty of water; they clean themselves thoroughly. Then they comb their hair...

The next illustration shows the children embracing their mother as they leave for school, and the text describes exactly what they say as they take their leave. On the way they never tarry but go directly to school, arriving exactly on time.

Another passage for reading and dictation is entitled "The sensible child" (*Uslu çoçuk*), and we see him depicted in a very simple pen-and-ink drawing, wearing a fez and sitting at a slanted-top desk with pen and inkpot as he pores over his book. More series of simple illustrations follow: "The Return from school" and "Recess and afternoon." In the latter the simple line drawings show male children, dressed in their school uniforms and wearing fezes playing games at recess.[54] Then they are shown back in their classroom, arranged in rows of communal desks and benches as the teacher looks on from his separate desk on the side. Finally the children are depicted filing out of the school at the end of the day. The accompanying questions prompt the reader with comprehension-based queries.

A subsequent section is called "In the classroom" and instructs the readers as to the proper deportment to be shown during lesson time. The teacher calls the roll and the students are to respond with "present" (*mevcud*). The teacher then poses questions to the students one by one about their previous lessons, before embarking on a new one. The simple drawings show a crowded but well-ordered late Ottoman-style classroom in which the teacher is firmly in control.

The last of the series detailing the idealized family's day is called simply "The evening." It shows the family at home after a day of study and work. The father returns from his work, enjoys listening to his children recite their lessons, and looks at their workbooks. The mother attends to providing them with their supper. Afterwards the father reads the newspaper while the mother sews. The children, called Behçet and Nazife in this episode, play a game before returning to their work. When it is time for bed they wish their parents a good evening.

This idealized vision is as much a creation of the text as it is of the accompanying illustration. Here we see text and image working in concert to portray a didactically guided vision of model childhood and domesticity. The illustrations, while not sophisticated, seem appropriate to the inexpensive reader in which they appear, and are clearly Ottoman in their vernacular visual referents. We have, in short, an adult's fantasy of the proper deportment expected from late Ottoman children.

The Republican era generated its own idealized version of children's behavior in much the same way, relying on a similar combination of text and illustration. The popular primer produced by Sadrettin Celal demonstrates the ways in which the Republican turn soon manifested itself in children's readers. His 1929 *Cümhuriyet Çocuklarına Sevimli Kırâat* (The Enjoyable Reader for Republican Children) is the text that presented its readers with an unmistakably Westernized image of the teacher mentioned in chapter 3, a fitting symbol of the Western-looking direction of the early Republic. But even this conspicuously Republican example draws, like its late Ottoman predecessors, on an interesting mixture of local and western images. After the passage entitled "The new teacher" comes a story titled "My Neighborhood and My School" which is illustrated with a picture, probably of local provenance given its rendering of her dress, of a girl reading at a table.[55] The third entry is emphatically local in depiction; the story titled "Death of the Lady Teacher" appears alongside an illustration that clearly reveals a local setting. A crowd of children and a few adults are laying wreaths at a gravesite in a cemetery featuring gravestones with the turbans typical of Ottoman period. The drawing is signed in the old-style script, while the story itself is listed as deriving from a foreign source. Clearly there is a strong degree of Turkification on display here. Subsequent reading selections draw on an eclectic mix of referents, local and foreign, revealing both a direct concern with the political agenda of the day as embodied in a poem about Mustafa Kemal here or a reference to the War of Independence there and an occasional and by contrast rather escapist retreat to the deracinated generic kiddieland, as seen in the oddly inserted passage "Winter and snow" in which two clearly northern European girls dressed in Santa-style hats build a snowman while outside the picture's frame a girl with a passing resemblance to Shirley Temple drinks from what appears to be a mug of hot chocolate. With time the borrowed images would decline and ultimately disappear to be replaced by unmistakably local production. For example, the state-supplied reader Okuma Kitabı 1 (Reading Book 1) published in 1935 confronted its young audience with a photograph of a statue of Atatürk's head. Inside the images are both local, as can be seen in the school smocks typical of the Turkish Republic, and modern, as evinced, for example, in an almost Bauhaus-like rendering of an idealized, modern detached house to accompany a passage called "Our House" (*Bizim Evimiz*). The book's final pages are highly suggestive of the republican version of the idealized world of children, reading and republic. In a passage entitled "Whom do you love the most" tells us that a young but remarkably self-reflective boy named Can pondered this question before he entered school. The initial answer, his mother, his father and his sibling, had to expand once he learned to read; now his loved ones included his teacher whom he loved "just as he loved his mother and father" and his schoolmates. On the very next page the political scope widens to include the relationship between children and their nation. At the top of the page an outline of the map of Turkey features a crescent and star. Below it two children gaze up at it while the text of the following dialogue appears to their right:

Gül – Turkey, my beautiful homeland. I love you very much. I am a Turk!

Can – Turkey, my beautiful homeland. I love you very much. I am a Turk!

Gül and Can – We are Turks! We all love you [Turkey] very much. Beautiful

Turkey, beautiful homeland. Hurray ... Hurray ... Hurray ...

On the next page of the book we have the familiar portrait of Atatürk in evening dress. Below him the following message appears:

Kamâl (sic) Atatürk
The father of our homeland.
The children love him very much.
We Turkish children also love him very much.
Hurray Atatürk.[56]

Thanks to the concerted application of text and image the world of the child has expanded beyond the home to embrace the nation and the state in a highly idealized fashion.

These images and the ways in which they are integrated with the surrounding text show that the attempts at visual certitude were part of a larger aim, namely, to illustrate right conduct in a variety of settings, both inside and outside of school, that obtained in both the late Ottoman and early Republican periods. A few general observations can be made. First, over time text and image were increasingly working together. The random insertion of pictures unrelated to the overall message of the text declines with time, despite the occasionally jarring reoccurrence of curious juxtapositions. Secondly, the books begin to assume an increasingly active role on the part of their young readers. The assumption of passive readers tends to give way as the texts pose questions, set texts for dictation and sometimes even go so far as to encourage their young readers to cut out shapes, questionnaires or competition entry forms. Interestingly, the expectation of an increasingly active readership is simultaneous with the understanding that the actual practice of reading ought to be internalized, i.e., accomplished without the moving of lips, the tracing of fingers or the making of sound. Yet the active stance of the readers is circumscribed by the carefully delineated and heavily didactic content of the texts and their accompanying images. Very few of the officially or semi-officially produced material intended for children are meant to do anything but instruct. Children may assume increasingly active roles but their activity is controlled. Words are placed in their mouths, the answers to questions are often supplied and the overall ethos is one of improvement and rectitude. This ambivalent attitude toward children – wanting them to assume a more active stance as they read and learn yet also wanting to control what they think – is symptomatic of both late Ottoman and early Turkish Republican attempts to foster literacy while maintaining strong centralized control over reading content. The active participation on the part of children is desired but only insofar as it adheres to the didactic and moral constraints being rigorously supplied by the voice of authority.

Diversity, diversion and satire

Further complicating this picture was the emergence of children's publications that offered material that directly challenged the authoritative voice of the state. While the state was expanding its educational system, the private publishing sector was also booming. Between 1869 and 1927 more than fifty Turkish-language children's periodicals appeared in the Ottoman Empire.[57] In spite of the close links between the two phenomena – a major reason for the growth of the publishing business was the patronage of the state as it sought to procure texts for its growing number of schools – we can nevertheless note both that private sector publications were on the rise and that their arrival produced tensions and competition with the state's agenda.

With time children's publications began to offer material that parodied or otherwise made light of state education – its teachers, lessons and surroundings. Given the overbearing seriousness and didacticism of the state educational enterprise as a whole, the publisher's task of finding a humorous target was hardly difficult. Let us now consider this turn to parody, at once both a radical, unexpected departure from the reverent norm and a natural turn of events suggested by the combined logic of the expansion of state education and literacy and the forces of market capitalism.

At times the recourse to humor was seemingly generic. There are numerous instances of children's articles that seem to have been included purely for their risible nature, for example a story about a horse that could write or a lamb that came to school. These attempts at lightheartedness often jarred with the more usual seriousness of children's publications. The contrast between the fluffy vision of childhood and the grave import with which learning to read was freighted is epitomized in a cover illustration from 1924. The main illustration shows a young girl playing the role of teacher to a class composed of her dolls. The caption says, "Teacher Nebahat is teaching a Turkish lesson." The stern visage of Mustafa Kemal looks over the scene from the upper right-hand corner[58] (Figure 4.3). Sometimes the search for levity could assume a darker tone. The magazine *Yeni Yol*, particularly notable in this regard, ran cartoons ridiculing one character for being overweight and making jokes about an African woman depicted in full racist caricature with her two children, named Daylight (*Gündüz*) and Cotton (*Pamuk*).

Sometimes this "humor" could be taken at the expense of the official line, actually encouraging disobedience. Children's journals eventually targeted schools and teachers as objects of derision, poking fun at them in an apparent attempt to form a closer bond with the students. Thus schools and teachers were portrayed as silly or irrelevant. Like their contemporaries in Western Europe in this period, publishers were attempting to cater to the tastes of younger readers.[59] The result was a shocking

Figure 4.3   Nebahat teaches her dolls

departure from the serious, duty-laden tone and material of the earlier texts. The new trend was toward the comic and the satirical. Naturally, the old *hocas* and their *mektebs*, or Qur'an schools, were a prime candidate for this abuse, but interestingly the new style schools were targeted as well. Consider the cover illustration of an edition of *Yeni Yol* dating from 1925[60] (Figure 4.4).

It features a member of the ulema teaching in a "new style" school, with the children seated in rows of desks and a map hanging on the wall. The scene resembles one of those children's games where the object is to spot all of the things that are wrong in the picture. The *hoca* looks on aghast over his charges; some of the boys are snickering and whispering to each other; some are busy folding paper into origami-like shapes;

Figure 4.4   The teacher aghast

one is standing to give an apparently unconvincing answer while a fist arrives from outside the frame and punches him in the back; others pore over a copy of *Yeni Yol*. The message is clear: the teacher has clearly lost control of the class, and none of the props of classroom teaching – the map on the wall or the blackboard with its Arabic declensions – can hold the boys' attention the way the magazine can.

Other examples show that this sort of satire was not only reserved for members of the ulema. A humorous piece in *Bizim Mecmua*, founded just prior to the establishment of the Republic, has some fun at the expense of a new-style teacher when the math problem he gives the class is converted into a joke by a cheeky retort: "The teacher: 'What do five kuruş bread, five kuruş tea, five kuruş cheese make?' Student: 'Breakfast, Mr. Teacher.'"[61] A final example, accompanied by an illustration, provides more evidence that the fez- and frock coat-wearing teacher is equally subject to ridicule. In this scene, another math lesson, the teacher is again made to look ridiculous:

> The Math Lesson:
> My son, what is ten take away ten?
> !!
>
> Why are you silent? For example, a man buys ten apples. He throws two away because they are rotten; he drops five; three are stolen by vagabonds; so now how many are left?
>
> A pear [slang for idiot].[62]

Figure 4.5   The math lesson

The crudely drawn illustration (Figure 4.5) makes it clear which side the magazine is on; one of the boys has a copy of *Yeni Yol* sticking out of his jacket pocket.

As in late eighteenth-century France, late Ottoman and early Republican-era popular texts delivered an unprecedented proliferation of images.[63] Some textual and some pictorial, they together changed the reading experience. Since the materials we have been considering here were intended for children, we can assume that they generated an even greater attraction and importance than they would for adults. By reinforcing and, less frequently, undermining official projections of correct deportment and affiliation, these images played a crucial role in extending the impact of the printed word.

While the attempts at humor described above may seem mild by today's standards, they contrast sharply against the background of overbearing didacticism and authority that characterized the environment in which late Ottoman and early Republican children were taught to read.[64] While it could be argued that such a milieu was inherently ripe for satire and undermining, it seems more probable that the explanation for such a marked divergence from past practice is to be found in the growing tension between the rhetoric of the state and the economic conditions of the publishing industry. It is to the latter subject that we turn in the next chapter.

5
Commodification and the Market

The importance of the physical appearance of the reading material leads to the question of commodification and the market, the subject to which we now turn. Drawing on recent research into the relationship between commodification and modernity, this chapter addresses the hidden but crucial socioeconomic aspects of reading and literacy. The starting point for this investigation is recognizing a basic but fundamental shift effected by the new-style educational dispensation that was responsible for the expansion of literacy in the late Ottoman and early Republican periods, namely, the abandonment of what had been an essentially consumption-free educational apparatus, based on oral transmission and writing on erasable surfaces, in favor of one that required the wide-scale production and consumption of an expanding variety of books and other printed materials. The seemingly insatiable demand for teachers and textbooks meant that many could now make (or substantially augment) a living by writing. It also changed the way nascent readers related to what they read; what had been a largely communal act involving a shared medium of writing and a largely oral/aural environment was replaced by an individual, frequently silent and increasingly commercial activity.

The growing ranks of individual young readers collectively constituted a market that publishers were quick to exploit. In order to set their offerings apart from the competition, the publishers of children's literature were soon tempted to resort to poking fun at the stiffly didactic nature of state-supplied education, especially as symbolized by its main target, the teacher, as we have just seen. This chapter proceeds to examine in more detail a number of aspects associated with the creation of a market for young readers, including the mechanics of distribution, serialization and what today would be labeled the "marketing" of reading materials for children.

A central aim of this study is to reveal the subtle but powerful ways in which the changes set in train by the ongoing educational transformation of the late Ottoman and early Turkish Republican periods both reflected and constituted modernity. The changes associated with reading, at once so profound and so "natural," both reveal the transformative changes associated with a radically realigned relationship between state and society in the modern era and indicate the less immediately visible but no less profound involvement of market forces in constituting the underlying mechanisms that enabled and perhaps even demanded the new socioeconomic dispensation. In other words, the rise in literacy in general and the specific environment in which reading was taught and practiced in the modern era meant that the act of reading both conformed to a model generated by an increasingly centralized and activist state and reflected the inherently less predictable but no less powerful mechanisms of a capitalist economy. What is crucial to uncover in this context is therefore nothing less than the relationship between commodification and modernity.[1]

Reading was central to both the new relationship between state and society and to that connecting the individual consumer to the wider matrix of market forces. It served as an instrument of the new approach to learning, promoted by the state and the private sector alike as the chief means of reaching out to the young generation. As we shall see, authors and educationalists in this period conceived of child readers both as receptacles ready to be filled with wholesome and salutary advice and as proto-independent thinkers who were deemed sufficiently competent to form their own opinions and exercise independent choice, especially insofar as purchasing reading material was concerned. Cumulatively, the market's response to the new and growing ranks of young literate consumers was constitutive of the new socioeconomic realities, reflecting as it did not only the expanding political but also the economic ramifications of literacy.

There are important tensions to recognize in this dual function of literacy. On the one hand we can sense an almost palpable conflict between reading as individual and as group behavior, that is to say between reading as something undertaken as a matter of personal choice and motive and reading as an activity that "happens" as a result of the broader and deeper forces operating on society as a whole. This is the process described by Ami Ayalon as taking place in late Ottoman and Mandate Palestine where "irreversible" forces were creating a reading society in the aggregate.[2] On the other hand we can see reading as reflecting a broader tension still, namely, that between social activity as dictated by the state and that initiated by discrete individuals for their own particular reasons, such as convictions, tastes, whims and so on. This last tension carries with it some extremely important implications for society as a whole. It is possible to see the provision of reading materials and their acceptance as a zone of contestation, as a kind of battleground. From the perspective of the state, the centrally planned educational system served as an efficiently convenient means of delivering a variety of messages concerning a range of attitudes ranging from personal morality to political identification, as previous chapters have illustrated in some detail. The state sector therefore, perhaps inevitably, pushed in the direction of convergence of message, of consistency and sameness of attitude and affect. Left to its own devices it would have produced a reading environment that was essentially didactic, almost entirely monotone, and imposed from above. Conversely, the very existence of this expanding apparatus for the commissioning and distribution of texts – mainly school textbooks, of course, but also incorporating other genres – ensured that there was both a ready source of writers and eager ranks of readers who might be seen in the broader sense to be pushing in the opposite direction. That is, the relatively stiff and pedantic reading fare on offer at school almost inevitably created the private sector reading market that was ready and able to provide and consume what emerged by contrast as a much more varied and often more vibrant body of reading material.

In other words, alongside their socioeconomic implications the changes taking place in the realm of reading inherently contained a fundamentally political tension. As Lovell demonstrated in the case of Russia and Ayalon in Palestine, the democratization of reading produces problems and tensions.[3] Access to reading expanded unevenly and therefore tended to exacerbate already irregular power relations. At the same time it could provide new, indeed unprecedented, avenues of participation in the public sphere, avenues that altered the socioeconomic and political equation of the newly literate societies. New career paths, new economic and social opportunities arrived with the spread of print literature. In the Ottoman/Turkish case, these changes chiefly benefited the state. After all, it was the government, first Ottoman and then Republican, which played the chief role in the expansion of literacy. But the lead that it thus garnered for itself was not unassailable. In part because of the state's reliance on the private sector for producing the high volume of material upon which its educational apparatus depended and in part because of the relative maneuverability of the independent operators, it soon became apparent that individual voices were going to make themselves heard – and seen – through the medium of print.

Commodification

A key link between the political and economic effects associated with the rise of literacy lies in the area of commodification. As Yael Navarro-Yashin has demonstrated, the articulation of Turkish culture and the Turkish political economy has depended heavily on the processes by which certain physical objects have become imbued with symbolic significance and feature as indicators of the production of societal, cutlural or national meaning.[4] The role of the market is crucial to this development. Navarro-Yashin has shown that both the religious and the secular movements in Turkey have essentially depended on the same market mechanism for the dissemination and implanting of their symbols throughout Turkish society. Ironically, both the symbolically laden and nearly ubiquitous image of Mustafa Kemal Atatürk and the equally evocative and prevalent headscarf represent two sides of the same process of manufacture and dissemination.[5]

Navarro-Yashin's findings concerning the crucial role played by commodification in Turkish politics in the 1980s and 1990s have an important resonance with the expansion of reading in the late Ottoman and early Turkish Republican periods, for they point toward the importance of recognizing the economic, political and ultimately symbolic role played by the book in this earlier era. Much of the following section of this chapter is devoted to the economic dimensions of the spread of reading but it bears underscoring here that a crucial feature of the new educational dispensation was its reliance on the individual purchase and subsequent ownership of reading material – largely books but also other important vehicles such as magazines and pamphlets. Another basic but easily forgotten observation is that the same technical manifestation, whether school textbook or subscription magazine, was available to essentially very different ideational strategies. In other words, the technology was subservient to and harnessed by a range of end uses, whether political, economic or social in conception. The same strategy aimed, say, at deploying children's reading material as a means of inculcating a particular set of values could, depending on their content and their audience, produce widely disparate results. Even countervailing discourses adopt a similar approach to commodification, whether of symbols, clothing or texts.

As one scholar has indicated, "Consumption involves the incorporation of the consumed item into the personal and social identity of the consumer."[6] It is to the strategies of such incorporation that we now turn. Since the objectives and mechanisms of the state sector directed at promoting reading among late Ottoman and early Republican children are fairly straightforward and relatively well known, it is the mechanics and strategies employed by the private sector that for the most part will occupy us here.

First of all, let us look at the mechanics involved in making reading material available to young readers in this period. While very little research has been conducted in this crucial area, it is nevertheless clear that a trend toward encouraging individualized consumption was in operation. Several avenues existed to encourage the consumption of the new reading materials, reflecting the range of socially and economically influenced options available. The new reading dispensation was dependent on – and thus clearly encouraged – the individual purchase of reading material. This could take the form either of buying a book or a subscription to a periodical publication. The physical possession of the reading material itself played an important role in promoting the commodification of the practice of reading in this period.

Purchase and possession

In Chapter 2 we saw the way in which a late Ottoman children's reader projected the bond between student and book. The story titled "The Book" valorized the role of the books in Zeki's mother's library as the proper vehicle for learning and awareness of the wider world. There were many similar examples. In a variety of changing contexts, each emphasizing a different aspect of identification whether public or private, national or universal, domestic or societal, the book remained central to the image of the child as being connected to his or her surroundings.

Having a book of one's own became crucial to attaining the advantages associated with literacy. Publishers of texts for both school and home depicted the humble but still relatively expensive book as a window on the world, a way of transporting the generic child of the simple line drawings into a range of destinations, national as well as international, realistic as well as fantastic. The book was thus a means to observe the world beyond the classroom or the home. But it was more than that because literacy was also presented as the very vehicle to participate in – and not merely regard – modern life. Literacy offered children access to a new territory. The means of coming into this new country was through reading and in its crudest sense the thing that allowed this travel was the physical presence of the reading material itself.

Several options allowed young readers to obtain their own reading material. The simplest was the purchase and individual consumption of a book or magazine. But as for most potential young readers the purchase or possession would have been a novel practice, it was first necessary to prepare them to desire them in the first place. Their schools would have played the prime role in making them accustomed to reading in the first place and to do so out of their own copies of the centrally mandated texts. But state control probably had a mixed effect on encouraging reading; it was doubtful that children wanted to continue on with the stilted material offered by the state outside of school hours.

But the campaign to encourage literacy was far larger than that generated by the state alone. We have seen the ways in which images of children were used to model and promote children's reading in previous chapters. Now let us consider another crucial component of the broadly based effort to encourage children to read, namely, that of valorizing the reading material itself. Efforts to inculcate respect and appreciation for books, magazines and, indeed, the humble pen and paper formed a conspicuous part of their reading and appeared in many forms and places. A few examples will illustrate the range involved.

Fictional literature played a prominent role, if an understandably self-serving one, in encouraging children to value books. Given his prolific publishing rate and the wide range of topics he covered, it is not surprising to find Ahmed Midhat involved. His typically didactic children's book entitled The Well-behaved Child (*Terbiyeli Çocuk*) of 1303 (1885–1856) presented a day in the life of the unnamed boy of the title. This idealized child's routine naturally features both home and school life. At school he always respects the property of others, including specifically their books, papers and pens, keeps his own things neat and tidy, always hangs up his book bag on its proper hook and knows where his books are.[7] A reader produced for girls in 1316 (1898–1899) encouraged them to appreciate the fact that books were relatively inexpensive when compared to the past when only the wealthy could afford them – further evidence for the popularization of reading being made possible by technological change and the expansion of commodification.[8] Ali İrfan's First reader (*Birinci kıraat*) picks up on this theme and expands on it, instructing his charges on the usefulness of paper and books and what we would today refer to as their democratic role. Books and paper, he asserts in one chapter, are a sign of progress (*terakki*) accumulated over the centuries during which the acts of writing and reading have become steadily easier and more widespread. A subsequent chapter explains how paper is made and another presents a fictional story of a boy who throws his book on the floor. This affords the author the opportunity to sermonize on the value of books and the need to preserve them.[9]

Ali İrfan employs a direct style – "Look at the book in your hand" – in his attempt to encourage his readers to identify with books, the way they are made and the development of the possibilities for reading over time. His reader also featured small illustrations of books indented in the margins of his text. More likely to engage with the tastes of young readers was the more enticing approach of Ali Nazima's reader, entitled Read, or The New Treatise on Morals and Children's Duties, mentioned in Chapter 2, which was doubtless more successful in attracting the attention of the young. In the story entitled "The Child Who Knows How to Read" ("*Okuma bilen çocuk*") the young Cevher is rewarded for her progress in reading by her parents in the form of money with which to buy new books. Her uncle also gives her a beautifully illustrated two-volume book as a present.[10] She is overjoyed and the author exhorts his readers to follow her example.

Here the progress of the state and the profits of the bookseller are happily aligned. All the while, the state was of course playing its part in encouraging the purchase of books. As we have seen, its large-scale orders for textbooks on an unprecedented array of topics was the engine driving much of the surge of children's literary production. It is also important to note that with time state educational institutions began to purchase a variety of general texts beyond those specifically required in their curricula. For example, the Primary School Regulation of 1929 specifically noted the important role that textbooks should play in reinforcing what was taught in lessons.[11] But interestingly it also decreed that classrooms should have their own libraries containing dictionaries, atlases and children's literature,[12] offering a further boost to the private publishing sector. Finally, as will be seen in the next chapter, the autobiographical literature demonstrates that this variegated campaign to valorize books and encourage their consumption was being reciprocated by its young audience. Children clearly were involved in what Gell has termed the "incorporation of the consumed item into the personal and social identity of the consumer."

But of course not all children could afford to buy books even if they were now inclined to. As we shall see shortly, costs could be prohibitive.

Two solutions presented themselves to circumvent or at least mitigate the economic problems associated with buying books and magazines of one's own. One was the practice of shared reading, typified by recourse to reading rooms (*kıraathane*) and lending libraries. The other was the emergence of journals to which readers could subscribe, thereby defraying the costs of reading material over time.

Shared reading or, in Ayalon's terms "accessing without buying,"[13] was an increasingly prevalent option in the late Ottoman and early Republican context. It built on the ongoing tradition of public or shared reading that flourished across the Ottoman centuries, especially at the popular level.[14] Whether gathering to read religious texts, historical or semi-historical epics, or love stories, the Ottoman public was accustomed to the shared consumption through public recitation of a fairly wide variety of materials. This tradition doubtless conditioned late Ottoman and early Republican readers to take up reading with its characteristic enthusiasm across a number of genres and styles.

The late nineteenth- and early twentieth-century incarnation of shared access to texts differed in two important respects. First, whereas shared reading in the past often meant more than one person reading or listening to the same copy of a certain text, now it meant that readers took it in turn to read the same text on their own in serial fashion. In other words, the new shared reading was no longer a communal process but simply one that reduced the financial barriers to individual reading. Secondly, more copies of each text were now available and the types of text available were changing with time. The shared reading of the types of text being produced in large numbers by educationalists and freelance authors depended largely on two institutions, the library and the reading room.

The library had both religious and secular antecedents in the classical period of the Ottoman Empire. But a crucial development occurred in the late nineteenth century with the opening of public libraries that were centrally located in the major cities. In Istanbul the first of these to appear was at Bayezid in 1884 and known as the public Ottoman Library (*Kütüphane-i Umumî-i Osmanî*). Another opened in Süleymaniye in 1918. They featured card catalogues, tables and chairs (and thus *alafranga* seating as opposed to their precursors with their low tables, cushions and folding book stands or *rahles*), and were open to the public five days a week.[15] Openness and accessibility were also features of privately supported lending libraries in the Ottoman provinces such as that of the Khalidi family of Jerusalem. When it opened around 1900 the Khalidiyyah was the first public library in Palestine. Its comfortable furniture and well-lit, tilted tables were intended to allow the reading public to consult its vast collections which ranged from the traditional Islamic subjects to contemporary literature, both scientific and fictional, both imported from Europe and neighboring Arab and Ottoman lands.[16] A public library opened in Izmir in 1912, the work of a committee of progressively minded citizens. Known as the National Library (*Millî Kütüphanesi*) it came into being due to close cooperation with and the assistance of the local branch of the Committee of Union and Progress.[17] Linked with a cinema and offering courses in languages and, for girls, sewing, it was part of a broader effort of local and national uplift in this important port city.[18] Its book and periodical holdings grew over the years, eventually becoming a national depository for books published in the Turkish Republic after a visit by Atatürk in 1933.[19]

While libraries were spreading throughout the empire, another informal means of providing the public with access to reading materials was developing. This development was an outgrowth of the arrival and spread of the *café* in the Ottoman Empire. Introduced in the mid-sixteenth century, the coffeehouse spread widely. By the nineteenth century one visitor to Istanbul remarked that the city looked like one big coffeehouse.[20] It was estimated that there were as many as 2500 such establishments in Istanbul: one out of every six or seven commercial shops was a coffeehouse.[21] But more interesting for our purposes was its gradual transformation into the institution known in Turkish as the *kıraathane*, literally "reading house," that was part coffeehouse and part reading room. This hybrid was a nineteenth-century phenomenon, appearing first in the middle of the century. By the 1890s there were six such establishments in the old section of Istanbul alone.[22] Tellingly, they were closely linked with the publishing industry and made the latest copies of the newspapers, both metropolitan and provincial, freely available to their customers. In their heyday they seem to have served as an important vehicle for intellectual and social life, a mix of the traditional café, a literary salon and a men's social club.[23]

For those who could not afford to accumulate libraries on their own access to books and reading was thus expanding, particularly in the urban areas. But crucially for our purposes this expansion was overwhelmingly directed at the adult – and usually male – population. Outside the school and the occasional mention of children's provision in public libraries there are hardly any references to children partaking in this new world of public literacy. For that we have to turn again to the private publishing sector, and to the emerging phenomenon of subscription-based children's magazine.

Subscription

As we have seen, publishers were quick to sense that the new educational system had created a ready market for children's literature. From the producers' point of view, the challenges lay in providing and then promoting a product that was affordable and attractive in terms of both appearance and content. Publishers pursued different strategies in addressing these challenges, as we shall see shortly, but it is clear that the rapidly expanding market guaranteed neither longevity nor profitability. Especially when venturing beyond simply providing texts for the state school system publishers had to rely on instinct as well as trial and error in order to find a viable solution. The emergence of the market in children's periodicals provides ample evidence that publishers had to learn to adjust to become successful in the emerging market.

The burgeoning presence of children's periodicals speaks both to the emergence of a young reading public, a product of educational expansion, and to the new possibilities available in the fields of production and dissemination. Instead of gathering readers in a coffeehouse or reading room, the publishers of periodicals could attract a communal but geographically dispersed readership, a community not dissimilar to Benedict Anderson's notion of "imagined communities." The expanding postal services made available in the nineteenth century allowed for publishers to reach an extremely diffuse audience.[24] The success or otherwise of these publishing ventures depended almost entirely on their ability to engage with their young readers and encourage them to identify with the products on offer, which as we have seen above, is the key to commodification.

What was crucial for the authors and publishers of the new materials was to develop both a rapport with their readership and a distinctive profile for their products. This they attempted, but often only rather clumsily. A first step was frequently to try to cement the bond between reader and reading matter by positioning themselves as constant companions, alive to the needs and wants of their young customers. One tactic employed here was for the editors to claim that they were putting out their publication in response to popular demand. For example, *Bizim Mecmua* (Our Magazine) addressed its readers on the occasion of its being reissued in a newer, larger format by stating that,

> We thought long and hard about reissuing Bizim Mecmua at a time when a lot of magazines for children are being published. But our young readers have grown so fond of and identified so much with

our magazine that they demanded absolutely that it be published ... So after understanding our children's sincere bonds of attachment to their magazine we decided to bring out Bizim Mecmua once again.[25]

Another approach was to try to present the publication as their trustworthy companion. For example, under the headline *"Musahabe,"* meaning "friendly chat," the editor of the children's journal *Yeni Yol* addressed its readers in the autumn of 1923:

> You find yourselves gathered together again in your schools after a two- or three-month holiday. You rested your tiny brains (mini mini dimağlarınız), which were tired after nine months of work and the examination period, under the shade of trees, by cold springs, upon cool summer pastures, and in green gardens[.] And today you have returned to your schools with energetic bodies, healthy minds, young hopes and high ideas.[26]

It then went on to refer to *Yeni Yol* as the readers' "most faithful and loyal friend" and as a journal that engages in conversation with them. It mentions improvements in the writing and illustrations but still cannot resist the urge to warn its young companions against the harmful practice of skipping school. Such ambivalence is indicative of the problems that publishers faced in their efforts to appeal to relatively unknown entity that was the market for young readers.

By comparison with other children's offerings *Yeni Yol* appears to have been more successful in appealing to the young. But given the patronizing tone and staid content of the competition, this is perhaps not saying terribly much. Even *Yeni Yol* struggled to find common cause with its youthful audience. Entering into its third year it attempted to get on the same level with its readership by printing a special issue and claiming that the magazine had recently celebrated its birthday, "just like you, we have birthdays." It also called attention to the sacrifices it had made in order to put out the journal, claiming, "When we started out we didn't have a penny."[27] (That this was the same issue that included some maladroit attempts at racial and obesity-driven humor, suggests again that the publication had some ways to go before it could claim to connect with its target audience in a meaningful and appropriate way.)

The biggest problem with this strategy, of course, was that it tended to elicit a blatantly condescending tone. The publishers were prone to patronizing their young audience, both in the way that they addressed their readers and in the choice of subject matter that they presumed would keep them entertained. Perhaps reflecting the uncomfortable position of attempting to reach out to children on their own terms, children's publications frequently resorted, as we have already seen, to what must have seemed to their publishers as the most effective strategy, namely, piggybacking on the increasingly widespread and intensive relationship between children and school. The paeans to the school, the teacher and the tearful parting at the beginning of summer vacation must have seemed a natural – to an adult mind at least – way of forging bonds with their prospective readership. Exceptions to the otherwise predictable condescension of educators *cum* publishers toward their young readers were nevertheless possible, as we have already seen in the form of *Yeni Yol*'s occasional efforts to side with the students against their teachers. Publishers were developing new strategies to attract the affections of young readers.

New strategies

These new techniques affected the content, the layout and even the price of the publications themselves, reflecting the extent to which the publishers of children's materials sensed the need to develop a rapport with their readers. Each technique was different but they all reflect the common impulse to form connections with their clientele. Perhaps due to the inherently passive aspects of reading, many such intended connections were conspicuously aimed at encouraging active participation. We have already seen several examples of magazine publishers addressing their readers, sometimes engagingly and sometimes conspicuously less so. Now we can see a concerted effort to try to raise a palpable response from their audience.

In both the late Ottoman and early Republican periods children's magazines employed a variety of devices to encourage participation. The main ones included printing readers' letters, arranging competitions that promised a variety of prizes, offering coupons and displaying the photographs that readers were encouraged to send in.

Competitions seem to have garnered considerable attention. Even the stately and well-funded late Ottoman-era Children's own Journal (*Çocuklara Mahsus Gazete*) was not above such a mechanism for connecting with its readers. In its second issue it announced:

> To those who answered the question in the previous issue: Ahmed Fuad Bey Efendi, a fifth-year student in the Şemsulmaarif Mektebi won the prize.

We liked the answer that Ahmed Fuad wrote in answer to the question very much. Ah, may his prosperity increase.

Let him come to our offices on Saturday evening and collect his prize.

We appreciate the efforts of all the other young men and women who responded to our question.

So many responses arrived at our offices that it took a long time to examine them. It is not possible to print the papers because the size of our newspaper is small. But we are carefully keeping all the answers received. We shall collect all that come for months and we shall produce an excellent collection in the name of the progress of our nation. And we ask God for success in publishing this collection in the future.[28]

Asking the winner to come in to receive his prize in person suggests that this Istanbul-based magazine concentrated its efforts on local readers. Such localism was the norm when such publications were starting up but, as we shall see, often yielded to a broader geographical outreach. The journal entitled *Çocuklara Rehber* (The Children's Guide), although published in Salonika (Selânik), clearly intended to reach a wider audience, as indicated by its two-tier subscription pricing. The contents of its first issue reveals its intention to attract and entertain its readership: sections included those entitled "Dear Reader," "Our Replies," "Jokes," "Puzzle" and "Our Questions."[29] The puzzle section for that issue featured riddles, one of which was: "Eyes has it none but it lives; It has no tongue but it speaks; It cannot be seen but what it says can be heard." The answer was given below: An echo. The second issue lists the winners of the competitions presented in the first issue and it is clear from their names and school affiliations that they were students at the preparatory (*idadî*) level, two boys and two girls. Other magazines, such as *Bizim Mecmua* (Our Journal) offered different competitions for both older and younger children.

Prizes were a sure way of encouraging a response. The prizes on offer were normally subscriptions to the magazines themselves, usually for six and twelve months, books, and for the third-place finishers, a post card. The early Republican *Çıtı Pıtı* offered the winner of its crossword competition, drawn from all the successful entries, a writing set; second prize was a pocket atlas; third, a handsome wallet; fourth, a chic drawing notebook; fifth through tenth each received a book; tenth though fiftieth places received a post card. But on occasion competitions offered other things besides books and magazines and sometimes even considerable sums of cash. *Yeni Yol* offered such inducements as *eau de cologne* and boy scout belts. One such contest sponsored by the same journal in 1925 offered a prize of five *lira* each to one hundred young readers, at this time a considerable sum of money for anyone, let alone a child.[30] The types of puzzles generally included the kinds where the readers were meant to connect dots, cut out coupons, fill in letters in crosswords and so on.

Children played along. A coupon cut out and filled in by hand by a certain student named Burhaneddin remains in a copy of *Yeni Yol* in my possession. On one side of the coupon is an illustration of a rural scene containing a woman standing with a pair of oxen before a simple house in the countryside. On the other side young Burhaneddin, who has also supplied his address and school identification number, has written down his answer to the puzzle, indicating on the other side of the coupon where the third ox is hidden in the drawing by circling the hidden beast in red ink.[31] It is not uncommon to come across issues of magazines where the coupons have been cut out, indicating that readers were responding to the publishers' attempts at expanding participation.

If further proof were needed of the allure of these types of promotion in the eyes of young readers, we can see that they are occasionally remembered with affection in the autobiographical literature. For example, the novelist Tarık Buğra (1918–1994), the son of an illiterate Türkmen mother and an Ottoman intellectual, describes his elation at winning a prize offered by the children's magazine *Çocuk Dünyası*.[32] Having learned to read before he entered school thanks to his father's predilection for reading in the evenings – another example of parental reading as a vehicle for literacy and a cozy introduction to literacy that we will see repeated often when we turn to biographical approach to learning to read in the following chapter – and marveling at his father's collection of books and journals, he soon wanted reading materials of his own. With the help of his father and his sisters he was soon able to work his way through a variety of texts and even began to spend a share of his pocket money on books instead of sweets, nuts or playthings. When he was in the third year of his primary school in Akşehir he took the weekly *Çocuk Dünyası* and, solving one of their puzzles, he sent in his solution.

A few weeks later I had suddenly become the most famous person in the Gazi Musafa Kemâl Paşa School. Because they had held a draw of the successful solutions submitted and the first prize had gone to Süleyman Tarık Efendi, third-year student in the Gazi Musafa Kemâl Paşa School of Akşehir.

When I got to school I was met by people shouting, 'Hey, hey' and putting on a display reminiscent of Japan. Those who took the magazine had spread the news as soon as it arrived.[33]

He goes on to describe the arrival of his prize of nine books, treated with great importance and ceremony, and was able to recall several of their titles when composing his memoirs as an old man. The "incident of the nine books" was, he says, a turning point in his life, drawing him further into the world of reading and ultimately encouraging him to become a writer himself.

Advertisements played a role in drawing in young readers and their parents alike. From the late nineteenth century onwards one can trace the emergence of an increasingly vivid and direct approach to the spending potential of this new market. Books and other printed materials were natural choices for promotion. The series or "library" of a set of texts became a common way of presenting children's publications. The first of these, The children's library (*Kütübhane-i etfâl*), appeared in 1873, and others soon followed. The Pocket Library (*Cep kütübahnesi*), the collaborative work of Mihran Nakkaşian and Şemseddin Sami produced 29 volumes in spite of their relatively high prices.[34] The "School Library" (*Mektep kütüphanesi*) and the "Children's Library" (*Çocuklar kütüphanesi*) were typical of this new way of packaging and presenting reading material intended for the young. It had the no doubt intended effect of underscoring the point that there was much to read and that reading widely was crucial to a child's intellectual and moral formation. Other types of advertisement appealed less to the budding intellect and more to entertainment and enjoyment. Purveyors of products such as ice cream, chocolate bars and other delights were a common feature of the periodical literature of this period. Not surprisingly, advertisements for these kinds of commodities tended to appear not in the periodicals intended for children – these are relatively rare in this period – but rather in those aimed at their parents, reflecting a realistic assessment of who controlled the means to buy the relevant items.[35]

Localization

As we have seen, children's publications frequently revealed a tendency to cater to what was depicted as a generic and generally undefined sense of childhood. This was a place of fluffy animals and candy, devoid of almost anything in the way of local character. It is difficult to say how far children accepted this generic presentation but it seems clear that it would pale in comparison with the more realistic, exciting frame of World War I and the national struggle for independence. But this changed with time. Publishers began to see the importance of aligning their offerings with the demands of their readership, which in turn was growing more selective and differentiated or segmented as time went on. Two important forces thus can be seen to have affected these publications. On the one hand publishers reacted to a rapidly growing and increasingly sophisticated readership by offering a variety of materials in the hopes of carving out a niche for themselves. This was a force pushing toward diversity and novelty and sometimes, as we have seen, even toward irreverence and satire. On the other hand the political pressures of the period had the effect of encouraging a smaller and more uniform worldview. This was, after all, the period of the provisional Anatolian government under Mustafa Kemal Paşa that was already showing signs of the radical nationalism that it would impose after the founding of the Turkish Republic in 1923. As we have seen in previous chapters the need to conform to the increasingly nationalist message is readily apparent in the foregrounding of the national and the local instead of the cosmopolitan. The impetus to refine their connections with their readership and with the ambient conditions of the period explains the emergence in time of a new concern with the local, the Turkish context.

A case in point is the tone set in the very late Ottoman period by the journal *Bizim Mecmua* (Our magazine). Whereas previous issues had conveyed an almost Disney-like visual impression through the inclusion of pictures of large elephants, dot-to-dot drawings, clowns and so on, from the middle of May 1922 a clear change occurs. With its seventh issue the magazine presents a recognizably Turkish scene. The generic visual vocabulary abruptly gives way to a localized depiction that includes scenes of mosques, fields, football games and lest anyone doubt, the occasional Turkish flag.[36] At roughly the same time, the children's periodical *Yeni Yol*, on commencing its second year of publication, firmly declares that it does not intend simply to mimic or translate Western journals (Figure 5.1).

We do not want to be the imitator or translator of European periodicals; we want to publish a periodical that is appropriate to the spirit, the level, and the learning of our own world, not the world of the West.[37]

Such localization assumed an even more precise focus over time, especially when children's publications began featuring photographs of the

Figure 5.1   Localization: Flags

readers themselves, thereby giving a specifically local dimension to the relationship between the publication and its readers. Some children's magazines had been in the habit of printing the exam results for a particular school.[38] While doubtless unpleasant for those with disappointing scores, this practice at least afforded children to see their names in print. This seems to be an important step in conveying the sense that child readers were actually individuals living in a local context and not generic children which is how, as we have seen, they were often imagined and portrayed. An even more personalized format appeared with photography. This began in the form of posed school or class pictures that were sent in by the children themselves, or perhaps their teachers, and printed as if to make permanent the relationship between publishers and the young readers. This type of outreach now stretched much further than Istanbul. For example, the students of İnönü Boys School are displayed in 1924, dressed in kalpaks, white shirts with kerchiefs scout-fashion, a flag containing the name of the school and four star-and-crescent symbols.[39] Within 18 months the same publication was publishing strips of individual photos of its readers on its back cover. Listing their hometown, the name of their school, their school identification numbers and their names, these photos reveal a variety of clothing, headgear, backdrop, age and attitudes towards the camera.[40] An issue a fortnight later continued this new motif but moved the pictures inside pages of the magazine and labeled them "The photographs of our hardworking youngsters."[41] A note to the students running at the bottom of the page refers to the fact that the magazine is unable to print all the photographs it had received in response to its request and states that the readers will need to wait to see their pictures appear in turn. The response reveals that the new strategies were working. The assembly of a group of geographically disparate yet communal readership seem to be a realization of the national clientele such publications were working so hard to establish.

Prices

The efforts of publishers to commodify and promote their products were clearly dependent on making their products affordable. At this they were largely successful. In this respect they were fortunate to benefit from the widening access to paper and printing presses. It has often been noted that the Ottoman Empire hardly reacted to the early eighteenth-century arrival of the Arabic-script printing press with alacrity or profusion – there was no "printing revolution" as in early modern Europe.[42] But focusing on Ottoman society's "failure" to rush to embrace the printing press certainly did not mean that it shunned books. A visitor to Istanbul in the late sixteenth century marveled that, "*Il y a des livres à Constantinople en quantités énormes. Les bibliothèques et les marchés en débordent. Il y arrive des livres de tous les pays du monde.*" As Frédéric Hitzel has noted, it may be difficult for us to imagine a highly literate society that largely ignored printing for a long time but the fact remains that the Ottoman Empire featured a vibrant book culture.[43]

Whatever its origins the earlier reticence to make use of the printing press was rapidly being abandoned by the late nineteenth century. As literacy spread a publishing industry developed and then thrived. Whereas only an estimated 439 titles had been published in Ottoman Turkish prior to 1839, in the less than two decades following 1876 over 3000 titles appeared in that language.[44] Key to this newfound profusion was the ability to lower the prices of published materials, a product of reduced costs for paper and type and of the emergence of a more reliable and speedier postal service.

The declining costs associated with publishing are clearly reflected in the prices of children's publications. The trend was clearly running in the buyers' favor. Most periodical publications in the last decades of the nineteenth century and the first decade of the twentieth century charged around twenty *para* for an individual copy. That was reduced first to ten and then to five *para* in subsequent years with the exception of the inflationary period surrounding World War I when prices rose dramatically to reach an average of five *kuruş*, a significant sum.[45] Regardless of the rate of inflation, the cover price remained relatively affordable. For comparison's sake we can refer to the daily expenses of an Istanbul bureaucrat in the first decade of the twentieth century. The daily outlay on bread for a family of six and several servants amounted to five *kuruş*, which was the same amount that he paid for lunch in a restaurant. (A French-Turkish lexicon cost forty *kuruş*.)[46] So a children's publication of twenty *para* would have been on a level with one fifth of the money that a well-to-do family would spend on its daily bread, or essentially small change for the emerging middle-class families of the cities.

Annual subscriptions were correspondingly accessible. The weekly *Çocuklara Rehber*, a magazine with relatively high production standards, charged twenty *para* for a single issue but subscribers paid twenty *kuruş* annually if they lived in Salonica or thirty *kuruş* if they lived elsewhere. Local subscribers thus saved six *kuruş*, or slightly less than 25 percent, of the retail price. As with most magazines, half-yearly subscriptions were also available. Naturally enough the magazines featuring more illustrations, sometimes even in color, charged more. Appearing in 1923, *Yeni Yol*'s annual subscription rate was 120 *kuruş* and the price per issue was five *kuruş*, meaning that those who were "*abone*" – the Turkish followed the French word for subscriber – saved more than half of the cover price.

Books naturally tended to be more expensive than magazines but not dramatically so. Some books were even less expensive than magazines produced at the same time. The volumes that formed the series organized by Ebuziya Tevfik, Kitabhane-i Ebuziya, which ran from 1882 to 1893, kept the prices as low as 1.5 *kuruş* per volume, a price hardly much more than the journal issues of the period.[47] Ali İrfan's *Birinci Kıraat* (First reader), published in 1328 (1910/1911) when most children's magazines were selling for around ten *kuruş*, went for two *kuruş*. Other books in the same series were priced from between one to three *kuruş*.

For this nominal fee young readers could enter into a new world. Much of the material was unremarkable or even mind-numbingly banal but frequently the fare was creatively arranged and dramatically illustrated. Even more exciting, no doubt, was the transporting quality of the texts themselves. They informed their readers about far away lands and radically new inventions. As we have seen, geographical curiosities and technological marvels featured frequently in the children's magazines and books of this period. Illustrations were crucial. Whether representing the aboriginal inhabitants of Africa, East Asia or North America, the drawings and eventually photographs offered young readers vivid glimpses of remote lands and peoples. When photography was either too expensive or impossible, for example, when accompanying a futuristic or other imaginary tale, drawings were used. The quality and provenance of such illustrations varied tremendously. Publishers seem to have felt themselves free to borrow from all sorts of images, many of them foreign. But increasingly children's publications featured purpose-drawn illustrations that naturally gave them a look that was more tailored to fit with Ottoman/Turkish, as opposed to Western European, audiences. This localization of the appearance of children's reading material worked hand in hand with the publishers' impetus to focus on more domestic considerations in line with the ambient trend toward national consciousness. But it also sat somewhat uncomfortably with the widening of horizons that was such a strong feature of the children's literature in this period. This tension between the local and the global is perhaps to be expected during this period when the forces of the market were encouraging the opening up of new avenues of communication and identification but the dominant political tendency ran conversely in the direction of a more narrow national consciousness.

Identification

The overall picture that emerges from the children's publishing scene in the late Ottoman and early Republican period is one of forging various types of overlapping identification. The most basic links, perhaps, were those forged between authors and their reading audience. But far from all texts were signed or otherwise identified their composers. The relationship between publishers and readers was therefore in many respects even more influential. As we have seen, the publishers of works for children employed a variety of strategies in order to solidify the identification between their readers and their products. Attractive and frequently participatory features such as puzzles, competitions and printing both group and individual photographs were the most tangible signs of the attempt on the part of publishers to forge lasting bonds with their audience. But the most basic bond was that between readers and the texts themselves. Frequently piggybacking on the spread of the school, children's publications strove to create a stronger bond with young children. Through various devices including behavior modeling, humor – sometimes pointedly directed at the educational establishment itself – and the provision of visually attractive and transporting, horizon-expanding subject matter, children's publishers were effectively marketing their product to a growing group of consumers. An unintended consequence of the new dispensation in reading was the creation of new relationships between and among fellow readers, links ultimately beyond the control of both the apparatus of the state and the publishers themselves but ones that were naturally crucial to the creation of the notion of a reading public in particular and civil society in general. This was in part what Anderson described as the creation of an imagined community based upon common readership. But it was more than that; as the publications for children took to reproducing the photographs, names and written contributions of its readers, their young peers could do far more than imagine the broader community that reading was helping to construct. They could now see and read evidence of this new extended family of reading.

As mentioned at the beginning of this chapter, the crucial task from the publishers' perspective was to effect "the incorporation of the consumed item into the personal and social identity of the consumer." Doing so meant engaging a number of strategies, frequently competitive, sometimes cajoling, and invariably selling that did not always sit easily alongside the increasingly strident attempts at political indoctrination that emanated from the state. How these mixed messages, these tensions and these increasingly variegated products were incorporated into the lives of those on both sides of these exchanges is the subject of the next chapter.

6
Lives of Reading and Writing

Before the relationship between individuals and texts intensified in the modern period, reading, writing and vocalization already played important roles in the lives of ordinary Ottoman subjects. From cradle to grave, textual and oral traditions mediated and informed daily existence in the pre-modern Ottoman empire. A number of clearly observed rituals marked the important stages and transitions in everyday life. Reading, whether textual or oral, and vocalization were crucial to almost all of them. Ottoman society and culture were predominantly oral but texts nevertheless enjoyed positions of prominence and surfaced at critical junctures.

Reading of one sort or another marked each stage of life. At birth prayers and injunctions were whispered into the ear of the newborn child. Learning to read and the commencement of schooling were, as we shall see, important milestones and celebrated as such. For males, the rite of circumcision featured the Arabic phrase *"Maşallah"* (literally, What [wonders] God has willed; How wonderful!) embroidered on the special suit of clothes worn for that celebrated occasion,[1] a practice that continues in Turkey to this day albeit in the Latin script. In times of illness popular remedies involved reading passages of the Qur'an.[2] Service in the military, the bureaucracy and the religious hierarchy both required and in turn generated diplomas, letters of investiture and other documents of various kinds. In the nineteenth century the number of documents generated by this ever more textual society increased dramatically. The central government kept tabs on the growing ranks of its civil servants by means of its personnel files, the *Sicill-i ahvâl defterleri*, which one scholar has likened to a series of state-produced autobiographies,[3] a source to which we shall return later in this chapter. In life's final hours the Qur'an would be read at the

175

deathbed.[4] One of the most enduring links between human lives and text appeared after death: Ottoman gravestones presented a mixture of the formulaic and the distinctive, mirroring the mélange of the common and the individual aspects of humanity.[5]

The cumulative effect of the uncoordinated but influential reading campaign that began in the late Ottoman period and continued with renewed vigor in the early Republic served to strengthen and intensify this relationship between the individual and reading. The drive toward greater literacy created a new series of relationships between individuals and texts; it added new contexts for reading to those already present in pre-modern Ottoman society. The general tendency was toward a more direct and a more individualized relationship between reader and text, gradually supplanting the communal aspect of traditional reading. This new dispensation came about, as we have seen, through a series of inter-related developments. Beginning at home and continuing at school, children were drawn into a more intense and a more frequent interaction with writing. Their books and, increasingly, their magazines addressed them directly.[6] Both their teachers and their journals enjoined them to read and otherwise engage with texts on a regular basis through homework assignments, quizzes, puzzles and competitions. Each in their own way, the schools and the private printing houses attempted to foster affection and loyalty to their institutions. They encouraged the purchase and reading of a variety of texts, for pleasure, for edification and for socialization and indoctrination. In this way reading came to play an increasingly prominent role in more and more young lives. The consequences of this shift remain for the most part unknown; as a solitary, even lonely, act, reading leaves few physical traces in its wake. It is only later and occasionally that the experiences of reading can be expressed in writing and so recorded for posterity. Memoirs depicting childhood reading provide us with evidence of the important place that reading held in numerous lives, both individually and collectively. As we shall soon see, the new reading dispensation opened up new worlds, offered new forms of earning a living and generally altered lives in innumerable ways, ranging from the most mundane to the most sublime.

This chapter examines the impact that this intensified relationship had on the individual lives of readers and writers. By focusing on biographical information it draws together a number of broader issues that have been addressed in previous chapters to examine the ways in which the changes taking place in the larger society affected specific individuals. It relies largely on memoirs, whenever possible in conjunction with other materials.[7] Under the best of circumstances autobiographical sources are problematic. When they seek to remember across a political divide such as that imposed between the end of the Ottoman Empire and the birth of the Turkish Republic with all of the attendant changes in cultural and ideological orientation that such a shift intended, they are naturally liable to be even trickier. Even the memoirs written by those born after 1923, the "children of the republic," traverse shifting territory, as the early Kemalist dream yielded to the reality of the later years of the republic.[8] But in their favor, of course, is the fact that memoirs provide the specific detail and emotional texture that most other sources simply cannot offer. Recovering this degree of specificity is crucial to our attempt to understand the ways in which reading changed the way people lived their lives.

Becoming readers

To begin, let us examine the ways in which readers encountered the written word. At times it appears as if it reached out and touched or changed these readers-turned-writers, such was the almost visceral pull of the text. Although reading is of course mainly an internal, cerebral process, the desire for reading is frequently expressed in physical terms. The sense of a hunger, an appetite, an almost febrile passion for and even an addiction to reading come through strongly in the autobiographical narratives. In some cases the child afflicted with the reading fever becomes almost insensate, oblivious to the normal demands of his or her everyday life. Almost all descriptions of learning to read and childhood reading include evocative descriptions of the physical ambience in which the reading took place. Whether curled up in the embrace of a parent, falling asleep by a flickering fire or stretched out on a carpet, young readers describe their early reading experiences in strongly physical, sometimes even sensual, ways. The physicality of reading is something we noted earlier in our discussion in Chapter 2 of the ways in which reading and literacy were depicted by educators and publishers keen to promote the activity. Now we shall see how the practice of learning to read was experienced, or at least remembered, by the children themselves.

The following biographical passages evoke the many ways and colorations associated with learning to read Turkish, just one of the many languages of the empire in this period. (If we were to try to trace the full range of learning to read in the Ottoman context, we would of course require far more in the way of scope, sources and linguistic competence than any one student of the period can offer.) Because each interaction between child and the world of reading is quite different, even within one linguistic range, it will be necessary to call on a sample of such experiences and to consider each one on its own terms. The individuals subjected to examination in this chapter have been chosen on the basis of their having produced memoirs that delve into the worlds of their late Ottoman and early Republican childhoods, thereby providing sufficient contextual background – some much more than others[9] – to permit explication of these crucial first encounters with reading.

In spite of the expectations produced by the usual treatment of the Ottoman-to-republican transition, what frequently comes to the fore is the connection between literacy and popular culture. The prevailing assumption has been that literacy in the Ottoman period was essentially a phenomenon of the thinnest of elites. The republican view of the language and literature of the *ancien régime* has generally tended to paint them as manifestations of an impossibly ornate, distant and outmoded world, overburdened by reliance on complicated poetic forms and religious superstition. By contrast the republican self-view was one that embraced, as we have seen, the peasant and the countryside, in spite of the fact that few of its leading cadres knew much more about that side of life than did their Ottoman precursors. The Republic saw itself – and wanted others to see it – as bestowing the gift of literacy on the nation and arranged spectacles and propaganda to get this point across. Most famously these featured Mustafa Kemal lecturing citizens of the Republic on the new, Latin-derived alphabet, an innovation that was justified on the grounds that it was more appropriate than the Arabic script for representing Turkish. Somewhat ironically given the ostensibly popular inspiration of the regime, new institutions such as the "People's Rooms" and the "Village Institutes" appeared in an effort to impart literacy, not to mention secularism and positivism and other Kemalist ideals, to the rural population. The army was also invoked as a national educator. Posters appeared under the slogan "The Army is the People's School" (*Ordu Bir Halk Mektebidir*) which showed pictures of the visible difference that this national training was making, for example, teaching citizens to wear western-style hats and forming ranks of well-drilled soldiers.[10] Of course the leading lights of the Republic inevitably owed their educational and literary formation to the previous era. So it is important to notice that many of the memoirs recalling first encounters with literacy in the late Ottoman period are already suffused with a strong popular bent, yet another sign of the frequently overlooked continuities in the Ottoman-to-republican transition.

Halide Edib [Adıvar]

The nationalist writer and political activist Halide Edib [Adıvar] (1882–1964) is one of the most recognized figures of the young republic. Partly because she wrote an English version of her memoirs and partly because of her involvement in and propagandizing for the independence struggle, her story is fairly well known outside Turkey. Reading is a central feature in her autobiographical writings, whether written in English or Turkish.[11] Her vivid accounts of the manner in which she entered into the world of literacy and reading have featured in earlier chapters as we focused on, for example, the mechanics of learning to read and the milieu in which reading took place. What I would like to draw attention to here is the mixture of elite and popular sources constituting her reading environment.

Halide Edib came from a well-to-do Istanbul family – her father served as first secretary to Sultan Abdülhamid II's privy purse at Yıldız Palace and her mother's father also had held positions in the palace – and was educated privately before being sent to the missionary-run American College in Üsküdar. Yet it is clear that some of her most important influences came not from the sophisticated world of elite letters but rather from the popular realm of legends and folktales. No doubt reflecting her nationalist predilection for the popular constituents of Turkishness, her memoirs contain several passages freighted with the importance of folk literature. However, it would be wrong to attribute their inclusion simply to a desire to project nationalist sentiment backwards onto her Ottoman-era childhood. For one thing, her remembrances have the ring of authenticity about them and for another they echo similar passages in the memoirs of her contemporaries, as we shall soon see. In other words, the republican emphasis on popular culture did not need to fabricate popular influences on learning to read; they were already there.

The first reference to literacy in the English version of her memoirs appears in connection with a young Circassian boy who was living in her house. He is described sitting at a table, "lost in his books, for he was getting ready for a school education." Halide Edib explains parenthetically, using the third person to refer to herself: "Her father had a mania for taking poor young men under his protection and sending them to school."[12] So although this young man does not relate to Halide directly, reading figures in the narrative both as a force for betterment and as a world into which one could be transported and through which one's life could be transformed. The second mention of literacy, or rather its opposite, relates to another figure in her family's extended household, an old man from Anatolia. This man is an illiterate Turk from the provinces but represents the conduit for one important source of inspiration for the young girl. He tells her stories about the wars with Russia in eastern Anatolia. Later in the narrative other Anatolians would serve as similar vehicles for the traditional Turkish legends such as that of Battal Gazi, to which we shall return below.

Halide Edib's initial account of her childhood includes a variety of influences, each representing a different strand of the interwoven religious and cultural environment of the Ottoman capital in the late nineteenth century. Western inspirations appear early on in the narrative in the form of her father's "admiration for the English and their way of bringing up children. He believed that the secret of their greatness was due to this, and so his method of bringing up his first-born [i.e., Halide's older sister] was strongly influenced by English ways as he had read of them in books."[13] The influence of the "minority" communities registers in her description of the three Greek spinsters who ran the kindergarten which young Halide attended, the only Turk among the other, mostly Armenian and Greek, children.[14] Here she learned enough Greek to be able to sing the "Kyrie Eleison" and to recite before the class. She "did not realize that she spoke two languages, one at school, and one at home. Language to her was a mere gesture, and one used one or the other according to the person who understood this or that way of expression."[15] This multilingual situation serves as a subtle reminder of what would be lost or at least greatly diminished in linguistic and cultural terms under the drive for national – and linguistic – homogeneity under the new regime.

Halide Edib's initiation into Turkish Islamic cultural world, in both its secular and religious manifestations, relied heavily on reading. As with most of her contemporaries, the Islamic dimension predominated early on in her life. While mention of her grandmother's penchant for writing "crude love stories and very old-fashioned verse" served as an example of the secular literary pursuits,[16] the religious dimension was represented by the persistent presence of a series of ulema, or *hocas* as they are more often known in Turkish. On one occasion the sight of some boys torturing a wounded dog produced a strong reaction in Halide. She was taken home where her grandmother summoned the *hocas* to restore her to health. "I patiently lay where I was and let the holy men in green turbans come and read the Koran in undertones and breathe its holy virtue into my face." But other potential cures were also invoked. The family's Circassian maid burnt incense in Halide's room, "made queer gestures, and bade the fairies (*peris*) to set me free." Her father's recourse was rather different: he summoned a "famous German doctor... who filled me with all sorts of disagreeable medicines."[17]

This diversified approach to healthcare was reproduced in Halide Edib's introduction to reading. Halide's narrative depicts the impetus to read as stemming from a largely secular impulse, linked as it was to an elegant palace lady who distributed presents of sweets and silk handkerchiefs when Halide's family went to visit her rooms in their extended household. "But what makes me remember that day especially was her bringing out picture-books to show us during our visit to her apartments. It was a strange sensation to me, those signs and the pictures out of which a new world suddenly spoke." The book in question was a volume on African travels and it reappears later in the narrative. This *"Auntie Teïzé"* clearly made a huge impression on young Halide: "From that moment I gradually began to find the palace lady very attractive. An uncontrollable desire to learn to read began with the African travels that day."[18] This sense of a "new world" awakened by reading and the geographical connection resonates with our discussion in Chapter 2 concerning the ways in which publishers were attempting to present their wares as windows on the wider world.

But if Halide Edib's inspiration for wanting to learn to read was kindled by a well-scented palace lady, her first encounters with learning to read were dominated by the men of Islamic letters, the ulema.

> One night about this time I begged granny to allow me to learn to read. "Thy father does not want thee to learn before thou art seven," she said. "It is stupid of him. *I* started at three, and in my days children of seven knew the Koran by heart." In spite of this I kept bothering her and even speaking to father about it, so that he at last consented, although I was not fully six yet. Thereupon the house began to get ready to celebrate my *bashlanmak*, my entrance into learning.[19]

As was the case with many of her contemporaries, Halide Edib presents her will to read not as something imposed from outside but rather as emanating within herself. But once fixed in the mind of the child such an impulse had to negotiate with the realm controlled by adults, with all of the conventions and cultural associations that had evolved over the centuries. In Halide Edib's case she had to overcome her father's "modern" instinct to delay her initiation into the world of reading until she was seven years old.

The "pretty ceremony" of initiation was conducted in a deeply religious vein: "A little girl was dressed in silk covered with jewels, and a gold-embroidered bag, with an alphabet inside, was hung round her neck with a gold-tasseled cord." She was placed in an open carriage with the schoolchildren of the neighborhood following behind and singing "the very popular hymn, 'The rivers of paradise, as they flow, murmur, "Allah, Allah." The angels in paradise, as they walk, sing, "Allah, Allah."' At the end of each stanza hundreds of little throats shouted, 'Amin, amin!'"[20]

After the hoca chanted a passage from the Qur'an, swaying back and forth to its rhythm, Halide Edib was made to kneel and to repeat the first letters of the alphabet before kissing the hoca's hand. Thereafter she took private lessons with the hoca at her home in the evenings. "Two candles therefore were placed on the table and burned under green shades, while I struggled with the Arabic writing of the book. Of course it was difficult to go on without understanding the meaning of the words one read, but the musical sound of it all was some compensation."[21]

Halide's progress at reading Qur'anic Arabic was only marginally helpful in her wish to become a reader of Turkish. Still, she persisted, gravitating to Teïzé's upstairs apartment and the allure of the book of African travels. In her narrative, this journey between the two types of text represents the distance between the secular and religious written traditions. Whenever she had the chance she would now go to the upstairs flat when the maid was dusting Teïzé's library.

> I would beg her to take out the book of African travels and open it for me on the floor. It was too large for me to handle, and when she had laid it down I stretched myself on the floor and tried to decipher it. In this position, resting on my elbows, I would struggle till my eyes ached. It was so different from the Koran, and the words, even when I could make them out, were such that I did not understand.[22]

While she tried to read the maid would be chatting away, relating stories of her childhood in the Caucasus and fanciful tales of the Circassian spirit world, adding a third, oral or folk dimension to the cultural associations which Halide Edib imbibed as she struggled to enter the world of reading.

Yet another aspect of the variegated reading culture of the late Ottoman period appeared in the form of a rather ghoulish book in manuscript form that she was given to read from Teïzé's library. Although the palace lady apparently did not think much of it, this text offered one very useful advantage for a reader-in-the-making such as Halide. "As it had the Arabic vowel signs inserted in the text, I could read it for myself, and most unfortunately for me I did read it. It was called 'The Adventures of Death.'"[23] Despite the negative effect on Halide's nerves and the nightmares that this macabre volume produced through its exploration of the process of death, described by the author as "having the imagination of Dante without his genius," in terms of learning to read it was a boon. As a half step between stumbling over the letters, guessing at their probable pronunciation and grammatical roles on the one hand and comfortable literacy on the other, this pre-vocalized text allowed Halide Edib to read with considerable retention, indeed rather more than the young girl's fragile constitution could comfortably handle.

All the while that this autodidactic process was taking its course, Halide continued to be taught by the hocas. But it was the succession of male household tutors who had a greater impact on her intellectual development at this stage. Each of these men had his methods and sources of inspiration. First there was a certain Süleyman Ağa who delighted Halide with his tales of Eastern Anatolia and of his personal adventures, including his relations with his three wives. He was eventually deemed to have overreached his station by presuming too much and taking on "such airs that he displeased Granny" and was dismissed. Next came Ahmed Ağa, "a man who could read and write and handle, or rather rule, his masters with psychological insight. From him I got a great deal of my early education." His lessons seem to have succeeded because of their informality and because he provided another channel to the deep reservoir of popular Anatolian tales. Over the course of almost three years before she would enter the American girls college she read the folk legends with Ahmed Ağa. This phase of her reading education began with the legend of Battal Gazi, the Turkish epic romance that adopted and embroidered earlier tales of heroism of the Arab conquests in an Anatolian context.

> I found Ahmed Ağa reading a big black book one day and asked him to tell me the story. He read something which charmed me so intensely that I got hold of the book and struggled on by myself, reading aloud and asking a thousand questions about things I did not understand.[24]

Moving back in time from Battal Gazi to Abu Muslim Khorasani, the hero of the Abbasid revolution which overthrew the Umayyad dynasty in 750 CE, and finally to Ali b. Abi Talib, the nephew and son-in-law of the Prophet, Halide Edib absorbed the heroics of Turkish and early Islamic legend.

What is striking in Halide Edib's memoir is the vividness with which she depicts the mélange of socio-cultural influences attending her introduction to the world of reading. By turns secular and religious, high and low, non-Muslim and Muslim, Turkish and Western and imparted through recitation, published books, manuscripts and orally recounted tales, the combined weight of these distinct strands nevertheless serves to form a more or less coherent background to her reading life, at once both situational and unified. From her "uncontrollable desire to learn to read" to her emergence as one of the most important figures of the early republic, Halide's memoir reveals the remarkably broad array of ambient influences operating in the late Ottoman period.

Şevket Süreyya [Aydemir]

Şevket Süreyya [Aydemir's] (1897–1976) origins represent in certain respects the antithesis of Halide Edib's. Born into a humble family that had fled, like so many others, the territories lost as the empire's borders shrank over the course of the nineteenth century, Şevket Süreyya grew up in the rough and tumble outskirts of Edirne, a former imperial capital transformed by century's end into a border town. Despite the differences in their material and geographical origins, he and Halide Edib shared similar influences in their development as readers. The future biographer of Atatürk describes his neighborhood of recently settled refugees from the former Balkan provinces as poor but orderly and self-respecting. In his account, the center of the quarter's life was his house and it was dominated by the figure of his mother. He describes her as an energetic, sensitive and religious woman who was continually consulted for her advice and practical solutions.

Literacy and reading were crucial to his mother's role in the community.

> ...the most frequent and most lively meetings in our border neighborhood took place in our house. Apart from us and not in a single house in the quarter was there anyone who could read these lithographed books. In contrast to my father who despite his accomplished and superior qualities was unable to read or write, my mother could read books on religion, story tales and epics. She taught the girls and women of the quarter how to pray and explained the prayer surahs.[25]

By "these lithographed books" he was referring to the poor quality publications that he had mentioned a few paragraphs earlier as forming part of the rich folk life of this poor quarter. This he describes as a mixture of refugee tales, war stories and accounts of gang activity (*çetecilik*), the yarns passed on from mouth to mouth, and the books in which could be read superstitions, the interpretation of dreams, fortune telling, love stories and heroic epics. Not high literature, to be sure, but these were the sorts of inexpensively produced books generated by the penny press of the late Ottoman Empire,[26] an important but overlooked dimension of the new reading scene.

However cheaply they were produced, these texts still required the ability to read and this was in short supply in impoverished circumstances such as war-torn Edirne. Şevket Süreyya explains how his stock in the world went up due to his mother's teaching him how to read. "With the passing of a little time and my mother's more or less teaching me to read, gradually I too became a young person who was sought after and respected in the quarter."[27]

His account is quite vague on the mechanics of learning to read, a clear point of contrast with the private tuition that Halide Edib's family could afford. In Şevket Süreyya's memoir he explains that he learned to read because his mother "more or less" taught him. This phrasing seems to suggest that a bright boy would naturally acquire the rare and useful talent deployed to such positive effect by his mother through a combination of instruction and osmosis. In fact, when he was later taken to school for the first time by his father, his mother having hung an ornamented cloth pouch around his neck containing the first section of the Qur'an before he set out, he already knew as much reading and writing as the local school could teach him.[28] He went through the abbreviated entrance ritual which contained none of the ceremony attending that experienced by Halide Edib, and began his schooling in spite of the fact that he should properly have gone on to a higher level school. Even so, it was the first step in his movement away from his neighborhood and toward his own remarkable life story.

A few pages later he describes the reverence with which the rare commodities of writing and literacy were held in his neighborhood. "To the people of our quarter, the school, the book and the person who could read were great and auspicious riches. In our neighborhood a piece of paper with writing on it would never be seen on the streets or on the ground." The reason for this was that writing was popularly associated with the sacred text of the Qur'an and therefore all writing might be holy. In his own house both the books of stories and those on religious subjects were kept on high shelves or an alcove. The Holy Qur'an would always be kissed when it was taken down and before being put away in its protected place.[29] It is precisely this idealized attitude toward text that was being transformed by the expansion of reading and the proliferation of reading materials upon which it depended.

Şevket Süreyya ventured forth outside his house with his reading skills so as to share his talents with others in the neighborhood.

> Sometimes towards a summer's evening I would climb out on a branch of the big mulberry tree in our garden and read in a loud voice the divans of Âşık Ömer and Âşık Garip. Sometimes during the evening meetings I would read aloud from war storybooks, the tales of genies and sprites or the epic and love stories to everyone.[30]

These works of Anatolian poetry share a similar provenance to those read and enjoyed by Halide Edib, showing that both ends of the socio-economic spectrum of the Turkish-speaking Ottoman population were inspired by similar influences.

However casually acquired, Şevket Süreyya's reading would take him on a remarkable journey. The first step along this path involved only moving as far as the *mekteb* that formed part of the Muradiye mosque complex in the center of Edirne. Next came military boarding school where he imbibed the heady atmosphere of Turkish nationalism that many such schools fostered. Military service during World War I followed during which he served as a reserve officer and was wounded in action on the Caucasus front. After the rout of the Ottoman army he remained in Russian Azerbaijan, working as a schoolteacher. Here he became inspired by the Bolshevik Revolution and eventually moved to Moscow to continue his studies. He moved "back" to Turkey after the founding of the Republic but was subsequently arrested on charges of subversive activities and imprisoned in 1925. While in jail he wrote a study that he submitted to the education ministry. This met with official approval; his sentence was curtailed and he was appointed to a series of official posts after pledging his support to Mustafa Kemal. Reading and writing remained vital throughout his life. He was among the founders of the influential if short-lived leftist literary *cum* ideological journal *Kadro* (Cadre), (founded in 1932 but banned two years later). After the 1960 coup he again took up writing and produced a torrent of books, the most well known of which are his three biographies of Atatürk, İsmet İnönü and Enver.

Rıza Nur

The memoirs of the medical doctor, political activist and diplomat Rıza Nur (1879–1942), depicting his childhood in the Black Sea coastal town of Sinop, emphasize reading and writing. One of the first things he mentions is that his father was literate,[31] and paid close attention to Rıza's education. In his father's strict understanding, echoing the fear of the "children of the neighborhood" encountered in Chapter 3, this meant that Rıza was forbidden to play or speak with people in the street. "From school to home, from home to school. Nothing else." Every day after school his father made him memorize something and required him to practice ten lines of calligraphy. His father's beatings were balanced with incentives such as money, new clothes and trips to Istanbul if he were to win prizes at school. This made him work hard and on prize days he collected more rewards than anyone else in the schools he attended. The prizes were books, wrapped in crêpe paper; ten books for ten prizes and a trip to the capital.[32]

Rıza Nur's childhood memories are written in a direct and vivid style that appears unmellowed by the passage of time and changes in taste or fashion. His first schooling began at the age of four in a "*mektep*" or Qur'an school run by two turbaned hocas. His matter-of-fact depiction of his memories of this institution are limited to a brief description of the school, later destroyed in the war, and its teachers and the fact that there were beatings with both cane and the bastinado. In spite of the punishment, the head teacher was "a very educated man. Everyone loved him." Young Rıza had perhaps more cause for affection than others for this teacher who from time to time would offer him sweets, saying, "Eat lots of sweets; they stimulate the mind." Later when Rıza had gone on to the advanced primary school the teacher called in Rıza's father and heaped high praise on the boy, "Your son is very clever. There are three hundred children in the school. If all of their intelligence were counted together it wouldn't amount to his. For goodness sake, in time send this child to Istanbul to study. He will become a great man. He will provide great services to the state and to the (religious) community. Beware that you don't neglect his education!" My father later told me this a few times. It means that Ahmed Efendi, God's mercy upon him, was an intelligent man."[33] However immodest, this frank approach is typical of Rıza Nur's account.

He does not refrain from commenting on both the positive and negative aspects of the many changes that his life witnessed. For example, he recalls fondly the games that he played – and naturally he was recognized as the ringleader – with children of varying ages in the streets of his neighborhood. After listing ten such games and describing how they were played he says, "These are our national games and sports... What a shame that they have all been abandoned... The Europeanizing reform movement totally destroyed them."[34]

If the nation may have been losing some of its cultural heritage in this period of acute Westernization, it was nevertheless a time of personal progress for the young Rıza. As a ten-year-old student he was the first in his class, thanks in part to his capacity for memorizing things after reading them three times.[35] Although it served him well, he criticizes the pedagogical penchant for unquestioning memorization and the problems it created, principally the lack of understanding.[36] As we encountered in our discussion of the problem of parroting in Chapter 4, this sort of rote learning was an integral part of the learning in both the late Ottoman and early Republican periods, a continuity against which educationalists would continue to fight in frustration.

But Rıza Nur's example shows that memorization did not necessarily suppress individuality, creativity or a passion for reading. He rebelled against the bastinado, developed a keen interest in bird keeping and, most apposite to our enquiry, a fervor for reading. He took up works like,

> Muhammediye, Ahmediye, Seyyid Battal Gazi, Kan Kalesi, Hayber Kalesi... I read these with great fondness and excitement. As I read them the zeal for heroism took hold of me. I understand that these works are what provided the Turks with the famous training to be heroes of old. What a shame it is that they have been devalued. They ought to be rewritten in a contemporary fashion.[37]

Reading thes tales of Turkish and Islamic heroism coincided with a period of religiosity in the future doctor's life:

> for a time I was quite devout. Thinking it more virtuous, I performed my prayers not at home but in the mosque. I would rise early and go to mosque for the morning prayers as well. My parents were well pleased. I confess that this was the happiest period of my life. I was in a place of divine happiness...[38]

The connection between his personal devotion and the heroic impulse derived from his reading is clear.

When I came across the stories of Battal Gazi, they awakened in me a great passion for valor, heroism and bravery. On reading phrases such as, 'He killed a thousand infidels with a single stroke of the sword,' I leapt with emotion. I would say to myself: If only I too could do such things. I wanted to cut down a thousand infidels by the sword.

Influenced by these books, the passion to become a powerful wrestler (*pehlivan*), a soldier and a commander arose within me. I began to wrestle with the children at school. My father wanted me to become a doctor. As for me, later on when I completed the military *rüşdiye* school in Istanbul I went and enrolled in the military *idadî* instead of the military medical *idadî* because of this passion.

How important these works were. To my mind there can be no doubt but that the lion's share of the upbringing (*terbiye*) which made the Turk become a hero and such a successful conqueror was found in these books. Indeed these were the first works about the Turkish conquests in Islam. If they were to be corrected and republished they would be of great service to national education.[39]

He claims elsewhere in his memoir that he planned to establish a library in Sinop,[40] the town where his life – and his passion for reading – began.

These "popular legends" were far more influential than is generally appreciated. We have now observed the impact they had on Halide Edib and Rıza Nur. Likewise the patriotic Turkish poet Mehmet Emin [Yurdakul] (1869–1944) underscores their influence upon him as a boy, recalling that his unschooled father had him read such tales as Battal Gazi and Kerem and Aslı and that he later read the poetry of Namık Kemal. "Our roof witnessed both good days and bad. Just as I grew up under that roof with my mother's folk lullabies (*halk ninnileri*), I also grew up with folk advice.[41] Under that roof I grew to understand that the people needed books that would explain their own lives, their own spirit, their own loves and their own sufferings in their own language."[42]

Hüseyin Cahit [Yalçın]

This popular impetus stands out clearly in the pathways of numerous Turkish authors whose lives traversed the Ottoman-to-republican transition. The Unionist writer, journalist, publisher, critic and politician Hüseyin Cahit [Yalçın] (1875–1957) was certainly one affected in this way.[43] His memoirs begin with a description of the ways in which folk tales and legends engendered in him a passion for books:

> When I look back to ascertain when my passion for books (*kitap meraki*) began, I feel the need to delve into my childhood. My first bookshelf was a shoebox that I had been able to get hold of somehow. The treasures hidden there with great pains and care were, I suppose, the epics (*destanlar*) and the stories of Aşık Garip and Kerem which were sold on the streets. Later on when I had a small bookshelf made by a carpenter I was small enough to climb inside it when playing.[44]

It would be hard to imagine a closer affinity for reading and books than climbing into the bookshelf to be with its contents. The notion of the "passion for books" is one that is often repeated among Turkish memoirists and conveys, even in retrospect, the excitement that the early encounter with the written word generated in young readers. He continues,

> Games and toys...I wasn't very satisfied with these. Today I even remember that my father had a hard time getting me to play. But there was no great difficulty in getting me to amuse myself with books. In the end my father, realizing that I didn't cause them any harm, trusted me to be left alone with his own books.

As with Rıza Nur, it was the folk epics that kindled his young imagination:

> The battles of his holiness Ali, Battal Gazi, Kara Davut...these were the books that I preferred over the stories of Aşık Garip and Kerem. Even the novels that were read in the evenings among the family failed to waken my enthusiasm as much as the tales of bravery such as that of his holiness Ali before the fort of Khaybar.[45]

In Hüseyin Cahit's memoirs family, folk tales, religious epics and reading mingle together to produce a cozy picture of the scenes that initiated him into the world of stories and adventure.

> The oldest memories I have of our life at home are mixed with these evening reading sessions. After the meal there would be a little talk with my father while he drank his coffee. Then at my father's sign my older sister would take up a book, sit down beside the gas lamp and, starting from the place where she had left off the previous evening, she would begin to read. While my mother and father

listened silently, I tried to follow the story, finally growing tired and falling into a deep sleep on a cushion.[46]

When the reading fare turned from popular legends to contemporary novels it is significant that the writer who remains vivid in his memory was the populist Ahmed Midhat Efendi whom we have encountered earlier.

> One of the first novels that I remember from those evening readings was *Felâtun Beyle Rakım Efendi*. My father rated the writer Ahmed Midhat Efendi very highly. 'Whatever he writes, he writes well,' he would say in praise. Seeing his books read with such care and followed with such interest and hearing him praised so highly, he rose to the status of a demigod in my imagination.

But Hüseyin Cahit's memoir informs us that already at this stage – he was perhaps six or seven years old at the time – he sensed that Ahmed Midhat Efendi's writings produced something of a disagreement between his parents. As he relates it, his mother objected to Ahmed Midhat's digressions and interjections. What's more, he remembered the way in which his writings influenced his young outlook. "I counted myself among Ahmed Midhat Efendi's loyal readers."[47]

As he grew older, the memoir continues, Hüseyin Cahit took to reading not just in the evenings but now increasingly in the daytime, developing the ability to finish books quickly. But he nevertheless found himself unable to penetrate those of his father's volumes treating on Islamic sciences and mysticism. "They seemed to be written in another language," he writes. Seen from the vantage point of the 1930s – Hüseyin Cahit [Yalçın] published his memoirs in 1935 – of course they were almost in another tongue and seemed to have emerged from another world, precisely the point of the Kemalist *Kulturkampf*. Certainly the kinds of books that proved impenetrable to the future journalist were those that had formed the core of the Islamic and Ottoman tradition and therefore those that the Kemalist project intended to disparage and to remove from mainstream discourse. The religious texts that Hüseyin Cahit mentions are Muhyiddin b. Arabi's *Fusus al-Hikam* and the "divan" poetry of such figures as Fuzulî, Nedim and Nabî, cornerstones of the Ottoman mystical and literary edifice respectively.

The attitude toward religion in Hüseyin Cahit [Yalçın]'s memoirs manifests a palpable tension, a tension that is symptomatic of the standard narrative of the Ottoman-to-republican transition. On the one hand he is absolutely clear that as a child he felt a strong affinity with Islam – "In my childhood I was filled with a powerful religious sentiment."[48] He recalls waiting impatiently as only a child can for one particular book that he had ordered from the Armenian book dealer Arakel, one of the first to seize the opportunity furnished by the rise in literacy and the first to publish a catalogue. From this catalogue Hüseyin Cahit had selected a number of texts including one called *Şevahidünnübüvve* which might be translated as Prophetic Witnesses, essentially a compendium of the miracles performed by the Prophet Muhammad. He neatly sums up his youthful appetite for these stories:

> The Prophet fed an army with a single date and quenched their thirst with a drop of water. But I was in no way satisfied. With a fresh, shaking and deep sensation, I always wanted more, always more. The braveries of his holiness Ali, the tales of Battal Gazi, the adventures of Kara Davut, the miracles of the Prophet, the greats of Nesimî...The proud feelings that all of these supernaturally lofty, beautiful things stirred inside me were thoroughly reconciled with the free life in Rumelia, recalling the Middle Ages [his family having moved to Serez]. I had a horse and a small rifle. I would wander in the summer pastures, the forests and the deserts, would be thrown into dangers and experience it all profoundly.[49]

On the other hand and in direct contrast with this harmonic depiction – "Looking back on my childhood now I see that my mind, my spirit and my body had developed in parallel and appropriate fashion. I realize that I owe my unfailing balance to this beautiful convergence"[50] – Hüseyin Cahit's account uses the metaphor of struggle to characterize his youthful but critical transition from reader to writer. In contrast with the depiction of bucolic harmony in Rumelia, there is a countervailing force within him that seeks expression through writing which, tellingly, is presented as a reaction against the religio-cultural milieu of the Ottoman era. This internal struggle is depicted as both natural – there was an irrepressible impetus within him to write – and "strange." When describing this transition the memoir then shifts directly to a discussion of Hüseyin Cahit's transition from reader to writer:

> One day a strange desire arose inside me. 'Let me try to write something,' I said but even as I thought of it I became embarrassed and abandoned the idea. Even so, something even stronger inside me never completely abandoned this plan. As my desire grew stronger, I tried to silence the voice that asked, 'How will I be able to write?'

Finally one day, I found a pencil in my hand. In a state of rebellion, it wanted to give birth to something on its own, no matter what.

He then proceeds to describe his first literary effort, of which he can only recall one line, composed in the classical Ottoman style of poetry, conjuring a sunrise on a plane in the Balkans. What is striking in Hüseyin Cahit's account is the interplay between the effect of his own reading environment and his internally driven compulsion to write. In a microcosm of the nature vs. nurture debate, he presents his young self as both deeply affected by Ottoman and Islamic popular literature and as driven to become a writer by a force deep inside him that he presents as acting at cross-purposes to his normal self. The possibility exists that his wish to separate the two influences derived from the strong anti-Ottoman cultural bias in force during the period when he was writing his memoirs.

What is clear is that in his subsequent literary activity, both as reader and writer, he turned away from the classical Ottoman literary genres and toward those originating in the West, such as the novel. He establishes a relationship with a purveyor of serialized novels from whom he receives individual treatment as he awaited the weekly arrival of new installments.[51] As a lycée student he began to read mostly crime novels such as those by Xavier de Montépin and Emile Gaborieau. He recalls that he became so absorbed in his reading of novels that he persisted even during lesson at school despite the attentions of his tutor. In this way Hüseyin Cahit aligns his life story as both reader and fledgling writer with the dominant narrative of the transition from the world of the late Ottoman Empire to that of the early Turkish Republic. His earliest reading memories were formed in the milieu of the religious and folk tales typical of the late Ottoman era. With time these were pushed aside in favor of the emerging and soon-to-be-dominant world of the imported literary production of the West.

Halide Nusret [Zorlutuna]

We encountered the future poet and novelist Halide Nusret [Zorlutuna] (1901–1984) in Chapter 4 in the context of our discussion of the mechanics of learning to read. Her rich memoir begins with a powerful description of her first experience with the written word. She recounts how at the traditional age of four years, four months and four days, she was made to repeat the Arabic phrases of the Qur'an while tracing her finger over the letters of the alphabet. What concerns us here is the manner in which she became first a reader and eventually a writer of Turkish, her mother tongue and the language in which all of her considerable writings appeared in both poetry and prose. But it is also important to remember that while Turkish was clearly the most important language of her formative years it was not the only one. Her encounters with both Arabic and Persian, not to mention the Sufi circles in which the men of her family traveled, clearly influenced her literary formation in the last years of the Ottoman Empire and remind us that this situation no longer obtained after the founding of the Turkish Republic.

Halide Nusret's account of her upbringing reflected considerable pride in the fact that hers was a reading family. Naturally enough for a girl whose father was imprisoned for part of her childhood, Halide Nusret took her cues from her mother whom she describes as "a natural teacher, a tender but at the same time an authoritarian woman. Had she been a teacher she would have been an ideal teacher."[52] The first memory connected to her family's return to Istanbul after its sojourn in Izmir is linked to her mother and the reading of newspapers.

> After the midday meal we would stretch out together on the bed and read the newspaper *İkdam* (Perseverence). In those days only a few families took newspapers but we had a subscription, the paper arriving every morning. My mother had become accustomed to it since my father's time. In those days, together with the morning paper *İkdam* we subscribed to *Servet-i Fünûn* (The Treasury of the Arts), *Musavver Malûmât* (Illustrated Knowledge) and *Hanımlara Mahsus Gazete* (The Ladies Own Journal).

This pride in cataloguing her family's literary activities and, of course, the fact that they could afford such a steady supply of reading material recalls a photograph found in the collection of late Ottoman portraits edited by Engin Çizgen. This portrait, taken of the photographer Ali Sami's own family, presents six of its members arrayed around a table. They conspicuously display the family's reading prowess by crowding as many different newspapers as possible into their portrait, each with its front pages displayed so as to be legible to the observer[53] (Figure 6.1).

Their evenings were spent in discussions concerning literature which were led by her mother. Her father had said that he hadn't time to read so that her mother should go ahead and read the work in question and he would learn about it from her description in the evenings.

> In this way she prepared literary topics, sweet topics of disputation. According to the way it was understood, my father was an "educator" (eğitimci). My mother was actually very clever, a woman who used

Figure 6.1 A family displays its zeal for reading

her mind. She didn't drink coffee or smoke cigarettes but she was a fearsome reading addict (okuma tiryakisi). This addiction held her until she was eighty years old. Only when she lost her eyesight, like it or not, did she give up reading.[54]

The notion of an addiction to reading is one with which contemporary readers can easily identify. It is a characteristically modern notion, first appearing in Western Europe in the late eighteenth century. Indeed the philosopher Fichte referred to reading as a "narcotic" and the subject of "reading mania" was frequently discussed there in this period.[55] Such an addictive pursuit presumes a steady supply of reading material to "feed the habit." Such a supply was, as we have seen, a feature of the new reading environment that was forming in first the Ottoman Empire from the second half of the nineteenth century and gathering pace during the early Turkish Republic. As these autobiographical accounts reveal, there was not shortage of genres or texts to attract and occupy young readers.

What did Halide Nusret read? She tells us that newspapers were crucial and that, thanks to her mother's tutelage ("one of the most beautiful memories of my childhood is reading the newspaper together with my mother"[56]), she could read them already at the age of six. "As I said, after the midday meal we would stretch out and read the paper. Most of the time she would read, but sometimes she would get me to read…At the age of six I could read the newspaper perfectly." She also says that she was addicted (*düşkün*) to literature in general and poetry in particular. But the sense of the poems she committed to memory were not always clear to her, sometimes only becoming so when she was a student in secondary school.

Novels played a crucial role in Halide Nusret's young reading life. Her memoir's first mention of the novel suggests a clear link between the world of reading and her everyday life, a harbinger of her subsequent and profound immersion in the life of the written word. Her mother had fashioned a playroom for her in a windowed balcony of their house and here Halide Nusret kept the precious dolls that her mother had made for her and that she describes as stunningly realistic. "So I would substitute the dolls for the heroes that featured in the installment novels (*tefrika romanlar*) that I read, completing the novels' endings in my mind on my own, speaking with them, making them speak, enraptured for hours on end. Later on I would make up my own plots and drag my dolls from adventure to adventure." Her friend Fahriye sewed costumes for the dolls and later went on to become a sewing instructor and a well-known tailor.[57] Although she does not mention it, what is left unspoken is the fact that Halide Nusret would go on to become a famous writer.

Other incidents appear like so many milestones along to the road that would lead her from an engaged reader of various literary genres to a writer in her own right. When her family moved to Kirkuk in what is today northern Iraq when her father, freed from prison after the Young Turk revolution of 1908, was appointed a district governor (*mutasarrıf*), she struggled with the rigors of Arabic but conversely had a very positive experience with Persian. Although she mentions that the town had several schools at that time, including a primary institution for girls,[58] she was taught privately, presumably because the level of instruction at that school would have been far too low for her or simply because private tuition was considered more acceptable for a family like hers. Her private teacher was a member of the ulema named Molla Hıdır Efendi whom she describes as "having a short, thick beard, wearing an embroidered turban, smiling, sweet tongued and respected."[59]

> Perceiving my weakness in the face of verse and poetry, he would for the most part begin our lessons with a couplet or a strophe from Mevlana [Rumi] or Sadi. At that moment it was as if the doors of my heart and my mind opened completely. Whatever my teacher said I listened to intently and learned it right away. From time to time he

set Persian composition assignments for me and he would be pleased with and praise what I wrote; he encouraged me to write.

In other words it was this respected teacher who discovered my strong desire and my capacity for writing.[60]

Halide Nusret was not alone in her penchant for Persian, the simpler grammar of which afforded relatively quicker progress. Many others shared her pleasure and some of whom developed a life-long and sustaining interest in that language even after the arrival of the Republic had put and end to the teaching of Persian to Turkish students.[61] In light of our earlier discussion of pedagogical methods it is interesting to note that Zorlutuna comments that her Persian teacher had no knowledge of the Principles of Instruction (*Usul-i Tedris*) or any Western educational methods, referring to him as a natural and successful teacher – one of those of whom God has said, Let him be a teacher.[62] The personal bond they developed – she later learned that he had named his daughter Halide Nusret – clearly proved crucial to fostering her interest in Persian and in writing in general. This was of course a feature of traditional education that modern methods would only struggle to reproduce.

Returning to Istanbul, her parents discussed the question of whether Halide Nusret should attend a school or be educated at home. Her mother supported the former option but lost the argument in the face of her husband's insistence that, having made progress with her personal instruction in Kirkuk, she continue to be taught at home. Her mother took up where Molla Hıdır Efendi had left off and Halide Nusret was soon immersed again in the masterpieces of Persian literature, her father supplying her with an armful of books.

Soon she received a surprise that furthered her passion for reading:

One day, I will never forget, returning home from a visit I saw that there was a book on each step of the staircase that led from the second to the third floor and in the face of such a big surprise I went delirious with delight. The truth is that I was surprised...I was surprised because in those days I would not have expected such a thing from my father whose serious mindedness had produced a timid respect in me...But, thinking about it now, for a 'child' who loved to read in a rather mad way, I can say that he could not have prepared a more beautiful surprise.[63]

This richly symbolic passage provides a further impetus into the world of reading. Soon thereafter she took to reading novels such as

Victor Hugo's *Les Miserables* to her father in the evenings but, realizing that she could not stand to wait for the following evening, took to reading all day long. "Now, I was carried away with the passion for reading. If I had a novel in my hand I would not eat, would not drink, would not sleep, I only would read. Other than reading, everything else seemed meaningless, unnecessary, ordinary."

She would only take a break from reading on those days when her friend Fahriye came over. But even then much of their conversation was given over to discussing novels, for Fahriye was also a committed reader. Inevitably, this reading mania was seen to be a problem. Her mother grew frustrated at Halide Nusret's passion for reading to the exclusion of everything else. She tried to teach the girls the domestic arts and Fahriye showed both inclination and capability but as for Halide Nusret she was "as incapable as a stone" and her mother despaired for her future. When Halide Nusret began to neglect other duties around the house such as dusting, ironing, putting things away and caring for her younger sibling, her mother took the drastic step of forbidding her from reading. In hindsight Halide Nusret knew her mother was right. "It was as if I were drunk, as if these people were strangers. Yes, my mother was correct; truly I was as she said I was. But I was pleased with my state and I felt so happy with myself in that drunken, sleepy state."

Banned from reading, Halide Nusret reacted in predictably dramatic fashion.

> What a pity! What would I do now? A child whose most prized toy had been taken from him or a man whose bread and soup had been taken away could not have been made more unhappy or hopeless than I was. The colorful, broad world that I had lived inside myself, the friends that I had lived with in my imaginary adventures had been taken out of my hands. It was as if, hands hanging at my sides, I had been left all alone in a strange world."[64]

It is difficult to imagine a more deeply felt attachment to reading than that shown by Halide Nusret in her memoir. Naturally enough, she managed to find a way to circumvent the ban on reading by working through a sympathetic relative who gave her a novel by an author, Recâîzâde Mahmud Ekrem, whom she knew Halide Nusret's mother admired. As the relative had hoped, mother and daughter read the book together. Her memoir continues, charting the rest of her life as a writer. But we will leave it here, noting the crucial influences on her reading, and eventually writing, life. Her first experience came through the medium of the Qur'an and later expanded to include poetry, prose, novels in particular, and the influences of other languages, especially Persian. She seemed palpably to feel that reading transported her to another world, a realm of imagination that she sensed so profoundly as to upset the routine of her daily life. This, we should recall, was precisely the effect that writers, publishers and educators were striving for in their efforts to expand the ranks of literate children. Halide Nusret's example may be unusual, perhaps even extreme, in the identification, nay, addiction, between reader and text, but it also rings true. Reading, we know, has the power to change lives and alter the way we think.

These memoirs show us that the new worlds that reading was opening up for children in the late Ottoman and early Republican periods, as of course it did in many other societies in this period, were deeply felt. Although virtually impossible to quantify in a meaningful way, the cumulative effect of the new reading dispensation amounted to a palpable change in childhood practices over the course of one or two generations. The intensification of the relationship between readers and text depended on the availability of a sufficiently wide variety of texts. The newly arrived genres clearly helped. Novels, short stories but also textbooks and magazines increased the chances that each potential reader would find reading material to suit his or her appetite and budget. The ability to consume these works, increasingly being treated as commodities, pushed the circle of readership still further. In these life stories the purchase and possession of books, for example, Hüseyin Cahit's catalogue order or those surprises that Halide Nusret's normally taciturn father placed on the stairs, clearly played a crucial role in the development of these figures as readers and, eventually, writers.

This string of biographical sketches could easily be expanded in scope and extended in time. The individuals whose learning to read we have explored were all born during the long reign of Sultan Abdülhamid II (1876–1909). If we were to include examples of those who were born in the Second Constitutional and early Republican eras, we might draw upon the lives of such individuals as Behçet Necatigil (1916–1979), who describes being rewarded with candy for his early efforts at writing, Tarık Buğra (1918–1994) or Ümit Yaşar Oğuzcan (1926–1984). We might also note the recent flood of memoirs mentioned by Özyürek that have epitomized the recent spate of alternately questioning and rendering nostalgic the early years of the Turkish state.[65] Their writings would show us that a variety of important but often overlooked continuities characterized the shift from empire to republic along with the more usually emphasized breaks. Space and time do not allow us to examine these autobiographical accounts which are perhaps more valuable as a barometer of political attitudes toward the Kemalist agenda. More useful perhaps is to evaluate the transition from young readers to writers. Although rarely commented upon, this shift was of course crucial to the expansion of reading.

From readers to writers

The transition from reader to writer appears in a variety of forms but all of them are presented in retrospect as a natural progression. The move from reader to writer is frequently portrayed as coming full circle or as forming a self-replicating loop. Somewhat paradoxically, young readers are drawn in by the attractiveness of both its individual and its participatory dimensions, something akin to Suraiya Faroqhi's notion of the "private yet written culture" which was a crucial precondition to the spread of popular literature in the nineteenth and twentieth centuries.[66] Young readers turned writers were responding to the encouragements given them at school or in the pages of magazines and more generally to the growing evidence that writing was assuming an increasingly important economic dimension. There were more and more jobs to be had for those who could write. Whether in the burgeoning civil service or in the private sector, opportunities for the actively literate were more visible than ever, a phenomenon recognized by encouraging parents and educators alike. In fact, the new possibilities that education and literacy were opening up enhanced the traditional mode of self-promotion through writing that was such a frequent feature of the Ottoman cultural past. The future nationalist poet Mehmed Emin [Yurdakul] sent his first publication, an essay entitled "Virtue and Nobility" ("*Fazilet ve asalet*"), to the Grand Vizier. He was suitably impressed to offer Mehmed Emin a position in the Ottoman customs office, the first step in a career that saw him appointed to several governorships, become president of the Turkish Hearth (*Türk Ocağı*) organization, and serve as a member of both the Ottoman and Turkish Republican parliaments. As Evelyn Waugh said of writing in another context, "In those days ... anyone who could write at all well could have a living."[67]

Indeed for its young practitioners, writing raised expectations of social as well as economic capital. For example, Halide Nusret [Zorlutuna] describes the effect of her winning first prize in a school competition organized by and published in *Talebe Defteri*, a students' journal edited by her teacher Muallim Ahmed Halid [Yaşaroğlu].[68] The symbolism of this milestone in her life story is heightened by the fact that the joy she felt from winning this prize for writing was juxtaposed with the grief she felt at the recent death of her father. "What a joy it was, my God, what a joy! From that day until today, I must have written quite a lot; my books have been published but I never again experienced such a joy in my life. My teacher, my friends and the school principal all congratulated me; my mother cried tears of joy."[69] One has to wonder if the economic dimension of her success was not mixed in with the personal and familial nature of this triumph.

Prospective writers who were not fortunate enough to have a teacher *cum* champion could look to books designed to encourage writing of various kinds. Once again, the market for printed materials recognized an opening and sought to fill it in different ways. We have already seen the varied ways in which texts for children modeled the importance of learning to write as well as to read. Stories in primers and magazines depict children composing letters to their parents, homework assignments and nascent attempts at fiction amidst the rest of their contents. Still more practical guides appeared. The traditional subject of composition (*inşa*) reemerged in a new guise, namely, that of a practical guide to writing updated for the modern age. The expanding demand for writing in everyday life lay behind the persistence of the old genre of composition into the modern period. In 1902 the celebrated writer Ahmed Rasım produced a volume entitled *İlaveli hazine-i mekâtib yahud mükemmel-i münşeat* (The supplemented treasury of letters or the complete exemplary letters) that quickly went through numerous printings.[70] The work was conceived on the conviction that the traditional form of composing letters in Ottoman Turkish was patently relevant if conceived in a "modern form" (*tarz-i cedid*).[71] What typified the modern mode was simplicity and directness of expression. The author stated that, "Everyone needs to write letters on many occasions during his lifetime. However great this need is, he should never deviate from simplicity."[72] The volume went on to provide samples of letters written for a variety of purposes, both official and unofficial. The latter category included model letters for sending holiday and birthday greetings, congratulations, condolences, thanks and so forth. From today's perspective the examples may appear rather sentimental in affection and syntactically less direct than what we are used to, but in the context of Ottoman letters they are decidedly modern in their use of shorter sentences, punctuation and a considerably less ornate and drawn out style than traditionally employed. Here is an example of a new year's letter to a friend:

> My dear friend,
>
> I congratulate you on the New Year. At such a time most people present their congratulations to one another. Men of true brotherhood (uhuvvet-i hakikiye erbabı) certainly ought not to be deprived of this honor. That which my pen writes is merely a portion of that which my heart feels. Our old friendship is witness to the sincerity of my congratulations. It is true that real friends do not require congratulations. But...may this year be auspicious; may your share be fortunate and blessed, Amen.[73]

This genre continued into the republican years in a variety of forms. Those needing to compose official correspondence to various branches of the bureaucracy could consult a volume such as Mehmed Sedad's 1905 text entitled "Practical principles of official correspondence."[74] Introduced with a *hadith* from Ali b. Abi Talib, the nephew and son-in-law of the Prophet Muhammad on the imperative of learning the art of correspondence, this text provided model letters to a range of officials from the chief scribe of the Ottoman palace to local bureaucrats. Given the importance of the formulaic forms of address such letters needed to take, such a book was doubtless useful for a wider audience than that of the preparatory-level student for which it was initially composed.

Writing textbooks was an important stimulus to authors. The remarkable growth of the state school system in the late Ottoman and early Republican periods created the demand for a wide range of texts. Beginning with Kayserili Doktor Rüşdü's *Nuhbet ül-etfal (elifba kitabı)* of 1857, a trail of texts can be traced which run parallel to the creation and growth of the Ottoman state school system. With the Education Regulation of 1869, the Ottoman state announced competitions for textbook composition.[75] The following year a competition was held which led directly to the appearance of Selim Sabit Efendi's *Rehnüma-yi muallimin-i sıbyan* (Guide for teachers of elementary pupils) of the same year. This text went on to play an influential role in Turkish primary education.[76] In the early 1870s the same author produced the *Elifba-yı Osmanî*, which provided a fillip to the instruction of reading and writing similar to that generated by the *Nuhbet ül-etfal.*[77] Eventually authors would grow accustomed to tailoring their writing to suit the various curricula produced by the Education Ministry. Even a brief glance at the titles published by late Ottoman writers demonstrates the importance of the textbook to authorial production in this period.[78] Istanbul was naturally the hub of this sort of literary production but there were also important contributions to the texts available to young readers from the provinces.[79] Wherever they lived young authors could see that writing could be a career. This is not the place for a detailed exploration of the opportunities that the expansion of reading were offering to young Ottoman and Turkish Republican writers but even a cursory view of several distinct career types clearly outlines the possibilities that reading was creating in this period of transition. The most obvious example of someone who made a career – and a name – for himself by his writing was the popular late Ottoman writer Ahmed Midhat Efendi whom we have already encountered. His colossal literary output, stretching to as many as 150 books, was such that he earned a very good living as an author or novels and short stories. Certainly it amounted to a massive leap up the socioeconomic scale from his rather humble origins as the son of a poor Istanbul draper.[80]

Writers of textbooks were less well known and presumably less well paid. Authors' fees are notoriously difficult to establish in the Ottoman and Turkish case,[81] but what is clear from several sources is that many teachers augmented their salaries by writing textbooks in both the late Ottoman and early Republican eras. Let us consider a relatively unknown character such as Ali İrfan [Eğribozu]. Born on the island of Eğriboz (Euboia) in 1286 A.H. (i.e., 1869–1870) Ali İrfan attended the Galatasaray lycée in Istanbul immediately before taking up his first teaching post in the preparatory school in Beirut. In his case and many others, therefore, the transition from student to teacher was rather abrupt. In Beirut and in subsequent postings to a number of provincial schools, including Rhodes, Diyarbekir and Mağnisa, he taught subjects ranging from history, geography, French, Turkish and composition to geometry, algebra and bookkeeping.[82] His monthly salary seems rarely to have increased very much and frequently declined when he took up a new post. Teachers could augment their salary considerably by teaching additional courses in certain subjects and Ali İrfan took full advantage to display his versatility in the classroom. For example, his salary as director of the *idadî* school in Beirut was 800 *kuruş*; he almost doubled this figure by teaching general history and geography classes which earned him a supplementary 750 *kuruş*. At the same time he managed to find time to write a number of textbooks on an almost equally wide range of topics. He published texts to accompany courses in trade, religion, morals, logic, Arabic and so on. More pertinent for our study, he wrote a number of texts designed to teach reading, some of which we have encountered in previous chapters. It is almost impossible to learn how much he might have earned from writing these texts but we know that several of them ran to several printings. He seems to have written more than fifteen textbooks and several other non-pedagogical works. But in comparison with some of the more prolific teachers/writers of textbooks, whom we shall encounter shortly, his production might almost appear scant. What seems clear is that state schoolteachers were in a good position to write such texts. They knew what types of books were required by the imperial curriculum, had a good sense of what proved effective in the classroom and, perhaps decisively, had the incentive to augment their salaries by composing the expanding range of texts.

While Ali İrfan's literary career seems to have been confined to the late Ottoman period, other authors continued on into the Republican period. One such figure was the educator and author Ahmed Cevad [Emre] (1876–1961). In the pre-Republican phase of his life he pursued a distinctly Ottoman and Islamic line in his writing for children. In works such as "The new ABC: I am reading the Qur'an," (*Yeni elifba: Kuranı okuyorum*), published from 1912 to 1926, or the 1912 "The true revolution through solid morals" Ahmed Cevat presents himself as a concerned Ottoman Muslim, praising *zakat*, referring to the Qur'an and endorsing a new *"cihad,"* an internal, moral campaign to liberate the empire from economic slavery.[83] He authored a characteristically wide range of textbooks for Ottoman schools, including works on Arabic, French, Ottoman and Persian grammar, civics and reading primers.

As early as 1916 Ahmed Cevad had brought out a volume entitled "The illustrated Turkish language" alongside his widely used book "The illustrated Ottoman language." He was thus well prepared for the semantic and cultural shift that the Republic effected. His interest in linguistic matters – and his political flexibility – was rewarded by Mustafa Kemal. The leader of the Republic appointed Ahmed Cevad to be chairman of grammar section of the Language Society. At first he seems to have been critical of the radical Turkification theories propounded by the Viennese Dr. Hermann Kvergiç and enthsuastically adopted by the circle of men surrounding Mustafa Kemal, theories that Ahmed Cevad dismissed as worthless. Later when Kvergiç's ideas became enshrined in the officially sanctioned Sun Language Theory, which held that Turkish was the origin of all the world's language, Ahmed Cevad "went overboard" in propagating it.[84] Like Sati al-Husri, another late Ottoman educationalist who partially reinvented himself to suit the post-imperial context in the Arab world,[85] Ahmed Cevad reflects the rapidly changing terrain of this period.

Like the new political circumstances, the new literacy situation allowed individuals to re-write their own lives, sometimes literally. In fact the very autobiographical sources on which we have relied in this chapter are themselves evidence of the growing importance of writing and individual lives. The wide variety of experiences that found their way into print is a fitting metaphor for both the diverse and yet common experience of reading and writing among this generation of Ottoman and Republican youth. Regardless of their differences, all readers shared the individual encounter with texts and all authors produced texts in a similar encounter with writing.

There is a palpable tension between diversity – in terms of region, ethnicity, religion, language, folkways and so on – and uniformity in the acculturation processes associated with learning to read. The tendency toward sameness and uniformity vied with the inherent diversity of experience among the readership itself. Put another way, the consumption of reading material disseminated from the larger urban areas necessarily assisted the process of homogenization. But the fact that many of the participants were not only passive receptacles of the texts but also with time became authors themselves and added to the available published fare, if only in a limited way, meant that these regional or marginal voices were also heard. The history of this period has, of course, tended to overemphasize the centralizing, homogenizing power of the center, whether in cultural or political terms. The lives of individual readers and writers forces us to retain an awareness of the tension between the diversity of the late Ottoman and early Republican experiences, be they regional, ethnic, linguistic and so on the one hand and central authority on the other.

As this chapter has shown, reading and then writing was increasingly crucial to the lived experience of a growing sector of late Ottoman and Turkish republican society. Schooling and a variety of newly available texts encouraged more and more children to read. The snowballing effect of the expanding state sector opened up a range of new educational and career paths that depended upon writing. This expansion of possibilities meant, in turn, that young readers found incentives, financial and otherwise, to become producers and not simply consumers of reading materials. The shift from reader to writer was embedded in the changing social, cultural, economic and political realities of the day. Despite still considerable differences in background more and more readers – and writers – were finding in the written word a common vehicle for their education, entertainment and career progression. Paradoxically, the individual nature of the act of reading and writing linked these young participants into a shared if still largely inchoate reading public.

7
Conclusion: Reading and Modernity

The preceding chapters have highlighted reading's importance in the late Ottoman Empire and the early Turkish Republic as well as its occasional elusiveness and unpredictability. We stated at the outset that it would be important to regard reading as an inherently neutral practice, despite the fact that many have seen it as a vehicle for a number of foregone conclusions. Indeed, the study of learning to read and reading underscores the importance of following the diverse practices and tastes of the population whether or not they conform to the dominant political or historiographical expectations, particularly those generated by the state. We have seen how the impulse to spread the practice of reading was pursued by those animated by diametrically opposing outlooks and concerns: imperial and national; cosmopolitan and local; Islamic and secular; dutiful and voluptuary; and individualistic and collective. Likewise, it is important to recall that different readers experienced reading in very different ways, according to distinct modes, moods and contexts. Recognizing the diverse approaches that informed both the motivations and the practices associated with literacy is important in any context, but perhaps especially so in the Ottoman/Turkish case where learning to read and reading have been so freighted with a number of weighty agendas.

This study has approached the subject of learning to read and reading from a variety of angles in order to emphasize its various distinct but related aspects. The introductory chapter highlighted the extent to which our ability to understand reading in the Ottoman/Turkish context, for all of its similarities with reading in other parts of the world, was enmeshed in the historiographical – and ideological – problem of the transition from empire to republic. Children's reading materials revealed that the advent of the Turkish Republic could both dramatically alter what they were expected to read and leave it largely unchanged. Seeing this period of transition through the lens of reading allowed us to note both the frequently noted ruptures and symbolic distancing effected by the republic as well as the less often observed continuities. Well before the alphabet change and linguistic engineering of 1928, important changes were in train that fundamentally altered the reading landscape. The rapid diffusion of public education in roughly the last four decades of the Ottoman period brought unprecedented numbers of children into formal schooling, provided them with standardized texts that unlike their Qur'an school analogs were created specifically with the pedagogy of reading in mind, allowed successive governments, both imperial and republican to model the benefits of reading, among other salutary behaviors, and initiated a chain of economic/literary activity that very quickly expanded beyond the remit of the burgeoning state. The Turkish Republic made important changes to the emphasis and content of children's reading materials but when seen across the usual chronological divide of 1923 it is striking how little the change in regime affected the world of children's reading.

Chapter 2 demonstrated the diversity inherent in the experience of learning to read in the late Ottoman and early Republican context. Focusing on the ways in which reading was represented to children allowed us to see the variety of referents, contexts, teachers and genres. But for all of the variety of experience, there was a clear directional trend. Children were increasingly shown that the path to success, both individual and collective and both moral and economic, ran through the state-supplied school. Different texts adopted different strategies but the common agenda was to demonstrate that in order to be properly taught and to be benefit from the expanding horizons that literacy offered, children needed to leave their families behind and benefit from that paragon of modernity, the new-style teacher. The emergence of new reading genres, in particular the children's magazine, meant that the new teachers – and the state they represented – would struggle to control young readers' attentions. Unfettered with some aspects of the state's meliorative and political agendas, these new publications could offer wider horizons and pursue a more personal, more entertaining relationship with their young customers.

The tensions that ran through the content to which young readers were being exposed as they began to read were the subject of Chapter 3. The discussion placed reading content along a spectrum that linked four binary pairings, the religious and the secular, the family and the nation state, the new and the old and the global and the local, in order to explore the dynamics of both certainty and ambiguity that children were confronting. At first glance it is the rigidity of the material that stands out; the young were given clear-cut examples of how to think, identify and behave. Closer examination, however, reveals the many uncertainties and contradictions occasioned by exposure to a rapidly changing world. Reading was therefore both symptomatic of and instrumental in complicating children's religious, political, social and geographical identities.

Since the messages children were receiving were complex and sometimes even contradictory, it is important to look at the way they were conveyed and the ways in which children actually read them, in other words, the mechanics of reading, the subject of Chapter 4. Focusing on the practical aspects of acquiring literacy, from learning the letters to the changing pedagogy of reading and the design of reading primers, this chapter probed some of the difficulties inherent in the push for large-scale literacy, such as the problems of "parroting" or reading without comprehension. It also explored some of the positive aspects of learning to read, including the pleasure derived from and for some even the passionate "addiction" to the pastime of reading. Both the pedagogical and the entertaining possibilities inherent in the use of illustrations informed the subsequent discussion of images in the service of literacy. New technologies afforded the incorporation of more and more images into the publishing mix, a development presenting both new opportunities and new challenges. Privately produced reading material could diverge dramatically from the official line as publishers followed their impulse to attract new readers *cum* customers.

Chapter 5 pursued the economic aspects of learning to read and reading more closely. Usually hidden from view, the economics of reading offer important insights into this period of transition. The discussion began with the state as the driver behind the biggest stimulus to literacy, the public educational system. Both by dramatically increasing the number of readers through its growing number of schools and by commissioning a seemingly endless supply of textbooks, the education ministries of this period spurred economic as well as intellectual activity. Books and other printer matter were the central commodities through which the new system operated – and around which considerable money changed hands. Each student in the new schools was meant to have his or her own copy of the books in question, a departure from the tradition of shared and consumption-free reading and one with considerable economic and social repercussions. As publishers sought to make their products attractive to readers who were growing accustomed to individual purchase and possession, they competed to develop more direct relationships with young readers, at times undermining the authority and message of the state.

The various aspects of reading considered in this book are important only as they affected individual people. Chapter 6 therefore plumbed the impact of the new reading dispensation on the human level. By tracing the biographical dimension of reading we are able to see how and to what effect literacy changed the way people lived. The ability to read and the practice of reading changed people's lives, sometimes dramatically. It brought them jobs that would have been unlikely or impossible only a generation or two earlier. It changed the way they thought, with important aesthetic, social and political connotations. Coming full circle, the chapter traced how certain individuals made the transition from readers to writers. Throughout the discussion of even a relatively small number of cases, the diversity of experience comes through clearly.

A central premise of this book has been that reading is both constructive and illustrative of modernity. Traversing the varied experiences of and paths to the modern, reading played a central role in the advent of many of the most important markers of modernity. By definition reading increased access to information; its rise ran parallel with and was heavily, although not completely, influenced by the expanding state; it depended upon and in turn facilitated the rapid assimilation of new technologies and modes of expression; its appearance reflected and, indeed, depended upon the importance of market-driven mechanisms of distribution, exchange and valuation; it enabled the direct relationship between the individual and the printed word, deemed so central to modern political and religious movements; in the aggregate it served as a vehicle for participation, at least indirectly, in larger currents of the day; and it opened unprecedented possibilities for socioeconomic advancement. Reading did not create the modern world on its own, of course, but it was crucial to several of its most salient features.

Certainly, this period witnessed the emergence of a new world of reading. The old reading dispensation, a world of low rates of literacy, the predominance of manuscripts, "high" literature and religious texts and communal reading, was rapidly yielding to a system of rising readership, popular literature and individualized consumption of reading material. Although religiously informed writing continued to be important (if understudied) the presumption that writing was sacred – the Hapsburg Ambassador to Istanbul Ghiselin de Busbecq in the middle of the sixteenth century noticed that people were quick to pick up scraps

of paper lest anyone step on them[1] – was disappearing under the prevalence of the printed word.

This changing scene saw experimentation, with genres, with voices,
with attempts to draw and sustain young audiences. There was no single path forward but publishers and readers were feeling their way. New
looks – illustrations were crucial here – and new formats emerged, new
products appeared in the form of magazines, novels and samplers and
after 1928 even new scripts. Underlying these changes we can see the
emergence and expansion of a world of reading that brought with it
immense political, economic, social and cultural ramifications, many
of which are crucial to understanding the eventual development of the
Turkish Republic up to the present day.

This book has attempted to show how reading was represented, how
its content was used to impart various but sometimes contradictory
messages, how it shadowed a number of changes and continuities that
both linked and separated empire from republic, how the practice of
learning to read and the look of reading were changing, how the market
affected reading and how reading changed people's lives in this transitional period.

A range of discursive practices, topics, illustration, forms of address
and affects combined to form an emerging field of readership for the
young, whether Ottoman or republican. There were important breaks
and shifts in this development but also numerous continuities, all the
more remarkable given the literature's and, after 1923, the new regime's
insistence on cleavage. Taking the long view, we can say that writing
and therefore reading was in the process of moving from a rare, highly
valued, sacred activity to one that is ubiquitous. Ironically, reading can
at times seem to be the victim of its own success, taken for granted
because of its increasing importance.

We paid special attention to the commodification of reading. This is
a process that allows for the easier exchange of things and one that can
occur with dramatic speed and scope. As we have seen, the commodification of reading in the late Ottoman and early Turkish republican
eras worked both to support and subvert the agenda of the state. But
the state's program, whether imperial or republican, was itself aimed
at transforming the dominant culture, especially those aspects which
it held to be retrograde. As one scholar has noted, the force of commodification (he calls it "commoditization") is met with resistance.
"The counterdrive to this potential onrush of commoditization is culture...Excessive commoditization is anticultural" because culture is
inherently based on discrimination.[2] The Ottoman/Turkish case is an

interesting one in the sense that the dominant culture was itself changing. Indeed, at times it found itself under a sustained and centrally planned onslaught. The state-driven version of modernism was heavily reliant on the printed word for disseminating its message but so also was the counter movement that emerged in the 1950s and 1960s heavily invested in advancing its cause through the written word. In short, much of the politico-cultural contest that has gripped Turkey would be inconceivable in the absence of an increasingly literate population.

Appadurai has noted the link between the emergence of Anderson's "print capitalism" and projects of ethnic affinity, pointing to the paradox of constructed primordialism that is particularly apposite in the Turkish Republican case.[3] But reading can be and was used for a variety of projects, not only ethno-political ones. Although they tend to be effaced by the volume and vociferousness of the Republican project, other modes of modernity also appeared in the period under discussion here. We have seen how late Ottoman textbooks could draw equally on Islamic as on national themes in their appeal to readers; print capitalism was by no means the sole preserve of secularists. Even in the early years of the Republic it was still possible for the previous types of appeal to be made, with only rather superficial changes being made to the message and forms of delivery. In short, reading was a neutral practice that could be bent to an almost infinite number of causes. Because reading was almost always seen as positive in societies that were only minimally literate, it behooved the advocates of each particular brand of modernity to act as if reading were exclusively their commodity.

Perhaps the most interesting development associated with reading in this period is its role in individualization. We have seen how readers became enamored of reading, sometimes even to the point of distraction. Books and magazines assumed a new and distinct identity as items to be bought, given, won, eagerly awaited in the post, in short, cherished as commodities. Texts were both read together in Anderson's and Appadurai's sense, but they were also read apart. That is, not everyone read the same texts or if they did, they read them in very different ways and contexts. These varied readings frequently served to further individualization and not collectivization. The intimate connection between the individual and the text – available to be bought, transported, curled up with – remains one of the most abiding relationships of the modern period.

But the physicality of reading – its very "bookness" – is challenged by the suggestion that modern consumption is ultimately based on pleasure.[4] As text increasingly moves away from our ability to hold it, as it moves on-line, on-screen and into the ether, its fleetingness seems paradoxically both logical and improbable. On the one hand it makes sense in the historical trajectory by which texts have moved from solid – carved in rock, inscribed in metal or penned on parchment – to less permanent forms like newspapers, chapbooks, pamphlets, magazines, also known as ephemera and eventually to the digital. The period examined in this book seems from today's perspective to have been one of transition. These cheaper, more widely available reading materials made possible the expansion of reading through the consumption of written material by unprecedentedly wide audiences. Learning to read became a passport to a seemingly ever-expanding world of text, opportunity and participation. What makes this vast-scale transition improbable is the fact that so much of the modern edifice of our text-based society rests on the flimsiest of physical foundations, the pages of a book. That might be a fitting point on which to end this story. Just as reading is known to be both incredibly important and extremely difficult to study so also is reading as one of the defining preconditions for modernity, both solidly attributed and physically ephemeral.

Notes

1 Introduction: Reading Empire, Reading Republic

1. Steven Roger Fischer, *A History of Reading* (London: Reaktion Books, 2003), 7.
2. Even those in so-called manual labor find text abundant on the job. The work order, instruction manual, LCD read-out, and, for the coffee break, the tabloid newspaper, are all common workday encounters.
3. Robert J. Barro, "Human Capital and Growth," *The American Economic Review* 91: 2 (May 2001): 12–17. In the Turkish case, see Sumru Altuğ, Alpay Filiztekin and Şevket Pamuk, "Sources of Long Term Economic Growth for Turkey, 1880–2005," *European Review of Economic History* 12 (2008), 393–430. I am grateful to Şevket Pamuk for these helpful references.
4. Benedict R. O'G. Anderson, *Imagined Communities: Reflections on the Origin and Spread of Nationalism* 2nd edn. (London: Verso, 1991). For a critical view, see Şerif Mardin, "Playing Games with Names," in Deniz Kandiyoti and Ayşe Saktanber, eds., *Fragments of Culture: The Everyday Life of Modern Turkey* (London: I. B. Tauris, 2002), 115 ff.
5. For an arresting example, drawn from the Albanian experience, of the link between nation and its reading material, see Nathalie Clayer, *Aux origines du nationalisme albanais; La naissance d'une nation majoritairement musulmane en Europe* (Paris: Éditions Karthala, 2007), 411–12.
6. Armando Salvatore and Dale Eickelman, *Public Islam and the Common Good* (Leiden: Brill, 2004), xi.
7. As cited by Roger Chartier, *The Cultural Origins of the French Revolution*, Lydia G. Cochrane, trans. (Durham, NC: Duke University Press, 1991), 20.
8. Yair Wallach, "Readings in Conflict: Public Text in Modern Jerusalem, 1858–1948," PhD Diss., University of London, 2008.
9. Ibid., 248.
10. Ibid.
11. As cited in Johann Strauss, "Who Read what in the Ottoman Empire (19th–20th centuries)?" *Arabic and Middle Eastern Literatures* 6:1 (2003), 39.
12. Martin Hartmann, *Der Islamische Orient: Berichte und Forschungen. Vol. 3: Unpolitische Brief aus der Türkei.* (Berlin: Verlag Rudolf Haupt, 1910), 66.
13. On the reading milieu in the late Ottoman Empire in general, see François Georgeon, "Lire et écrire à la fin de l'Empire ottoman: quelques remarques introductives," in *Oral et écrit dans le monde turc-ottoman*, Nicolas Vatin, ed., REMMM 75–76 (1995), 169–79; Frédéric Hitzel, "Manuscrits, livres et culture livresque à Istanbul," REMMM 87–88 (1999), 19–34; Johan Strauss, "Who Read What."
14. See A. Tietze, ed., *Akabi Hikayesi: İlk Türkçe Roman (1851)* (Istanbul: Eren, 1991).
15. N. a. *Kitab iftitah al-qira'at* (Izmir: n.p., 1264[1848]). The author was almost certainly Nassif Mallouf who published over thirty books, many aimed at children, in the mid-nineteenth century.
16. N. a., *Yeni kıraat* (n.p.: n.d.), 3. Thanks to Ioannis Moutsis for making this text available to me from his family's collection.

17. See, for example, Arakel Karamadtiosyan, *Miftah-i kıraat-i huruf-i ermeniye fi lisan-i osmanî* (Istanbul (?): n.p., n.d.) for an Ottoman-Armenian version and N Sasun, *Musevilere mahsus elifba-yi osmanî* (Istanbul: İsak Gabay Matbaası, 1321[1905]). My thanks to Eyal Ginio for bringing this latter work to my attention.
18. Alberto Manguel, *A History of Reading* (New York: Penguin, 1996); Fischer, *History.*
19. Manguel, 138–9.
20. Philippe Ariès, *Centuries of Childhood: A Social History of Family Life,* Robert Baldrick, trans. (New York: Vintage, 1962), 138.
21. Geroge Makdisi, *The Rise of Colleges: Institutions of Learning in Islam and the West* (Edinburgh: Edinburgh University Press, 1981).
22. See, for example, Yahya Kemal as quoted in Cüneyd Okay, *Osmanlı Çocuk Hayatında Yenileşmeler, 1850–1900* (Istanbul: Kırkambar Yayınları, 1998), 34.
23. Ariès, 141.
24. Chartier, *Cultural Origins.*
25. For Paris see Ibid. and the work of Robert C. Darnton, e.g., "The Forbidden Bestsellers of Prerevolutionary France," *Bulletin of the American Academy of Arts and Sciences* 43: 1 (October 1989), 17–45; for provincial France, see Eugen Weber, *Peasants into Frenchmen: the Modernization of Rural France, 1870–1914* (Stanford, CA: Stanford University Press, 1976), especially chapters 18 and 27.
26. See, for example, Elizabeth L. Eisenstein, "An Unacknowledged Revolution Revisited," *The American Historical Review* 107:1 (February 2002), 87–105 and Richard Wittmann, "Was there a Reading Revolution at the End of the Eighteenth Century?," in Cavallo and Chartier, eds., *A History of Reading in the West,* 284–312.
27. François Furet and Jacques Ozouf, *Reading and Writing: Literacy in France from Calvin to Jules Ferry* (Cambridge: Cambridge University Press, 1982).
28. Johan Strauss, "Romanlar, Ah! O Romanlar! Les débuts de la lecture moderne dans l'empire ottomane (1850–1900)," *Turcica* 26 (1994), 126–7.
29. Jeffrey Brooks, *When Russia Learned to Read: Literacy and Popular Literature, 1861–1917* (Princeton, NJ: Princeton University Press, 1985), 214 ff.
30. Stephen Lovell, *The Russian Reading Revolution: Print Culture in the Soviet and Post-Soviet Eras. Studies in Russia and East Europe* (Houndmills: Macmillan, 2000), 10 ff.
31. Erik J. Zürcher, *Turkey: A Modern History* 3rd edn. (London: I B Tauris, 2004), 197. For the public similarities with the Soviet Union (and other totalitarian regimes), see Sandrine Bertaux, *Ulusu Tasarlamak;1920'ler ve 1930'larda Avrupa Devletleri/Projecting the Nation: European States in the 1920s and 1930s* (Istanbul: Osmanlı Bankası Arşiv ve Araştırma Merkezi, 2006).
32. Li Yu, "Learning to Read in Late Imperial China," *Studies on Asia,* series III 1:1 (Fall 2004): 10 ff.
33. Ibid., 11.
34. Victor Mair, as cited in Ibid., 12.
35. Charles W. Hayford, *To the People: James Yen and Village China* (New York: Columbia University Press, 1990), 32 ff. Thanks to Chris Gerteis for this reference.
36. Ibid., 44–5.

37. E. J. Hobsbawm, *Nations and Nationalism since 1780: Programme, Myth, Reality* (Cambridge: Cambridge University Press, 1990), 93–4.
38. Martyn Lyons, "New Readers in the Nineteenth Century: Women, Children, Workers," in Guglielmo Cavallo and Roger Chartier, eds. *A History of Reading in the West* L. G. Cochrane, trans. (Amherst, MA: University of Massachusetts Press, 1999), 324 ff.
39. Furet and Ozouf, *Reading and Writing*.
40. William H. McNeill, "A Short History of Humanity," *New York Review of Books* XLVII: 11 (29 June 2006), 11.
41. On this process, see Gavin D. Brockett, *How Happy to Call Oneself a Turk: Print Culture and the Negotiation of a Muslim National Identity in Modern Turkey* (Austin, TX: University of Texas Press, forthcoming).
42. Michael Meeker, *A Nation of Empire: The Ottoman Legacy of Turkish Modernity* (Berkeley, CA: University of California Press, 2002).
43. Elizabeth Frierson, "Gender, Consumption and Patriotism: The Emergence of an Ottoman Public Sphere," in Salvatore and Eickelman, eds., *Public Islam*, 102–3.
44. Mehmet Ö. Alkan, "Modernization from Empire to Republic and Education in the Process of Nationalism," in Kemal Karpat, ed., *Ottoman Past and Today's Turkey* (Leiden: Brill, 2000), 47–132.
45. For an intriguing discussion of this concept in Iran, see Monica M. Ringer, "Rethinking Religion: Progress and Morality in the Early Twentieth-Century Iranian Women's Press," *CSSAAME* 24: 1 (2004), 49–57.
46. Among the many writings on this topic are: Geoffrey Lewis, *The Turkish Language Reform: A Catastrophic Success* (Oxford: Oxford University Press, 1999); Tahsin Yücel, *Dil Devrimi ve Sonuçları* (Istanbul: İyi Şeyler Yayıncılık, 1997) and Uriel Heyd, *Language Reform in Modern Turkey* (Jerusalem: Israel Oriental Society, 1954).
47. François Georgeon, "Lire et écrire," 170–1.
48. His figures measure illiteracy and range from about 50 percent to as low as 10 percent in Istanbul. Even allowing for some natural reluctance to be counted as illiterate, these figures are dramatically different from most other estimates. Kemal H. Karpat, "Reinterpreting Ottoman History: A Note on the Condition of Education in 1874," *International Journal of Turkish Studies* 2 (1981–1982), 94–5.
49. On the contradictions inherent in the Republic's attempt to present discontinuity as continuity, see Deniz Kandiyoti, "Identity and its Discontents: Women and the Nation," in Patrick Williams and Laura Chrisman, eds., *Colonial Discourse and Post-Colonial Theory: A Reader* (New York: Harvester Wheatsheaf, 1993), 379; and Yael Navaro-Yashin, *Faces of the State: Secularism and Public Life in Turkey* (Princeton, NJ: Princeton University Press, 2002), 10–12.
50. Alkan, 126.
51. Yeşim Bayar, "The Dynamic Nature of Educational Policies and Turkish Nation Building: Where Does Religion Fit in?," *CSSAAME* 29: 3 (2009), 362.
52. Ibid., 367–8.
53. Robert Darnton, "Introduction," in Robert Darnton and Daniel Roche, eds., *Revolution in Print: The Press in France 1775–1800* (Berkeley, CA: University of California Press, 1989), xiii.

54. Elizabeth B. Frierson, "Unimagined Communities: Women, Education, and the State in the Late Ottoman Empire," *Critical Matrix* 9 (1995), 58–9.
55. Ibid.; Deniz Kandiyoti, "End of Empire: Islam, Nationalism, and Women in Turkey," in Deniz Kandiyoti, ed., *Women, Islam and the State* (London: Macmillan, 1991), 22–3.
56. Frierson, "Unimagined Communities"; Yeşim Arat, "Nation Building and Feminism in early Republican Turkey," in C. Kerslake, K. Öktem and P. Robins, eds., *Turkey's Engagement with Modernity: Conflict and Change in the Twentieth Century* (Houndmills: Palgrave Macmillan, 2010), 38–51.
57. See Cüneyd Okay, *Eski Harfli Çocuk Dergileri* (Istanbul: Kitabevi, 1999).
58. Lewis, *Turkish Language Reform*, 2–4.
59. Navaro-Yashin, *Faces of the State*, 31.
60. On the process of repairing the tears in the historical-religious fabric created by the suppression of the Ottoman-Islamic tradition in favor of a national-secular program, see Brian Silverstein, "Islamist Critique in Modern Turkey: Hermeneutics, Tradition, Genealogy," *Comparative Studies in Society and History* 47 (2005), 134–60.
61. Mustafa Kemal himself abandoned the practice of making speeches in the newly concocted language because it was, ironically given the rationale for altering Ottoman Turkish in the first place, largely unintelligible to his audiences. Nazan Çiçek, "The Project of Creating True Turkish Children: The Children's Magazines in Turkey circa the Foundation of the Republic." Paper presented at the annual meetings of the British Society for Middle Eastern Studies, Birmingham, July 2006, 11. My thanks to Dr Çiçek for sharing her valuable work on this subject.
62. For two recent studies, see Velat Zeydanlioğlu, "Kemalism's Others: The Reproduction of Orientalism in Turkey" (PhD Diss., Anglia Ruskin University 2007), chapter 4; and Başak İnce, "The Construction and Redefinition of Citizenship in Turkey," PhD Diss., University of London, 2008.
63. Roderic Davison, "Atatürk's Reforms: Back to the Roots," in Roderic Davison, *Essays in Ottoman and Turkish History, 1774–1923* (Austin, TX: University of Texas Press, 1990), 243.
64. I return to the important question of the roles played by images and iconography in children's reading materials in Chapter 4.
65. Thanks to Palmira Brummett's research into the rich satirical literature of the Young Turk period, we can correlate the changes in literature for children against that for grown-ups. It is interesting to note that the binary juxtapositions emerging in Brummett's account of the revolutionary imagery seem grounded in many of the themes that had been emerging in less dramatic fashion in the preceding Hamidian period. Palmira Brummett, *Image and Imperialism in the Ottoman Revolutionary Press, 1908–1911* (Albany, NY: State University of New York Press, 2000), 22.
66. Paul Dumont, "La littérature enfantine Turque," in P. Dumont, ed., *Turquie Livres d'hier livres d'aujourdhui* (Strasbourg and Istanbul: Études Turques, 1992), 79. On the strident militancy of the literature developing in the period after Italy's 1911 invasion of Tripolitania, particularly that featured in the journal *Genç Kalemler* (The Young Pens) see Murat Belge, "*Genç Kalemler* and Turkish Nationalism," in C. Kerslake, K. Öktem and P. Robins, eds., *Turkey's Engagement with Modernity: Conflict and Change in the Twentieth Century* (Houndmills: Palgrave Macmillan, 2010), 27–37.

67. On Köprülü, see Halil Berktay, *Cumhuriyet İdeolojisi ve Fuad Köprülü* (Istanbul: Kaynak Yayınları, 1983).
68. Köprülüzade Mehmed Fuad, *Cumhuriyet Çocuklarına Yeni Millî Kıraat* (Istanbul: Kanaat, 1926). The same author, who would soon drop the patronymic suffix from his family name, also wrote a school textbook entitled *Yeni Millî Tarih* (New National History) for the same publisher. The anti-Ottoman tenor of these works is all the more striking for the fact that their author was one of the foremost historians of the Ottoman Empire in Turkey; his radical attitude cannot be explained by ignorance of the empire and its history.
69. Cf. Çiçek, "Creating True Turkish Children," 6.
70. Ibid., 8–9.
71. For a succinct summary of the Kemalist policy of sidelining political rivals, see Zürcher, *Turkey*, 168–74.
72. Ahmed Cevad, *Cumhuriyet Çocuklarina Türkçe Kıraat* 1:1 (Istanbul: Hilmi, 1929), 88–91.
73. Dumont, "Littérature enfantine," 79.
74. *Yeni Yol* 53 (4 Kanun-ı evvel 1340[4 December 1924]).
75. Brinkley Messick, *The Calligraphic State: Textual Domination and History in a Muslim Society* (Berkeley, CA: University of California Press, 1993), chapter 4.
76. "Kitapçı" Arakel, *Talim-i kıraat: malumat-i ibtidaiye ve nasayih-i nafia*. vol. 1 (Istanbul: Kitapcı Arakel Matbaası, 1303[1887]), 7.
77. Niyazi Berkes, *The Development of Secularism in Turkey* 2nd edn. (New York: Routledge, 1998), 282.
78. Serdar Öztürk, "Efforts to Modernize Chapbooks during the Initial Years of the Turkish Republic," *European Historical Quarterly* 40 (2010), 7–34.
79. Richard W. Bulliett, "First Names and Political Change in Modern Turkey," *IJMES* 9 (1978), 489–95.
80. For a discussion of Ottoman cartographic policy see Benjamin C. Fortna, "Change in the School Maps of the Late Ottoman Empire," *Imago Mundi: The International Journal of the History of Cartography* 57 (2004), 23–34. For the Republican period, see Étienne Copeaux, *Espaces et temps de la nation turque: Analyse d'une hisotoriographie nationaliste, 1931–1993* (Paris: CNRS, 1997) and *idem, Une vision turque à travers les cartes de 1931 à nos jours* (Paris: CNRS, 2002).
81. Asım Karaömerlioğlu, "The People's Houses and the Cult of the Peasant in Turkey," *Middle Eastern Studies* 34:4 (October 1998): 67–91.
82. See, for example, *Yeni Yol*, 50 (13 Teşrin-i sani 1340[13 November 1924]).
83. P. Xavier Jacob, *L'enseignement religieux dans la Turquie moderne* Islamkundliche Untersuchungen Band 67 (Berlin: Klaus Schwarz Verlag, 1982), 61.
84. *Atatürk'ün Söylev ve Demeçleri*, 245. It is interesting to note that, as Xavier Jacob has pointed out, the Turkish Education Minister Hasan Âli Yücel eliminated the term "religion" (din) in his 1939 pamphlet entitled *Atatürk's Directives on Education*. Jacob, 62, n. 135.
85. Köprülüzade, *Cumhuriyet Çocuklarına Yeni Millî Kıraat*, 9–10.
86. Ibid., 11. The Turkish reads:
    Şu kavgalı görültülü şehirlerden uzakta [amended from urakta]
    Semaları sis görmeyen o mübarek toprakta
    Ne şenlikli ömür sürer iyi kalbli çiftçiler...
87. Ibid., 147–8.

88. Ibid., 105. The original text reads:
    Düşmanlar İzmir'de; memleket yanmış!
    Hainler, milleti mahv oldu sanmış!
    Lakin bu milletin imanı büyük,
    Kurtulmak isterdi hep büyük küçük...
89. Ibid., 134
90. On the similarities and differences between military and civil schooling the late Ottoman period, see Benjamin C. Fortna, *Imperial Classroom: Islam, the State, and Education in the Late Ottoman Empire* (Oxford: Oxford University Press, 2002), 193.
91. For a study that pursues the gendered dimension of education in Turkey up to the present era, see Tuba Kancı and Ayşe Gül Altınay, "Educating Little Soldiers and Little Ayşes: Militarised and Gendered Citizenship in Turkish Textbooks," in Marie Carlson, Annika Rabo and Fatma Gök, eds., *Education in 'Multicultural' Societies" Turkish and Swedish Perspectives* (Stockholm: Swedish Research Institute in Istanbul, 2007), 51–70.
92. Köprülüzade, *Cumhuriyet Çocuklarına Yeni Millî Kıraat*, 86–7.
93. Ahmed Rasım, *Doğru usûl-i kıraat* (Istanbul: İkdam, 1926), 29–30. Interestingly, this author's emphasis on the Turkish element predated the founding of the Republic by more than two decades. His 1307 (1899–90) *Osmanlı Tarihi* (Ottoman History), a text written for students at the three lowest levels of state education in the late Ottoman period begins with an account of "The Turks" (Türkler) before continuing on with Ertuğrul Bey and his son Osman, the eponymous founder of the Ottoman state. He takes his account up to the reign of Abdülmecid (r. 1839–61) and wisely stops there. Ahmed Rasım, *Osmanlı Tarihi* (Istanbul: İstepan Matbaası, 1307).
94. Köprülüzade, *Cumhuriyet Çocuklarına Yeni Millî Kıraat*, 56.
95. On the selective appeal of official discourse in the early years of the republic and the post-World War II process of reincorporating the Ottoman past, see Brocket, *How Happy...*, Chapter 6.
96. A. İnan, *Medeni Bilgiler ve M. Kemal Atatürk'ün El Yazıları* (Ankara: Atatürk Araştırma Merkezi, 2000), 149–50, as cited in Zeydanlioğlu, 137–8.
97. It also skilfully sidelined or suppressed a number of other competing voices, ethno-national as well as religious.

2   Reading Represented

1. Fischer, *History*, 12.
2. See Fortna, "Education and Autobiography at the End of the Ottoman Empire," *Die Welt des Islams* 41:1 (2001), 8–10. For accessible, English translations that convey the traditional environment in which reading was encountered, or at least remembered to have been encountered, in this period, see İrfan Orga, *Portrait of a Turkish Family* (London: Victor Gollancz, 1950) and Halide Edib, *Memoirs of Halidé Edip* (London: John Murray, 1926).
3. Halide Nusret [Zorlutuna], *Bir Devrin Romanı* (Ankara: Kültür Bakanlığı, 1978), 9–10.
4. Halid Ziya Uşaklıgil, *Kırk Yıl* (Istanbul: İnkilap ve Aka Kitabevleri, 1969), 6–7.

5. Fortna, "Education and Autobiography," 9.
6. Halil Hâlid, *Diary of a Turk* (London: Black, 1903), 19.
7. As cited in Mehmet Nuri Yardım, *Tanzimattan Günümüze Edebiyatçılarimizin Çocukluk Hatıraları* (Istanbul: Timas, 1998), 31.
8. Akşin Selçuk Somel, *The Modernization of Public Education in the Ottoman Empire, 1839–1908; Islamization, Autocracy and Discipline* (Leiden: Brill, 2001), 108 ff.
9. Ali İrfan, *Çocuklara İstifade*[:] *Tehzib-i Ahlâk ve Malûmat-ı Nafia* (Istanbul: Şirket-i Murettibiye Matbaası, 1304), 21–5.
10. Ali İrfan, *Şiven Yahud Hatırat-i Şebabim* (Izmir: Ahenk Matbaası, 1315), 3.
11. Ariès, *Centuries of Childhood*, 212.
12. Dale Eickelman, "The Art of Memory: Islamic Education and its Social Reproduction," *Comparative Studies in Society and History* 20 (1978), 485–516.
13. On Persian, see Klaus Kreiser, "Persisch als Schulsprache bei den osmanischen Türken: Von der Tanzîmât-Zeit zur frühen Republik," in Jens Peter Laut and Klaus Röhrborn, eds, *Sprach- und Kulturkontakte der türkischen Völker. Materialien der zweiten Deutschen Turkologen-Konferenz* (Wiesbaden: Harrassowitz, 1993), 124.
14. For the language situation in this period, see Fortna, "Education and Autobiography," 26–30.
15. On the presence of the ulema in the burgeoning state schools, see Fortna, *Imperial Classroom*.
16. Bekir Onur, *Türkiye'de Çocukluğun Tarihi* (Ankara: Imge Kitabevi, 2005), 297–8.
17. Michael Meeker notes the semantic shift in the term "hoca" away from its designation as a religious instructor in the Ottoman period to a generic term for any kind of teacher in the Republican period. Meeker, *A Nation of Empire*, 40 note.
18. Ömer Seyfettin, "Falaka," in *Ömer Seyfettin: Bütün Eserleri. Vol. 8 Falaka* (Ankara: Bilgi Yayınevi, 1971), 42–3.
19. Ahmed Rasım, *Doğru usûl-i kıraat* 5. kısım (Istanbul: İkdam Matbaası, 1926), 44–5.
20. Like most stories of this period, this one was not specifically intended for children. It was not part of a reading primer but its simple style and its school-based plot increased the likelihood that it found its way to an audience of both young and old.
21. Sadrettin Celal, *Cümhuriyet Çocuklarına Sevimli Kırâat* (Istanbul Kanâat Kütüphânesi, 1928), 100.
22. Ibid., 101.
23. For the Egyptian case, see Gregory Starrett, *Putting Islam to Work: Education, Politics and Religious Transformation in Egypt* (Berkeley, CA: University of California Press, 1998), 35 ff.
24. See my "Education and Autobiography," 22 ff.
25. Sadrettin Celal, *Cümhuriyet Çocuklarına Sevimli Kırâat* (Istanbul Kanâat Kütüphânesi, 1928), 4–8.
26. Sadrettin Celal, *Cümhuriyet Çocuklarına Sevimli Kırâat*, 7. Readers of Turkish will note the unusual orthography in this text. The author and/or the typesetter seem to be struggling with the demands of the recently enacted

language law requiring the use of a modified Latin alphabet to render the Turkish that had previously been written in the Arabo-Persian script.

27. *Çocuklara Mahsus Gazete* 14 (17 Rebiülevvel 1314[26 August 1896]), 7.

28. Ahmed Rasım, *İbtidaî kıraat* (Dersaadet [Istanbul]: Şems matbaası, 1328–1330[1910–1912]), 9–10.

29. This text, entitled "Muallim hanımın vefâtı" (The schoolmistress's death), is interesting for several reasons. Unlike the illustration accompanying the story of The New Teacher, the picture supplied here is clearly domestically produced; it shows a group of mourners standing around the gravesite with rows of distinctly Ottoman-style headstones, some capped with carved turbans, in the background, and it is signed in the recently discarded Ottoman script by a certain Malik. Also interesting is the way that the late teacher's students are identified by the schools and classes in which she taught them. Thus, some students arrive with a wreath dedicated to her memory in the name of students of the fourth class. Finally, and most touchingly, we learn that she had left all of her fairly limited inheritance to her students. This amounted to her books, an inskstand (hokka), and a writing board (levha). Sadrettin Celal, *Cümhuriyet Çocuklarına Sevimli Kırâat*, 12–15.

30. Ibid., 9–11.

31. Ibid., 9–10.

32. Muallim Cevdet [İnanç], *Çocuklar için...Hayat bilgisine uygun yazılar ve temsiller* ([Balıkesir:] Türk Dili, 1943), 24. Similar letters devised to model the children's love for their teachers and even their textbooks are fairly common in this literature.

33. *Çocuklara Kiraat* 1 (1883), 1–2.

34. For a study of school textbooks in the late Ottoman period, see Nuri Doğan, *Ders Kitapları ve Sosyalleşme (1876–1918)* (Istanbul: Bağlam, 1994).

35. Okay, *Eski Harfli*, 216–7.

36. Hitzel, "Manuscrits," 31–2; Ayalon, *Reading Palestine*, 93 ff.

37. *Çocuklara Mahsus Gazete* 3 (29 Zilhicce 1313[11 June 1896]), 1.

38. Lest any readers get the wrong idea, the Kurdish leader is clearly depicted as trembling; a fly buzzes in the background.

39. Robert DeMaria, Jr., *Samuel Johnson and the Life of Reading* (Baltimore, MD: The Johns Hopkins University Press, 1997), 4 ff.

40. See, for example, the cover illustration, probably appropriated from a Western publication, of Ruşen Eşref, Mitat Sadullah and Necmettin Sadık, *Cümhuriyet Kıraati*. Kısım 3 (Istanbul: Tefeyyüz Kitaphanesi, 1928). It shows a boy in a suit with shorts and a white collar, standing beside his seat, who appears to be reading aloud from the book he holds in his hands. In the desk behind him a girl wearing a dress and a hair ribbon seems to be following along in her copy of the book that lies open on her desk.

41. Hailde Edip, *Memoirs*, 91 ff.

42. Halide Nusret [Zorlutuna], *Bir Devrin Romanı*, 17.

43. Ibid., 18.

44. Ibid., 83.

45. *Yeni Yol* 50 (13 Teşrin-i sani 1340[13 November 1924]), 417.

46. For the influence of Smiles's work, both East and West, see C. A. Bayly, *The Birth of the Modern World, 1780–1914: Global Connections and Comparisons* (Oxford: Blackwell, 2004), 319.

3 Context and Content

1. Cüneyd Okay, *Eski Harfli Çocuk Dergileri* (Istanbul: Kitabevi, 1999), 23–4.
2. This information is taken from the catalogues of the Seyfettin Özege Collection at the Atatürk University Library, Erzurum.
3. [Bedros] Zeki, *Rehnüma-yı kıraat ve tercüme*. Üçüncü sene. (Istanbul: Arak Garoyan Matbaası, 1327[1911]). This translation of Canevas's guide to reading and translation was one such exception.
4. N.a., *Rehber-i salat yahud sual ve cevablı ilm-i hal* (Dersaadet [Istanbul]; 1328[1912]).
5. Ahmed Cevad, *Yeni elifbâ[:] Kuranı okuyorum* (Istanbul: Matbaa-i Amire, 1342[1926]).
6. Robert G. Landen, "The Ottoman home front: a German correspondent's remarks, 1917," in Camron M. Amin, Benjamin C. Fortna and Elizabeth B. Frierson, eds., *The Modern Middle East: A Sourcebook for History* (Oxford: Oxford University Press, 2006), 441–43.
7. For the details, see Geoffrey Lewis, *Turkish Language Reform*.
8. *The Times*, 23 January 1932.
9. Zürcher, *Turkey: A Modern History*, 193.
10. *Islam Dünyası* 10 (13 Şaban 1331[18 July 1913]), 155.
11. Frédéric Hitzel, "Manuscrits, livres et culture livresque à Istanbul," *REMMM* 87–88 (1999), 24.
12. Johann Strauss, "Romanlar..." 128–9, citing Rıza Nur, *Hâtıratım* I, 73; and François Georgeon, "Les cafés à Istanbul au XIXe siècle," *Etudes turques et modernes*. Documents du travail, 1 (Mars 1992): 14–40. Cengiz Kırlı, "Coffeehouses: Public Opinion in the Nineteenth Century Ottoman Empire," in Dale Eickelman and Armando Salvatore, eds., *Public Islam and the Common Good* (Leiden: E J Brill, 2004), 75–98 and "Kahvehaneler ve Hafiyeler: 19. Yüzyıl Ortalarında Osmanlı'da Sosyal Kontrol," *Toplum ve Bilim* 83 (Winter), 58–79.
13. Carter V. Findley, *Ottoman Civil Officialdom: A Social History* (Princeton: Princeton University Press, 1989), 22–3.
14. Martyn Lyons, "New Readers in the Nineteenth Century: Women, Children, Workers," in Cavallo and Chartier, eds., *A History of Reading in the West*, Linda G. Cochrane, trans. (Amherst, MA: University of Massachusetts Press, 1999), 327.
15. Even for Arabic speakers, there was of course a considerable gap between the language of the Qur'an and everyday speech.
16. For the details, see Fortna, *Imperial Classroom*, especially chapter 3.
17. Kitapçı Arakel, *Talim-i kıraat*. See, e.g., 31.
18. Ahmed Rasım, *Kıraat kitabı* (Istanbul: 1314[1898]), 2–4.
19. Ali İrfan [Eğribozu], *Vatanı seven okusun* (Dersaadet: Mahmud Bey Matbaası, 1324[1908]), 3–4.
20. For the details, see Fortna, *Imperial Classroom*, especially chapter 6.
21. Ahmed Midhat, *Terbiyeli çocuk Mubtediler için kıraat kitabı* (Istanbul: Kırkambar Matbaası, 1303[1887]), 4.
22. Ibid.
23. Ibid., 2.
24. Cf. Arakel, *Talim-i kıraat*.

25. Ibid., 10.
26. M. Safvet, *Kıraat* (Kostantiniye: Matbaa-yi Ebuzziya, 1308[1892]), 5.
27. Faik Reşat, *Kıraat* (Istanbul: Karabet, 1313[1897]).
28. Ahmed Rasım, *Kızlara mahsus kıraat kitabı* (Istanbul: Karabet, 1316[1900]), 21–2.
29. Arakel, *Talim-i kıraat*, 8.
30. Ali İrfan, *Ma'lumat-i diniye* (Istanbul: Şirket-i Muretibbiye Matbaası, 1329[1911]), 1.
31. Okay, *Eski Harfli*, 126.
32. Erol Köroğlu, *Türk Edebiyatı ve Birinci Dünya Savaşı (1914–1918): Propagandadan Millî Kimlik İnşasına* (Istanbul: İletişim, 2004), 135–7.
33. Nazan Çiçek, "The Project of Creating True Turkish Children: The Children's Magazines in Turkey circa the Foundation of the Republic." Paper presented at the annual meetings of the British Society for Middle Eastern Studies, Birmingham, July 2006. My thanks to Dr Çiçek for making this available to me.
34. Jessica Selma Tiregöl, "The Role of Primary Education in Nation-state-building: The Case of the Early Turkish Republic," (PhD Diss., Princeton University, 1998), 114–16. I am grateful to Şükrü Hanioğlu for bringing this work to my attention.
35. Tiregöl, "The Role of Primary Education," 114–16.
36. Ibid., 117.
37. Leyla Neyzi, "Object or Subject? The Paradox of 'Youth," in Turkey *IJMES* 33 (2001), 416.
38. *Çocuklara kıraat* 1 (1 Safer 1299[23 December 1881]), 3.
39. Ali İrfan, *Birinci kıraat* (Istanbul: İkbal Kütüphanesi/Şems Matbaası, 1328–1330[1910–1912]), author's preface.
40. Ibid., 6–7.
41. Ibid., 8.
42. Ibid., 8.
43. Navaro-Yashin, *Faces of the State*, 47.
44. Paul Dumont, "La literature enfantine turque," in Paul Dumont, ed., *Turquie: Livres d'hier livres d'aujourd'hui* (Istanbul: Isis, 1992), 79.
45. *Yeni Yol* 20 (17 Kanunusâni 1340[17 January 1924]), 274.
46. Ibid., 275.
47. Mustafa Kemal Atatürk, *Nutuk* (Istanbul: Bordo Siyah Klasik Yayınlar, 2007), 798–9.
48. *Yeni Yol* 10 (8 Teşrin-i sâni 1339[8 November 1923]), 153.
49. Ibid.
50. Fortna, "Education and Autobiography," 12–15.
51. Ariès, *Centuries of Childhood*, 215. Whereas the eighteenth-century French case he describes involves a mother's insistence that her son be educated outside the home in a Latin school run by a priest, in the nineteenth-century Ottoman empire the struggle is usually between either a military or civil or a religiously- or state-supplied school.
52. Fortna, "Education and Autobiography," 12 ff.
53. Ali Nazima, *Oku yahud yeni risale-i ahlâk ve vezaif-i etfal* (Read, or the new treatise on morals and children's duties) (Istanbul: Kasbar Matbaası, 1320[1904]), 4. An interesting feature of this particular text is its juxtaposition of regular

printed type (kitap yazı) with a handwritten text (mektup yazı) on facing pages. Some sections appear entirely in the *rıka* script, the most common handwriting style of the late Ottoman period. It seems that the author, himself an assistant director at the School of Civil Administration (Mülkiye Mektebi) and the Imperial University, was seeking to encourage the practical literacy of his readers by presenting them with a printed example. The preoccupation with the mechanics of writing, already apparent in the late Ottoman period, would become much more assertive in the early Republic.

54. Ali Nazima, *Oku*, 6.
55. Tiregöl, 92.
56. T. C., *İlmektepler Talimatnamesi* (Ankara: Bakanlık, 1929) 3; 13.
57. Ahmed Cevad, *Cumhuriyet çocuklarına Türkçe kıraat*. İlk mektep, birinci sınıf. (Istanbul: Marifet Matbaası, 1929), 3.
58. Ibid., 6.
59. Ibid.
60. Ibid, 9.
61. Ibid., 12. Accompanying the poem is an illustration of a boy and a girl saluting the flag. The boy is wearing a kerchief akin to those worn by the Boy Scouts.
62. Ibid., 17.
63. Ibid., 18.
64. Tiregöl, 79.
65. Navaro-Yashin, *Faces*, 11.
66. Paul Dumont, "La literature enfantine turque," in Paul Dumont, ed., *Turquie: Livres d'hier livres d'aujourd'hui* (Istanbul: Isis, 1992), 79.
67. Ibid.
68. Büşra Ersanlı Behar, *İktidar ve Tarih: Türkiye'de "Resmi Tarih"Tezinin Oluşumu* (Istanbul: AFA Yayınları, 1992); Navaro-Yashin, *Faces*, 48.
69. Navaro-Yashin, *Faces*, 48.
70. Ahmed Cevad, *Cumhuriyet Çocuklarına Türkçe kıraat* 1:1, 85–6.
71. Kazım Sevinç, *Türk Yavrularına Yurt Bilgisi*. Sınıf 5, 28, as cited in İnce, "Citizenship," 163.
72. Tiregöl, 93, note.
73. Ahmed Rasım, *İbtidaî Kıraat* (Dersaadet [Istanbul]: Şems Matbaası, 1328–1330[1910–1912]), 16.
74. Ahmed Rasım, *Doğru usûl-i kıraat* 5. Kısım (Istanbul: Kanaat Kitaphanesi, 1926), 55–7.
75. On the subject of cartography and political affiliation in the Ottoman and Turkish context, see Etienne Copeaux, *Espaces et temps de la nation turque: Analyse d'une historiographice nationaliste, 1931–1993* (Paris: CNRS Editions, 1997) and Fortna, "Change in the School Maps of the Late Ottoman Empire," *Imago Mundi* 57:1 (2005), 23–34.
76. Sadrettin Celal, *Cümhuriyet Çocuklarına Sevimli Kıraat* (Istanbul: Kanaat Kütüphanesi, 1928), 4–8.
77. Sadrettin Celal, 8. The not-yet-standard spellings in the title and text reflect the uncertainties ushered in with the alphabet change.
78. Brummett, *Image and Imperialism*, 22.
79. On the symbolism of the sailor suit in the British context, see Clare Rose, "Imperialism and consumerism in the late Victorian sailor suit," *Journal of*

Maritime Research (forthcoming). In the Ottoman context, this style of dress seems to convey modernity and a sense of being part of the international scene.

80. Cüneyd Okay, *Osmanlı Çocuk Hayatında Yenileşmeler, 1850–1900* (Istanbul: Kırkambar Yayınları, 1998).
81. Guzine Dino, *La genèse du roman turc au XIXe siècle.* (Paris: Publications Orientalistes de France, 1973), 45 and Güzine Dino, "Le cycle urbain de la Hikaye," in R Dor and M Nicolas, eds., *Quand le crible était dans la paille...Homage à Pertev Naili Boratav* (Paris: Maisonneuve et Larose, 1978), 152.
82. Somel, 250.
83. Lyons, 327.
84. Serdar Öztürk, "Efforts to Modernize Chapbooks during the Initial Years of the Turkish Republic," *European Historical Quarterly* 40 (2010), 7–34.
85. Strauss, "Who Read What," 50.
86. Ibid., 50–1.
87. Ibid., 51.
88. Seyhan Kübra Esmer, "Cumhuriyet Dönemi'nin İlk Yıllarında (1923–1928) Yayımlayan Çocuk Dergilerindeki Tahkiyeli Metinlerin Çocuklara Değer Aktarımı Açısından Değerlendirilmesi" MA Thesis. (Gazi University, 2007), 131. Interestingly, the forever-unattainable figure of Leyla reappears metaphorically at the time of Republic's seventy-fifth anniversary celebrations as a symbol for a poet's dream of the Republic that remains equally elusive. Leyla Neyzi, "Object or Subject?," 425–6.
89. *Haftalık Resimli Gazetemiz* 1 (13 Teşrin-i sani 1340[13 November 1924]): 1; 2 (20 Teşrin-i sani 1340[20 November 1924]): 3, as cited in Esmer, 272–3.
90. See, for example, the following cover illustrations: *Çocuk Dünyası* 10 (16 Mayıs 1321[29 May 1905]) (airplanes); *Çocuk Duygusu* 9 (1 Ağustos 1321[14 August 1905]) (hot air balloon) and *Mini Mini* 6 (19 Haziran 1330[2 July 1914]) (the telephone).
91. *Yeni Yol* 43 (25 Eylul 1340[25 July 1924]). Inside, an article in the "scientific section" encourages the young readers to ponder a series of remarkable future inventions.
92. Paul Dumont, "Si Evliya Çelebi visitait le turquie d'aujourd'hui...," in Paul Dumont, ed., *Turquie: Livres d'hier livres d'aujourd'hui* (Istanbul: Isis, 1992), vi–vii. There will be more to say about the ways in which printed books supplanted manuscripts in Chapter 5.
93. On printing in the Ottoman Empire, see Klaus Kreiser, *The Beginnings of Printing in the Near and Middle East: Jews, Christians and Muslims* (Wiesbaden: Harrassowitz in Kimmission, 2001), Sinan Kuneralp, "Les debuts de l'imprimerie à Istanbul, 1800–1908," in Paul Dumont, ed., *Turquie: Livres d'hier, livres d'aujourd'hui* (Istanbul: Editions Isis, 1992), 1–4.
94. M. Şükrü Hanioğlu, *A Brief History of the Late Ottoman Empire* (Princeton: Princeton University Press, 2008), 29 ff. In Hanioğlu's sampling of the inheritance (tereke) registers for the Hicrî years 1164 (1750–1751) and 1215 (1800–1801), only one person bequeathed more than ten books and many, including the only teenager listed, had none.
95. Frédéric Hitzel, "Manuscrits, livres et culture livresque à Istanbul," *REMMM* 87–88 (1999), 31.

96. Strauss, "Who Read What," 47.
97. Hitzel, 28–9. For similar changes at institutions such as the Khalidiyya Library in Jerusalem, see Ayalon, 94 ff.
98. Ahmed Rasım, *İlaveli hazine-i mekâtib yahud mükemmel münşeât* (Istanbul: Feridiye Matbaası, 1318[1902]).
99. Ibid., 307.
100. *Yeni Yol* 22 (31 Kanunisâni 1340[31 January 1924]).
101. Ahmed Rasım, *Doğru usûl-i kıraat*, 62.
102. *Yeni Yol* 8 (25 Teşrin-i evvel 1339[25 October 1923]), 4. *Kızılelma* was the title of a collection of poetry written by Ziya Gökalp and published in 1914.
103. Murat Ateş, "Ziya Gökalp ve Çocuk Edebiyatı," www.sosyalbil.selcuk.edu.tr/sos_mak/makaleler%5CMurat%20ATEŞ%5C95–114.pdf
104. Esmer, 210.
105. *Yeni Yol* 25 (23 Şubat 1340[23 February 1924]).
106. Arakel, *Talim-i kıraat*, 62.
107. Ahmed Cevad, *Çocuklara sarf ve nahv dersleri: Turkçe okuyorum* (Istanbul: Matbaa-i Hayriye, 1326[1910]), 3–4.
108. Ibid., 12.
109. Tüccarzâde İbrahim Hilmi, *Altın Kitab[:] Çocuklara ilk kıraat* (Istanbul: 1327[1911]), 3, 9, 10.
110. Esmer, 22.
111. *Yeni Yol* 13 (29 Teşrin-i sani 1339[29 November 1923]).
112. *Yeni Yol* 15 (13 Kanunelevvel 1339[13 December 1923]).
113. For a more detailed treatment of maps in the service of late Ottoman education, see Fortna, "Change in the School Maps of the Late Ottoman Empire," *Imago Mundi: The International Journal for the History of Cartography* 57:1 (2005): 23–34.
114. Ahmed Rasım, *Kıraat kitabı*. Birinci sene. (Istanbul: Karabet Matbaası, 1313[1897]), 6.
115. *Birinci kıraat*, 5.
116. Faik Sabri [Duran], *Çocuklara ilk coğrafya kıraatları* (Istanbul: Marifet Matbaası, 1926).
117. Tüccarzâde İbrahim Hilmi, *Altın Kitab[:] Çocuklara ilk kıraat* (Istanbul: Kitabhane-i Askeri: 1327[1911], 35.
118. Ibid., 37.

4 Mechanics: Text and Image

1. Stephen Lovell, *The Russian Reading Revolution: Print Culture in the Soviet and Post-Soviet Eras* (Houndmills, Basingstoke: Macmillan, 2000), 1 (citing Manguel, 27–39).
2. Maryanne Wolf, *Proust and the Squid: The Story and Science of the Reading Brain* (Cambridge: Icon Books, 2008), 3–10. Thanks to Sarah Fortna for this reference.
3. As cited in Wolf, 19.
4. Fischer, *History*, 11.
5. Halide Nusret [Zorlutuna], *Bir Devrin Romanı* (Ankara: Kültür Bakanlığı, 1978).

6. After 1928 and the Republic's adoption of a Latin-based script, they would of course even have appeared equally odd even to those whose mother tongue was Arabic.

7. The sense of the Arabic is: I seek refuge in God from the cursed Devil. In the name of God, the merciful, the compassionate.

8. Ibid., 9.

9. Ibid., 10.

10. Martyn Lyons, "New Readers in the Nineteenth Century: Women, Children, Workers," in Chartier and Cavallo, eds., *A History of Reading in the West* (Amherst, MA: University of Massachusetts Press, 1999), 326.

11. The first letter of the Arabic alphabet, a single vertical stroke.

12. Zorlutuna, 10.

13. Cf. a range of other experiences with first reading, e.g., İrfan Orga, *Portrait of a Turkish Family* (London: Victor Gollancz, 1950; repr. Eland, 1988); Halide Edip, *Memoirs of Halidé Edib* (London: John Murray, 1926).

14. Sabiha Zekeriya Sertel, *Yeni Kıraat* (Istanbul: Resimli Ay Matbaası, 1928), 3.

15. Sertel, *Yeni Kıraat*, 4–5.

16. Brooks, *When Russia Learned to Read*, chapter IX.

17. Aziz Berker, *Türkiyede İlk Öğretim, 1839–1908* (Ankara: Millî Eğitim Basımevi, 1945), 133.

18. Ibid., 133.

19. Ibid., 133–4.

20. Ibid., 135.

21. Ibid., 136.

22. *Gürbüz Türk Çocuğu* (23 April 1927).

23. İbrahim Alaettin Gövsa, *Türk Meşhurları Ansiklopedisi* (Istanbul: Yedigün, 1938), 350.

24. Selim Sabit, *Rehnüma-yı muallimin: Sıbyan mekteblerine mahsus usûl-i tedrisiye* (Istanbul: Matbaa-i Amire, n.d.), 7.

25. On the "jadid" movement, see Adeeb Khalid, *The Politics of Muslim Cultural Reform: Jadidism in Central Asia* (Berkeley, CA: University of California Press, 1998).

26. Selim Sabit, *Rehnüma-yı muallimin*, 10. It is interesting to note the linkage between teaching the alphabet and teaching the Qur'an. As Aziz Berker has remarked, late Ottoman primary school schedules persistently allocate prime instructional hours to these two subjects, 12 out of 22 hours per week in the first year. Berker, *Türkiye'de İlk Öğretim*, 152.

27. Selim Sabit, *Rehnüma-yı muallimin*, 10–11.

28. Servet Safi, *Nev usûl elifbâ-yi osmanî* (Dersaadet: Kasbar, 1310[1894]).

29. Ibid., 4–5.

30. Ibid., 5.

31. Ibid., 7.

32. Ibid., 14.

33. Ibid., 24 ff.

34. N.a, *Elifbâ: Qura mekatib-i ibtidaiyesinde okutturulmasını* (Istanbul: Matbaa-i Amire, 1317[1901]).

35. *Elifbâ*, 16.

36. Ali İrfan, *Birinci kıraat*, 56–7.

37. Ahmed Cevad, *Resimli osmanlı lisanı* (Dersaadet: Kütüphane-i İslam ve Askeri, 1332[1916]), 3.

38. Ibid., 70.
39. [Encümen-i ilmî], *Yeni harflarla elifbâ* (Istanbul: Matbaa-yi hayriye ve şürekası, 1333[1917]).
40. Ali İrfan [Eğribozu], *Son Elifbâ-yı Osmanî* (Istanbul: Şems Matbaası, 1328–30[1910–1912]).
41. [T. C. Dil Encümeni], *Yeni Dil Encümeni Alfabesi* ([Istanbul]: Devlet Matbaası, 1928), 5.
42. Ibid., 6, 12.
43. Ali İrfan, *Son Elifbâ-yı Osmanî*, 7.
44. Ahmed Cevad, *Altın Alfabe* (Istanbul: Hilmi Kitabhanesi, 1928), 5.
45. M. Turan, *Öz Türk dilile Kolay okutan Alfabe* (n.p.: Maarif Kitabevi, 1935–1936).
46. Symbol of the party's six principles: republicanism, secularism (laiklik), nationalism, populism, statism and revolutionism. For the details, see Zürcher, *Turkey*, 181–2.
47. M. Turan, *Öz Türk*, 31–2.
48. İsa Yavuz and Nezahat Yavuz, *Harfli Alfabe* (Istanbul: Emek İş Yayınevi, 1973).
49. Wolf, 8–9.
50. Brummett, *Image and Imperialism*, 23.
51. Ahmed Cevad, *Resimli Osmanlı Lisanı*, 35.
52. Ibid., 44.
53. Ibid., 70.
54. Ibid., 80–1.
55. Sadrettin Celal, *Cümhuriyet Çocuklarına Sevimli Kırâat. Üçüncü sınıf.* (Istanbul: Kanâat Kütüphanesi, 1929).
56. T. C. Kültür Bakanlığı, *Okuma Kitabı.* Birinci Sınıf (Istanbul: Devlet Basımevi, 1935), 21–3. For an analysis of early Republican textbooks devoted to cementing the correlation between Turkishness, Turkey and the Turks, see Ince, "Citizenship."
57. Cüneyd Okay, "Eski Harfli Çocuk Dergileri" *Türkiye Araştırmaları Literatür Dergisi* 4:7 (2006), 511–18.
58. *Yeni Yol* 46 (16 Teşrin-i evvel 1340[16 October 1924]).
59. Martyn Lyons, "New Readers in the Nineteenth Century: Women, Children, Workers," in Chartier and Cavallo, eds., *A History of Reading in the West* (Amherst, MA: University of Massachusetts Press, 1999), 332.
60. *Yeni Yol* 57 (1 Kanun-i Sani 1341[1 January 1925]).
61. *Bizim Mecmua* 2 (12 April 1922), 4. The term of address for the teacher, Muallim Bey, marks him as a secularly trained teacher, and not a member of the ulema.
62. *Yeni Yol* 66 (5 Mart 1341[5 March 1925]).
63. James Leith, "Ephemera: Civic Education through Images," in Robert Darnton and Daniel Roche, eds., *Revolution in Print: The Press in France, 1775–1800* (Berkeley, CA: University of California Press, 1989), 270.
64. For a fuller treatment of this phenomenon and a discussion of its potentially radical effects, see my "Reading, Hegemony and Counterhegemony in the Late Ottoman Empire and Early Turkish Republic," in John Chalcraft and Yaseen Noorani, eds., *Counterhegemony in the Colony and Postcolony* (Houndmills: Palgrave Macmillan, 2007), 141–54.

5   Commodification and the Market

1. On the role of capitalism in transforming the timeless exchange of commodities into the distinctively modern form of commodification, see Charles Tripp, *Islam and the Moral Economy: The Challenge of Capitalism* (Cambridge: Cambridge University Press, 2006), 3–4.
2. Ami Ayalon, *Reading Palestine: Printing and Literacy, 1900–1948* (Austin, TX: University of Texas Press, 2004).
3. Lovell, 7 ff.; Ayalon, 156–7.
4. Navarro-Yashin, *Faces of the State*, 78.
5. Ibid., 79.
6. Alfred Gell, "Newcomers to the World of Goods: Consumption among Muria Gonds," in Arjun Appadurai, ed., *The Social Life of Things: Commodities in Cultural Perspective* (Cambridge: Cambridge University Press, 1986), as quoted in Navarro-Yashin, *Faces of the State*, 111, note 32.
7. Ahmed Midhat, *Terbiyeli Çocuk. Mubtediler icin kıraat kitabı* (Istanbul: Kırkambar Matbaası, 1303), 8–9. This book was part of series called Çocuklar kütüphanesi (The children's library).
8. A. Rıza, *Kızlara mahsus kıraat kitabı* (Istanbul: Karabet, 1316[1900]), 22.
9. Ali İrfan, *Birinci Kıraat* (Istanbul: Şems Matbaası, 1328–1330[1910–12]), 56 ff.
10. Ali Nazima, *Oku yahud yeni risale-i ahlâk ve vezaif-i etfal* (Istanbul: Kasbar Matbaası, 1320[1904]), 4–6.
11. T.C., *İlkmektepler Talimatnamesi* (Ankara: Bakanlık, 1929), 18–19.
12. Ibid., 50–1.
13. Ayalon, 103.
14. Zehra Öztürk, "Osmanlı Döneminde Kıraat Meclislerinde Okunan Halk Kitapları," *Türkiye Araştırmaları Literatür Dergisi* 5: 9 (2007), 401–45.
15. Hitzel, "Manuscrits, livres et culture livresque à Istanbul," *REMMM* 87–88 (1999): 29.
16. Ayalon, 46–7, 95.
17. Erkan Serçe, *İzmir'de Kitapçılık (1839–1928)* 2nd edn. (İzmir: İzmir Büyükşehir Belediyesi Kültür Yayını, 2002), 76 ff.
18. The connection between cinema and the nation, identified by Elizabeth Thompson in the context of Syria, but the Turkish case awaits a full treatment. Elizabeth Thompson, *Colonial Citizens: Republican Rights, Paternal Privilege, and Gender in French Syria and Lebanon* (New York: Columbia University Press, 2000), chapter 12.
19. Serçe, 85.
20. François Georgeon, "Les cafés à Istanbul à la fin de l'Empire ottoman," in Hélène Desmet-Grégoire and François Georgeon, eds., *Cafés d'Orient revisités* (Paris: CNRS, 1997), 39.
21. Cengiz Kırlı, "Coffeehouses: Public Opinion in the Nineteenth-Century Ottoman Empire," in Armando Salvatore and Dale Eickelman, eds., *Public Islam and the Common Good* (Leiden: Brill, 2004),
22. Hitzel, "Manuscrits," 32.
23. Ibid.
24. For the importance of postal subscription to the development of the Greek press in the empire, see Marina Marks, "The Ottoman Greek Press (1830–1862)" PhD diss., University of London (forthcoming).

25. *Bizim Mecuma* 2nd run (18 March 1925), 1.
26. *Yeni Yol* 10 (8 Teşrin-i sani 1339[8 November 1923]), 146.
27. *Yeni Yol* 65 (1341[1925]).
28. *Çocuklara Mahsus Gazete* 2 (22 Zilhicce 1313[4 June 1896]).
29. *Çocuklara Rehber* 1 (20 Zilkade 1314[22 April 1897]).
30. Okay, *Eski*, 176.
31. *Yeni Yol* 33 (19 Nisan 1340) 149–50.
32. Tarık Buğra, *Güneş Rengi Bir Yığın Yaprak* (Istanbul: Ötüken, 1996), 43 ff.
33. Ibid., 51.
34. Johann Strauss, "Romanlar, Ah! O Romanlar! Les débuts de la lecture moderne dans l'Empire ottoman (1850–1900)" *Turcica* 26 (1994): 135.
35. Okay, *Osmanlı Çocuk*, 103–106.
36. *Bizim Mecmua* 7 (18 Mayıs 922[18 May 1922]).
37. *Yeni Yol* 25 (23 Şubat 1340[23 February 1924]).
38. See, for example, *Çocuklara Mahsus Gazete* 4 (7 Muharrem 1314[18 June 1896]), 62–3, listing exam results for student in years one through three at the Mirmiran Hasan Paşa Mekteb-i Feyziyesi in Istanbul.
39. *Yeni Yol* 18 (3 Kanun-i sani 1340[3 January 1924]).
40. *Yeni Yol* 103 (1 Nisan 1926[1 April 1926]).
41. *Yeni Yol* 104 (15 Nisan 1926[15 April 1926]).
42. Klaus Kreiser, "Causes of the Decrease of Ignorance? Remarks on the Printing of Books in the Ottoman Empire" in Klaus Kreiser, ed., *The Beginnings of Printing in the Near and Middle East: Jews, Christians and Muslims* (Wiesbaden: Harrassowitz, 2001), 16. Presses producing books in other scripts, such as Hebrew, Greek and Armenian, had been active for much longer.
43. Hitzel, "Manuscrits," 20.
44. Ibid., 15–16
45. Okay, *Eski*, 20–21. NB: In this period the *lira* was divided into 100 *kuruş*; the *kuruş* was in turn worth 40 *para*. For an overview of the Ottoman monetary system in this period, see Şevket Pamuk, "Money in the Ottoman Empire, 1326–1914" in Halil İnalcık with Donald Quataert, eds., *An Economic and Social History of the Ottoman Empire, 1300–1914* (Cambridge, Cambridge University Press, 1994), 970 ff.
46. Paul Dumont, "Said Bey – The Everyday Life of an Istanbul Townsman at the Beginning of the Twentieth Century" in Albert Hourani et al, eds., *The Modern Middle East: A Reader* (Berkeley, CA: University of California Press, 1993), 272.
47. Strauss, "Romanlar!," 135–6.

6 Lives of Reading and Writing

1. İrfan Orga, *Portrait of a Turkish Family* (London: Victor Gollancz, 1950), 31.
2. Orga, *Portrait*, 268.
3. Olivier Bouquet, "L'Autobiographie par l'État ches les derniers ottomans," *Turcica* 38 (2006): 251–79.
4. Orga, *Portrait*, 15.
5. Edhem Eldem, "L'écrit funéraire ottoman: création, reproduction, transmission," *REMMM* 75–6 (1995) *Oral et écrit dans le monde turco-ottoman*, 65–6.

6. See, for example, Ahmed Midhat, *Diplomalı kız. Letaif-i rivayat.* (Istanbul: Kırkambar Matbaası, 1307[1891]), 4, for just one of thousands of examples.
7. For a similar approach to the relationship between autobiography and learning to read, see Gretchen R. Galbraith, *Reading Lives: Reconstructing Childhood, Books, and Schools in Britain, 1870–1920* (Houndmills: Palgrave Macmillan, 1997).
8. On the life stories of the "children of the republic," see Esra Özyürek, *Nostalgia for the Modern: State Secularism and Everyday Politics in Turkey* (Durham, NC: Duke University Press, 2006), 29 ff.
9. It is interesting to note that not all memoirs say much about reading. For example, Orga's narrative, written in English and published in London, includes very few descriptions of reading, a remarkably unusual circumstance in the reminiscences of a future writer.
10. For a photograph of one of these posters in place during the early 1930s, see Bertaux, *Ulusu Tasarlamak/Projecting the Nation*, 273. The accompanying posters champion the virtues of civil marriage over the now presumably outmoded religious ceremony and of the infrastructural development achieved during the first decade of the Republic.
11. Her English memoirs, written when, having run afoul of Mustafa Kemal, she was in self-imposed exile in England, appeared in 1926. Her Turkish-language account of her childhood, *Mor Salkımlı Ev* (The House of Wisteria), was published in 1963.
12. *Memoirs of Halidé Edib* (London: John Murray, 1926), 11 (a passage later omitted in the Turkish version).
13. Ibid., 23.
14. Ibid., 24–5. On the ethnic pattern of life in Istanbul, see Çağlar Keyder, "A Brief History of Modern Istanbul," in Reşat Kasaba, ed., *The Cambridge History of Turkey Vol. 4: Turkey in the Modern World* (Cambridge: Cambridge University Press, 2008), 504–23.
15. Edib, *Memoirs*, 28.
16. Ibid., 59.
17. Ibid., 35.
18. Ibid., 79.
19. Ibid., 85–6.
20. Ibid., 86. For a full – and lyrical – German translation of this thirteenth-century poem of Yunus Emre, see Klaus Kreiser, *Istanbul: Ein Historicher Stadtführer* 2nd edn. (Munich: C. H. Beck, 2009), 232.
21. Edib, *Memoirs*, 88–9.
22. Ibid., 89–90.
23. Ibid., 91. As discussed in Chapter 4, Ottoman Turkish, like Arabic and Persian, is generally written without these vocalization marks inserted in the text. The work referred to here is thus an exception to the norm but it is a work that has proved impossible to trace.
24. Ibid., 116.
25. Şevket Süreyya [Aydemir], *Suyu Arayan Adam* 10th edn. (Istanbul: Remzi Kitabevi, 1997), 23.
26. A similar but much better understood phenomenon existed in neighboring Russia. Cf. Brooks, *When Russia Learned to Read.*
27. Aydemir, 23–4.

28. Ibid., 31.
29. Ibid., 30–1.
30. Ibid., 23–4.
31. Dr. Rıza Nur, *Hayat ve Hâtıratım* vol. 1 (Istanbul: Altındağ Yayınevi, 1967), 54,
32. Ibid., 60.
33. Ibid., 63.
34. Ibid., 65.
35. Ibid., 69.
36. Ibid., 70. Cf. Sertel, *Yeni Kıraat*, 3–5.
37. Dr Rıza Nur., 72.
38. Ibid.
39. Ibid., 73.
40. Ibid., 61.
41. Both his parents transmitted a "rich store of oral folk literature" to their son who was further influenced by the time he spent in northeastern Anatolia among his wife's family observing the lifestyle of the Turkish peasants. Fahir İz, "Mehmed Emīn." *Encyclopaedia of Islam* 2nd edn. Vol. VI, 986–7.
42. As cited in Mehmet Nuri Yardım, *Tanzimattan Günümüze Edebiyatçılarımızın Çocukluk Hatıraları* (Istanbul: Timas, 1998), 75.
43. For a neat synopsis of his life and work, see Cemil Koçak's prefatory comments, entitled "Hüseyin Cahit [Yalçın] ve Portreler Üzerine Bazı Notlar," in the volume Hüseyin Cahit [Yalçın], *Tanıdıklarım* (Istanbul: Yapı Kredi Yayınları, 2001), 7–19.
44. Hüseyin Cahit [Yalçın], *Edebiyat Anıları* (Istanbul: Türkiye İş Bankası Kültür Yayınları, 1975), 15.
45. Ibid. The author here refers to the exploits of Ali b. Abi Talib, the cousin and son-in-law of the Prophet Muhammad, in the Muslim conquest of the town of Khaybar in the Hijaz region of Arabia during the early days of Islamic history.
46. Ibid.
47. Ibid., 16.
48. Ibid., 17.
49. Ibid., 17–18.
50. Ibid., 18.
51. Ibid., 18–19.
52. Halide Nusret [Zorlutuna], *Bir Devrin Romanı* (Ankara: Kültür Bakanlığı, 1978), 17.
53. Engin Çizgen, *Photographer/Fotoğrafçı Ali Sami, 1866–1936* (Istanbul: Haşet, 1989), 76–7.
54. Zorlutuna, 17.
55. Reinhard Wittmann, "Was there a Reading Revolution at the End of the Eighteenth Century?," in Guglielmo Cavallo and Roger Chartier, eds., *A History of Reading in the West* (Amherst, MA: University of Massachusetts Press, 1999), 300.
56. [Zorlutuna], 18.
57. Ibid., 18–19.
58. Ibid., 49–50.
59. Ibid., 63.

60. Ibid.
61. On this issue, see Fortna, "Education and Autobiography," 28–9 and Kreiser, "Persisch als Schulsprache."
62. Zorlutuna, 63–4.
63. Ibid., 83.
64. Ibid., 84–5.
65. Özyürek, *Nostalgia for the Modern*, 29–30.
66. Suraiya Faroqhi, *Subjects of the Sultan: Culture and Everyday Life in the Ottoman Empire* (London: I B Tauris, 2005), 283.
67. *The Guardian*, "Waugh at the BBC," 15 April 2008, 9.
68. This would place the event in the year 1913, or when Halide was 12 years old. Okay, *Eski Harflı Çocuk Dergileri*, 119.
69. Zorlutuna, 97–8.
70. T.C. Kültür Bakanlığı, Millî Kütüphane Başkanlığı, *Türkiye Basmaları Kataloğu: Arap Harflı Eserler, 1729–1928* (Ankara: Millî Kütüphane Basımevi, 1990), 277.
71. Ahmed Rasım, *İlaveli hazine-i mekâtib yahud mükemmel-i münşeat* (Istanbul: Feridiye Matbaası, 1318[1902]), 2.
72. Ibid., 5–6.
73. Ibid., 17.
74. Mehmed Sedad, *Ameli usul-ü kitabet-i resmiye* (Dersaadet: Asır Matbaası, 1323[1907]).
75. Berker, 134.
76. Ibid., 134–5.
77. Ibid., 135.
78. T.C. Kültür Bakanlığı, Milli Kütüphane Başkanlığı, *Türkiye Basmaları Toplu Kataloğu, Arap Harflı Türkçe Eserler 1729–1928* 1. Cilt; 1. Bölüm (Ankara: Milli Kütühane Basımevi, 1990).
79. Strauss, "Romanlar," 134.
80. Bernard Lewis, "Ahmad Midhat." *Encyclopaedia of Islam.* Edited by: P. Bearman, Th. Bianquis, C.E. Bosworth, E. van Donzel and W.P. Heinrichs. Brill, 2008. *Brill Online.* S.O.A.S (soas). Accessed 2 April 2008.
81. Burcu Akan Ellis, personal communication, April 2008.
82. BOA, D.SAID (Sicill-i Ahvâl Komisyonu Defterleri) 141/187.
83. Ahmed Cevad, *İnkilab-i hakikam metin ahlâk ile olur* (Dersaadet[Istanbul]: Kader Matbaası, 1328[1912]).
84. Lewis, *Turkish Language Reform*, 60.
85. William L. Cleveland, *The Making of an Arab Nationalist: Ottomanism and Arabism in the Life and Thought of Sati` al-Husri* (Princeton, NJ: Princeton University Press, 1971).

7   Conclusion: Reading and Modernity

1. Ahmet Emin Yalman, *The Development of Modern Turkey as Measured by Its Press* (New York: Columbia University Press, 1914), 19–20.
2. Igor Kopytoff, "The Cultural Biography of Things: Commoditization as Process," in Arjun Appadurai, ed., *The Social Life of Things: Commodities in Cultural Perspective* (Cambridge: Cambridge University Press, 1986), 73.

3. Arjun Appadurai, "Disjunction and Difference in the Global Cultural Economy," in Patrick Williams and Laura Chrisman, eds., *Colonial Discourse and Post-Colonial Theory* (New York: Columbia University Press, 1994), 325.
4. Arjun Appadurai, *Modernity at Large: Cultural Dimensions of Globalization* (Minneapolis: University of Minnesota Press, 1996), 83–4.

Bibliography

A. Rıza. *Kızlara mahsus kıraat kitabı*. (Istanbul: Karabet, 1316[1900]).

Ahmed Cevad. *Altın Alfabe*. (Istanbul: Hilmi Kitabhanesi, 1928).

——. *Çocuklara sarf ve nahv dersleri: Turkçe okuyorum*. (Istanbul: Matbaa-i Hayriye, 1326[1910]).

——. *Cumhuriyet Çocuklarina Türkçe Kıraat*. İlk mektep, birinci sınıf. (Istanbul: Hilmi [also Marifet], 1929).

——. *İnkilab-i hakikam metin ahlâk ile olur*. (Dersaadet [Istanbul]: Kader Matbaası, 1328[1912]).

——. *Güzel Kıraat*. (Istanbul: Kutubhane-i İslam ve Askeri Ibrahim Hilmi, 1335[1919]).

——. *Resimli osmanlı lisanı*. (Dersaadet: Kütüphane-i İslam ve Askeri, 1332[1916]).

——. *Yeni elifbâ[:] Kuranı okuyorum*. (Istanbul: Matbaa-i Amire, 1342[1926]).

Ahmed Midhat. *Diplomalı kız. Letaif-i rivayat*. (Istanbul: Kırkambar Matbaası, 1307[1891]).

——. *Terbiyeli çocuk; Mubtediler icin kıraat kitabı*. (Istanbul: Kırkambar Matbaası, 1303[1887]).

Ahmed Rasım. *Doğru usûl-i kıraat*. 5. Kısım. (Istanbul: İkdam (and Kanaat), 1926).

——. *Falaka*. (Istanbul: Hamid Matbaası, 1927).

——. *İbtidaî kıraat*. (Dersaadet [Istanbul]: Şems matbaası, 1328–1330[1910–1912]).

——. *İlaveli hazine-i mekâtib yahud mükemmel münşeât*. (Istanbul: Feridiye Matbaası, 1318[1902]).

——. *Kıraat kitabı*. Birinci sene. (Istanbul: Karabet, 1313[1897] and 1314 [1898]).

——. *Kızlara mahsus kıraat kitabı*. (Istanbul: Karabet, 1316[1900]).

——. *Osmanlı Tarihi*. (Istanbul: İstepan Matbaası, 1307[1890]).

Ali İrfan [Eğribozu]. *Birinci kıraat*. (Istanbul: İkbal Kütüphanesi/Şems Matbaası, 1328–1330[1910–1912]).

——. [Eğribozu]. *Çocuklara İstifade[:] Tehzib-i Ahlâk ve Malûmat-ı Nafia*. (Istanbul: Şirket-i Murettibiye Matbaası, 1304[1888]).

——. [Eğribozu]. *Ma'lumat-i diniye*. (Istanbul: Şirket-i Muretibbiye Matbaası, 1329[1911]).

——. [Eğribozu]. *Şiven Yahud Hatirat-i Şebabim*. (Izmir: Ahenk Matbaası, 1315[1899]).

——. [Eğribozu]. *Son Elifbâ-yı Osmanî*. (Istanbul: Şems Matbaası, 1328–1330[1910–1912]).

——. [Eğribozu]. *Vatanı seven okusun*. (Dersaadet: Mahmud Bey Matbaası, 1324[1908]).

Ali Nazima. *Oku yahud yeni risale-i ahlâk ve vezaif-i etfal*. (Istanbul: Kasbar Matbaası, 1320[1904]).

Alkan, Mehmet Ö. "Modernization from Empire to Republic and Education in the Process of Nationalism," in Kemal Karpat, ed., *Ottoman Past and Today's Turkey*. (Leiden: Brill, 2000), 47–132.

Altuğ, Sumru, Alpay Filiztekin and Şevket Pamuk, "Sources of Long Term Economic Growth for Turkey, 1880–2005," *European Review of Economic History* 12 (2008), 393–430.

Anderson, Benedict R. O'G. *Imagined Communities: Reflections on the Origin and Spread of Nationalism*. 2nd edn. (London: Verso, 1991).

Appadurai, Arjun. "Disjunction and Difference in the Global Cultural Economy," in Patrick Williams and Laura Chrisman, eds., *Colonial Discourse and Post-Colonial Theory*. (New York: Columbia University Press, 1994), 324–39.

Appadurai, Arjun. *Modernity at Large: Cultural Dimensions of Globalization*. (Minneapolis: University of Minnesota Press, 1996).

Arakel, "Kitapçı" *Talim-i kıraat: malumat-i ibtidaiye ve nasayih-i nafia*. vol. 1 (Istanbul: Kitapcı Arakel Matbaası, 1304[1887]).

Arat, Yeşim. "Nation Building and Feminism in early Republican Turkey," in C Kerslake, K Öktem and P Robins, eds., *Turkey's Engagement with Modernity: Conflict and Change in the Twentieth Century*. (Houndmills: Palgrave Macmillan, 2010), 38–51.

Ariès, Philippe. *Centuries of Childhood: A Social History of Family Life*. Robert Baldick, trans. (New York: Vintage, 1962).

Atatürk, Mustafa Kemal. *Nutuk*. (Istanbul: Bordo Siyah Klasik Yayınlar, 2007).

Ateş, Murat. "Ziya Gökalp ve Çocuk Edebiyatı" www.sosyalbil.selcuk.edu.tr/ sos_mak/makaleler%5CMurat%20ATEŞ%5C95–114.pdf.

Aydemir, Şevket Süreyya. *Suyu Arayan Adam*. 10th edn. (Istanbul: Remzi Kitabevi, 1997).

Ayalon, Ami. *Reading Palestine: Printing and Literacy, 1900–1948*. (Austin, TX: University of Texas Press, 2004).

Barro, Robert J. "Human Capital and Growth," *The American Economic Review* 91: 2 (May 2001).

BOA, D.Said (Sicill-i Ahvâl Komisyonu Defterleri).

Bayar, Yeşim. "The Dynamic Nature of Educational Policies and Turkish Nation Building: Where Does Religion Fit In?," *CSSAAME* 29: 3 (2009), 360–70.

Bayly, C. A. *The Birth of the Modern World, 1780–1914: Global Connections and Comparisons*. (Oxford: Blackwell, 2004).

[Bedros] Zeki. *Rehnüma-yı kıraat ve tercüme*. Üçüncü sene. (Istanbul: Arak Garoyan Matbaası, 1327[1911]).

Belge, Murat. "*Genç Kalemler* and Turkish Nationalism," in C. Kerslake, K. Öktem and P. Robins, eds., *Turkey's Engagement with Modernity: Conflict and Change in the Twentieth Century*. (Houndmills: Palgrave Macmillan, 2010), 27–37.

Berker, Aziz. *Türkiyede İlk Öğretim, 1839–1908*. (Ankara: Millî Eğitim Basımevi, 1945).

Berkes, Niyazi. *The Development of Secularism in Turkey*. 2nd edn. (New York: Routledge, 1998).

Berktay, Halil. *Cumhuriyet İdeolojisi ve Fuad Köprülü*. (Istanbul: Kaynak Yayınları, 1983).

Bertaux, Sandrine. *Ulusu Tasarlamak:1920'ler ve 1930'larda Avrupa Devletleri/ Projecting the Nation: European States in the 1920s and 1930s*. (Istanbul: Osmanlı Bankası Arşiv ve Araştırma Merkezi, 2006).

Bizim Mecmua.

Bouquet, Olivier. "L'Autobiographie par l'État ches les derniers ottomans," *Turcica* 38 (2006): 251–79.

Brockett, Gavin D. *How Happy to Call Oneself a Turk: Print Culture and the Negotiation of a Muslim National Identity in Modern Turkey.* (Austin, TX: University of Texas Press, forthcoming).

Brooks, Jeffrey. *When Russia Learned to Read: Literacy and Popular Literature, 1861–1917* (Princeton: Princeton University Press, 1985).

Brummett, Palmira. *Image and Imperialism in the Ottoman Revolutionary Press, 1908–1911.* (Albany, NY: State University of New York Press, 2000).

Buğra, Tarık. *Güneş Rengi Bir Yığın Yaprak.* (Istanbul: Ötüken, 1996).

Bulliett, Richard W. "First Names and Political Change in Modern Turkey," *IJMES* 9 (1978), 489–95.

Cavallo, Guglielmo and Roger Chartier, eds. *A History of Reading in the West.* L. G. Cochrane, trans. (Amherst, MA: University of Massachusetts Press, 1999).

Celal, Sadrettin. *Cümhuriyet Çocuklarına Sevimli Kırâat.* (Istanbul Kanâat Kütüphânesi, 1928).

Celal, Sadrettin. *Cümhuriyet Çocuklarına Sevimli Kırâat.* Üçüncü sınıf. (Istanbul: Kanâat Kütüphanesi, 1929).

Chartier, Roger. *Cultural History: Between Practices and Representations.* Lydia G. Cochrane, trans. (Cambridge: Polity, 1988).

Chartier, Roger. *The Cultural Origins of the French Revolution.* Lydia G. Cochrane, trans. (Durham, NC: Duke University Press, 1991).

Çiçek, Nazan. "The Project of Creating True Turkish Children: The Children's Magazines in Turkey circa the Foundation of the Republic." Paper presented at the annual meetings of the British Society for Middle Eastern Studies, Birmingham, July 2006.

Çıtı Pıtı.

Çizgen, Engin. *Photographer/Fotoğrafçı Ali Sami, 1866–1936.* (Istanbul: Haşet, 1989).

Clayer, Nathalie. *Aux origines du nationalisme albanais; La naissance d'une nation majoritairement musulmane en Europe.* (Paris: Éditions Karthala, 2007).

Cleveland, William L. *The Making of an Arab Nationalist: Ottomanism and Arabism in the Life and Thought of Sati` al-Husri.* (Princeton, NJ, Princeton University Press, 1971).

Çocuk Dünyası.

Çocuklara Kıraat.

Çocuklara Mahsus Gazete.

Çocuklara Rehber.

Copeaux, Étienne. *Espaces et temps de la nation turque: Analyse d'une hisotoriographie nationaliste, 1931–1993.* (Paris: CNRS, 1997).

Copeaux, Étienne. *Une vision turque à travers les cartes de 1931 à nos jours.* (Paris: CNRS, 2002).

Darnton, Robert C. "The Forbidden Bestsellers of Prerevolutionary France," *Bulletin of the American Academy of Arts and Sciences* 43: 1 (October 1989), 17–45.

Darnton, Robert. "History of Reading," in Peter Burke, ed., *New Perspectives on Historical Writing.* (Cambridge: Polity, 1991).

Darnton, Robert. "Introduction," in Robert Darnton and Daniel Roche, eds., *Revolution in Print: The Press in France 1775–1800*. (Berkeley, CA: University of California Press, 1989).

Davison, Roderic. "Atatürk's Reforms: Back to the Roots," in Roderic Davison, *Essays in Ottoman and Turkish History, 1774–1923*. (Austin, TX: University of Texas Press, 1990).

DeMaria, Robert, Jr. *Samuel Johnson and the Life of Reading*. (Baltimore, MD: The Johns Hopkins University Press, 1997).

Dino, Guzine. *La genèse du roman turc au XIXe siècle*. (Paris: Publications Orientalistes de France, 1973).

Dino, Güzine. "Le cycle urbain de la Hikaye," in R Dor and M Nicolas, eds., *Quand le crible était dans la paille... Homage à Pertev Naili Boratav*. (Paris: Maisonneuve et Larose, 1978).

Doğan, Nuri. *Ders Kitapları ve Sosyalleşme (1876–1918)*. (Istanbul: Bağlam, 1994).

Dumont, Paul. "La littérature enfantine Turque," in P. Dumont, ed., *Turquie Livres d'hier livres d'aujourd'hui*. (Strasbourg and Istanbul: Études Turques, 1992).

Dumont, Paul. "Said Bey – The Everyday Life of an Istanbul Townsman at the Beginning of the Twentieth Century," in Albert Hourani et al., eds., *The Modern Middle East: A Reader*. (Berkeley, CA: University of California Press, 1993), 271–87.

Dumont, Paul. "Si Evliya Çelebi visitait le turquie d'aujourd'hui...," in Paul Dumont, ed., *Turquie: Livres d'hier livres d'aujourd'hui*. (Istanbul: Isis, 1992).

Edib, Halide. *Memoirs of Halidé Edip*. (London: John Murray, 1926).

Eickelman, Dale. "The Art of Memory: Islamic Education and its Social Reproduction," *Comparative Studies in Society and History* 20 (1978), 485–516.

Eisenstein, Elizabeth L. "An Unacknowledged Revolution Revisited," *The American Historical Review* 107:1 (February 2002), 87–105.

Eldem, Edhem. "L'écrit funéraire ottoman: création, reproduction, transmission," *REMMM* 75–6 (1995) *Oral et écrit dans le monde turco-ottoman*, 65–78.

[Encümen-i ilmî]. *Yeni harflarla elifbâ*. Istanbul: Matbaa-yi hayriye ve şürekası, 1333[1917].

Ersanlı Behar, Büşra. *İktidar ve Tarih: Türkiye'de "Resmi Tarih" Tezinin Oluşumu*. (Istanbul: AFA Yayınları, 1992).

Esmer, Seyhan Kübra. "Cumhuriyet Dönemi'nin İlk Yıllarında (1923–1928) Yayımlayan Çocuk Dergilerindeki Tahkiyeli Metinlerin Çocuklara Değer Aktarımı Açısından Değerlendirilmesi." MA Thesis, Gazi University, 2007.

Eşref, Ruşen, Mitat Sadullah and Necmettin Sadık. *Cümhuriyet Kıraati*. Kısım 3. (Istanbul: Tefeyyüz Kitaphanesi, 1928).

Faik Reşat. *Kıraat*. (Istanbul: Karabet, 1313[1897]).

Faik Sabri [Duran]. *Çocuklara ilk coğrafya kıraatları*. (Istanbul: Marifet Matbaası, 1926).

Faroqhi, Suraiya. *Subjects of the Sultan: Culture and Everyday Life in the Ottoman Empire*. (London: I B Tauris, 2005).

Findley, Carter Vaughn. "Knowledge and Education in the Modern Middle East: A Comparative View" in Georges Sabagh, ed., *The Modern Economic and Social History of the Middle East in its World Context*. (Cambridge: Cambridge University Press, 1989).

Findley, Carter Vaughn. *Ottoman Civil Officialdom: A Social History*. (Princeton: Princeton University Press, 1989).

Fischer, Steven Roger. *A History of Reading.* (London: Reaktion Books, 2003).

Fortna, Benjamin C. "Change in the School Maps of the Late Ottoman Empire," *Imago Mundi: The International Journal of the History of Cartography* 57 (2004), 23–34.

Fortna, Benjamin C. "Education and Autobiography at the End of the Ottoman Empire," *Die Welt des Islams* 41:1 (2001), 1–31.

Fortna, Benjamin C. *Imperial Classroom: Islam, the State, and Education in the Late Ottoman Empire.* (Oxford: Oxford University Press, 2002).

Fortna, Benjamin C. "Reading, Hegemony and Counterhegemony in the Late Ottoman Empire and Early Turkish Republic," in John Chalcraft and Yaseen Noorani, eds., *Counterhegemony in the Colony and Postcolony.* (Houndmills: Palgrave Macmillan, 2007).

Frierson, Elizabeth B. "Gender, Consumption and Patriotism: The Emergence of an Ottoman Public Sphere," in Salvatore and Eickelman, eds., *Public Islam and the Common Good.* (Leiden: Brill, 2004).

Frierson, Elizabeth B. "Unimagined Communities: Women, Education, and the State in the Late Ottoman Empire," *Critical Matrix* 9 (1995), 54–90.

Furet, François and Jacques Ozouf. *Reading and Writing: Literacy in France from Calvin to Jules Ferry.* (Cambridge: Cambridge University Press, 1982).

Galbraith, Gretchen R. *Reading Lives: Reconstructing Childhood, Books, and Schools in Britain, 1870–1920.* (Houndmills: Palgrave Macmillan, 1997).

Gell, Alfred. "Newcomers to the World of Goods: Consumption among Muria Gonds," in Arjun Appadurai, ed., *The Social Life of Things: Commodities in Cultural Perspective.* (Cambridge: Cambridge University Press, 1986).

Georgeon, François. "Les cafés à Istanbul au XIXe siècle" *Etudes turques et modernes.* Documents du travail, 1 (Mars 1992), 14–40.

Georgeon, François. "Les cafés à Istanbul à la fin de l'Empire ottoman," in Hélène Desmet-Grégoire and François Georgeon, eds., *Cafés d'Orient revisités.* (Paris: CNRS, 1997).

Georgeon, François. "Lire et écrire à la fin de l'Empire ottoman: quelques remarques introductives," *REMMM* 75–76 (1995), 169–79.

Goody, Jack. "Questions of Interface in Turkey," *REMMM* 75–76 (1995), 11–16.

Göçek, Fatma Müge. *Rise of the Bourgeoisie, Demise of Empire: Ottoman Westernization and Social Change.* (New York: Oxford University Press, 1996).

Gövsa, İbrahim Alaettin. *Türk Meşhurleri Ansiklopedisi.* (Istanbul: Yedigün, 1938).

The Guardian.

Gürbüz Türk Çocuğu.

Haftalık Resimli Gazetemiz.

Hâlid, Halil. *Diary of a Turk.* (London: Black, 1903).

Hanioğlu, M. Şükrü. *A Brief History of the Late Ottoman Empire.* (Princeton: Princeton University Press, 2008).

Hartmann, Martin. *Der Islamische Orient: Berichte und Forschungen. Vol. 3: Unpolitische Brief aus der Türkei.* (Berlin: Verlag Rudolf Haupt, 1910).

Hayford, Charles W. *To the People: James Yen and Village China.* (New York: Columbia University Press, 1990).

Heyd, Uriel. *Language Reform in Modern Turkey.* (Jerusalem: Israel Oriental Society, 1954).

Heywood, Colin [M.]. *A History of Childhood: Children and Childhood in the West from Medieval to Modern Times.* (Cambridge: Polity Press, 2001).

Hitzel, Frédéric. "Manuscrits, livres et culture livresque à Istanbul," *REMMM* 87–88 (1999), 19–34.

Hobsbawm, E. J. *Nations and Nationalism since 1780: Programme, Myth, Reality*. (Cambridge: Cambridge University Press, 1990).

[İnanç], Muallim Cevdet. *Çocuklar için ... Hayat bilgisine uygun yazilar ve temsiller*. [Balıkesir:] Türk Dili, 1943.

İnce, Başak. "The Construction and Redefinition of Citizenship in Turkey." PhD Diss., University of London, 2008.

İslam Dünyası.

İz, Fahir. "Mehmed Emīn" *Encyclopaedia of Islam* 2nd edn. Vol. VI, 986–7.

Jacob, P. Xavier. *L'enseignement religieux dans la Turquie moderne*. Islamkundliche Untersuchungen Band 67. (Berlin: Klaus Schwarz Verlag, 1982).

Kancı, Tuba and Ayşe Gül Altınay. "Educating Little Soldiers and Little Ayşes: Militarised and Gendered Citizenship in Turkish Textbooks," in Marie Carlson, Annika Rabo and Fatma Gök, eds., *Education in 'Multicultural' Societies" Turkish and Swedish Perspectives*. Sockholm: Swedish Research Institute in Istanbul, 2007, 51–70.

Kandiyoti, Deniz. "End of Empire: Islam, Nationalism, and Women in Turkey," in Deniz Kandiyoti, ed., *Women, Islam and the State*. (London: Macmillan, 1991).

Kandiyoti, Deniz. "Identity and its Discontents: Women and the Nation," in Patrick Williams and Laura Chrisman, eds., *Colonial Discourse and Post-Colonial Theory: A Reader*. (New York: Harvester Wheatsheaf, 1993).

Karamadtiosyan, Arakel. *Miftah-i kıraat-i huruf-i ermeniye fi lisan-i osmanî*. Istanbul (?): n.p., n.d.

Karaömerlioğlu, Asım. "The People's Houses and the Cult of the Peasant in Turkey" *Middle Eastern Studies* 34:4 (October 1998), 67–91.

Karpat, Kemal H. "Reinterpreting Ottoman History: A Note on the Condition of Education in 1874," *International Journal of Turkish Studies* 2 (1981–82), 93–100.

Keyder, Çağlar. "A Brief History of Modern Istanbul," in Reşat Kasaba, ed., *The Cambridge History of Turkey Vol. 4: Turkey in the Modern World*. (Cambridge: Cambridge University Press, 2008), 504–23.

Khalid, Adeeb. *The Politics of Muslim Cultural Reform: Jadidism in Central Asia*. (Berkeley, CA: University of California Press, 1998).

Kırlı, Cengiz. "Coffeehouses: Public Opinion in the Nineteenth Century Ottoman Empire," in Dale Eickelman and Armando Salvatore, eds., *Public Islam and the Common Good*. (Leiden: E J Brill, 2004), 75–98.

Kırlı, Cengiz. "Kahvehaneler ve Hafiyeler: 19. Yüzyıl Ortalarında Osmanlı'da Sosyal Kontrol" *Toplum ve Bilim* 83 (Winter), 58–79.

Koçak, Cemil. "Hüseyin Cahit [Yalçın] ve Portreler Üzerine Bazı Notlar," in Hüseyin Cahit [Yalçın], *Tanıdıklarım*. (Istanbul: Yapı Kredi Yayınları, 2001), 7–19.

Köprülüzade, Mehmed Fuad. *Cumhuriyet Çocuklarına Yeni Millî Kıraat*. (Istanbul: Kanaat, 1926).

Kopytoff, Igor. "The Cultural Biography of Things: Commoditization as Process," in Arjun Appadurai, ed., *The Social Life of Things: Commodities in Cultural Perspective*. (Cambridge: Cambridge University Press, 1986), 64–91.

Köroğlu, Erol. *Türk Edebiyatı ve Birinci Dünya Savaşı (1914–1918): Propagandadan Millî Kimlik İnşasına*. (Istanbul: İletişim, 2004).

Kreiser, Klaus. *The Beginnings of Printing in the Near and Middle East: Jews, Christians and Muslims*. (Wiesbaden: Harrassowitz, 2001).

Kreiser, Klaus. "Causes of the Decrease of Ignorance? Remarks on the Printing of Books in the Ottoman Empire," in Klaus Kreiser, ed., *The Beginnings of Printing in the Near and Middle East: Jews, Christians and Muslims*. (Wiesbaden: Harrassowitz, 2001).

Kreiser, Klaus. *Istanbul: Ein Historischer Stadtführer*. 2nd edn. (Munich: C. H. Beck, 2009).

Kreiser, Klaus. "Persisch als Schulsprache bei den osmanischen Türken: Von der Tanzîmât-Zeit zur frühen Republik," in Jens Peter Laut and Klaus Röhrborn, eds., *Sprach- und Kulturkontakte der türkischen Völker*. Materialien der zweiten Deutschen Turkologen-Konferenz. (Wiesbaden: Harrassowitz, 1993).

Kuneralp, Sinan. "Les debuts de l'imprimerie à Istanbul, 1800–1908," in Paul Dumont, ed., *Turquie: Livres d'hier, livres d'aujourd'hui*. (Istanbul: Editions Isis, 1992).

Landen, Robert G. "The Ottoman Home Front: A German Correspondent's Remarks, 1917," in Camron M. Amin, Benjamin C. Fortna and Elizabeth B. Frierson, eds., *The Modern Middle East: A Sourcebook for History*. (Oxford: Oxford University Press, 2006), 441–3.

Leith, James. "Ephemera: Civic Education through Images," in Robert Darnton and Daniel Roche, eds., *Revolution in Print: The Press in France, 1775–1800*. (Berkeley, CA: University of California Press, 1989).

Lewis, Bernard. "Ahmad Midhat," *Encyclopaedia of Islam* Edited by: P. Bearman, Th. Bianquis , C.E. Bosworth , E. van Donzel and W.P. Heinrichs. Brill, 2008. *Brill Online*. S.O.A.S (soas). Accessed 02 April 2008.

Lewis, Geoffrey. *The Turkish Language Reform: A Catastrophic Success*. (Oxford: Oxford University Press, 1999).

Lovell, Stephen. *The Russian Reading Revolution: Print Culture in the Soviet and Post-Soviet Eras*. Studies in Russian and East Europe. (Houndmills: Macmillan, 2000).

Lyons, Martyn. "New Readers in the Nineteenth Century: Women, Children, Workers," in Guglielmo Cavallo and Roger Chartier, eds. *A History of Reading in the West*, Linda G. Cochrane, trans. (Amherst, MA: University of Massachusetts Press, 1999).

M. Safvet. *Kıraat*. (Kostantiniye[Istanbul]: Matbaa-yi Ebuzziya, 1308[1892]).

McNeill, William H. "A Short History of Humanity," *New York Review of Books* XLVII: 11 (29 June 2006), 9–11.

Makdisi, Geroge. *The Rise of Colleges: Institutions of Learning in Islam and the West*. (Edinburgh: Edinburgh University Press, 1981).

Manguel, Alberto. *A History of Reading*. (New York: Penguin, 1996).

Mardin, Şerif. "Playing Games with Names," in Deniz Kandiyoti and Ayşe Saktanber, eds., *Fragments of Culture: The Everyday Life of Modern Turkey*. (London: I. B. Tauris, 2002).

Mardin, Şerif. *Religion and Social Change in Modern Turkey: The Case of Bediüzzaman Said Nursi*. (Albany, NY: State University of New York Press, 1989).

Marks, Marina. "The Ottoman Greek Press (1830–1862)." PhD Diss., University of London (forthcoming).

Meeker, Michael. *A Nation of Empire: The Ottoman Legacy of Turkish Modernity* (Berkeley, CA: University of California Press, 2002).

Mehmed Sedad. *Ameli usul-ü kitabet-i resmiye*. (Dersaadet: Asır Matbaası, 1323[1907]).

Messick, Brinkley. *The Calligraphic State: Textual Domination and History in a Muslim Society*. (Berkeley, CA: University of California Press, 1993).

Mini Mini.

Navaro-Yashin, Yael. *Faces of the State: Secularism and Public Life in Turkey*. (Princeton, NJ: Princeton University Press, 2002).

Neyzi, Leyla. "Object or Subject? The Paradox of 'Youth' in Turkey," *IJMES* 33 (2001), 411–32.

N.a. *Elifbâ: Qura mekatib-i ibtidaiyesinde okutturulmasını*. (Istanbul: Matbaa-i Amire, 1317[1901]).

N. a. *Kitab iftitah al-qira'at*. Izmir: n.p., 1264[1848].

N. a. *Rehber-i salat yahud sual ve cevablı ilm-i hal*. (Dersaadet [Istanbul]: 1328[1912]).

N. a. *Yeni kıraat* (n.p.: n.d.).

Nur, Dr. Rıza. *Hayat ve Hâtıratım*. vol. 1. (Istanbul: Altındağ Yayınevi, 1967).

Okay, Cüneyd. *Eski Harfli Çocuk Dergileri*. (Istanbul: Kitabevi, 1999).

Okay, Cüneyd. "Eski Harfli Çocuk Dergileri," *Türkiye Araştırmaları Literatür Dergisi* 4:7 (2006), 511–18.

Okay, Cüneyd. *Osmanlı Çocuk Hayatında Yenileşmeler, 1850–1900*. (Istanbul: Kırkambar Yayınları, 1998).

Onur, Bekir. *Türkiye'de Çocukluğun Tarihi*. (Ankara: İmge Kitabevi, 2005).

Orga, İrfan. *Portrait of a Turkish Family*. (London: Victor Gollancz, 1950).

Öztürk, Serdar. "Efforts to Modernize Chapbooks during the Initial Years of the Turkish Republic," *European Historical Quarterly* 40 (2010), 7–34.

Öztürk, Zehra. "Osmanlı Döneminde Kıraat Meclislerinde Okunan Halk Kitapları," *Türkiye Araştırmaları Literatür Dergisi* 5: 9 (2007), 401–45.

Özyürek, Esra. *Nostalgia for the Modern: State Secularism and Everyday Politics in Turkey* (Durham, NC: Duke University Press, 2006).

Pamuk, Şevket. "Money in the Ottoman Empire, 1326–1914," in Halil İnalcık with Donald Quataert, eds., *An Economic and Social History of the Ottoman Empire, 1300–1914* (Cambridge, Cambridge University Press, 1994).

Ringer, Monica M. "Rethinking Religion: Progress and Morality in the Early Twentieth-Century Iranian Women's Press," *CSSAAME* 24: 1 (2004), 49–57.

Rose, Clare. "Imperialism and consumerism in the late Victorian sailor suit," *Journal of Maritime Research* (forthcoming).

Salvatore, Armando and Dale Eickelman. *Public Islam and the Common Good*. (Leiden: Brill, 2004).

Sasun, N. *Musevilere mahsus elifba-yi osmanî*. Istanbul: İsak Gabay Matbaası, 1321[1905].

Selim Sabit. *Rehnüma-yı muallimin: Sıbyan mekteblerine mahsus usûl-i tedrisiye*. Istanbul: Matbaa-i Amire, n.d.

Serçe, Erkan. *İzmir'de Kitapçılık (1839–1928)*. 2nd edn. (İzmir: İzmir Büyükşehir Belediyesi Kültür Yayını, 2002).

Sertel, Sabiha Zekeriya. *Yeni Kıraat*. (Istanbul: Resimli Ay Matbaası, 1928).

Servet Safi. *Nev usûl elifbâ-yi osmanî*. (Dersaadet: Kasbar, 1310[1894]).

Seyfettin, Ömer. "Falaka," in *Ömer Seyfettin: Bütün Eserleri. Vol. 8. Falaka*. (Ankara: Bilgi Yayınevi, 1971).

Silverstein, Brian. "Islamist Critique in Modern Turkey: Hermeneutics, Tradition, Genealogy," *Comparative Studies in Society and History* 47 (2005), 134–60.

Somel, Akşin Selçuk. *The Modernization of Public Education in the Ottoman Empire, 1839–1908; Islamization, Autocracy and Discipline.* (Leiden: Brill, 2001).

Starrett, Gregory. *Putting Islam to Work: Education, Politics and Religious Transformation in Egypt.* (Berkeley, CA: University of California Press, 1998).

Strauss, Johan. "Romanlar, Ah! O Romanlar! Les débuts de la lecture moderne dans l'empire ottomane (1850–1900)," *Turcica* 26 (1994), 125–63.

Strauss, Johann. "Who Read What in the Ottoman Empire (19th-20th centuries)?," *Arabic & Middle Eastern Literatures* 6:1 (2003), 39–76.

Szyliowicz, Joseph. *Education and Modernization in the Middle East.* (Ithaca: Cornell University Press, 1973).

Thompson, Elizabeth. *Colonial Citizens: Republican Rights, Paternal Privilege, and Gender in French Syria and Lebanon.* (New York: Columbia University Press, 2000).

Tietze, A. ed., *Akabi Hikayesi: İlk Türkçe Roman (1851).* (Istanbul: Eren, 1991).

The Times.

Tiregöl, Jessica Selma. "The Role of Primary Education in Nation-State-Building: The Case of the Early Turkish Republic." PhD Diss., Princeton University, 1998.

Tripp, Charles. *Islam and the Moral Economy: The Challenge of Capitalism.* (Cambridge: Cambridge University Press, 2006).

Tüccarzâde İbrahim Hilmi. *Altın Kitab[:] Çocuklara ilk kıraat.* (Istanbul: 1327[1911]).

Turan, M. *Öz Türk dilile Kolay okutan Alfabe.* N.p.: Maarif Kitabevi, 1935–1936.

T. C. *İlmektepler Talimatnamesi.* (Ankara: Bakanlık, 1929).

[T. C. Dil Encümeni]. *Yeni Dil Encümeni Alfabesi.* ([Istanbul]: Devlet Matbaası, 1928).

T. C. Kültür Bakanlığı, Millî Kütüphane Başkanlığı. *Türkiye Basmaları Kataloğu: Arap Harfli Eserler, 1729–1928.* (Ankara: Millî Kütüphane Basımevi, 1990).

T. C. Kültür Bakanlığı. *Okuma Kitabı.* Birinci Sınıf. (Istanbul: Devlet Basımevi, 1935).

Uşaklıgil, Halid Ziya. *Kırk Yıl.* (Istanbul: İnkilap ve Aka Kitabevleri, 1969).

Wallach, Yair. "Readings in Conflict: Public Text in Modern Jerusalem, 1858–1948." PhD Diss., University of London, 2008.

Weber, Eugen. *Peasants into Frenchmen: the Modernization of Rural France, 1870–1914.* (Stanford, CA: Stanford University Press, 1976).

Wittmann, Richard. "Was there a Reading Revolution at the end of the Eighteenth Century?" in Cavallo and Chartier, eds., *A History of Reading in the West*, L. G. Cochrane, trans. (Amherst, MA: University of Massachusetts Press, 1999), 284–312.

Wolf, Maryanne. *Proust and the Squid: The Story and Science of the Reading Brain.* (Cambridge: Icon Books, 2008).

[Yalçın], Hüseyin Cahit. *Edebiyat Anıları.* Istanbul: Türkiye İş Bankası Kültür Yayınları, 1975.

———. *Tanıdıklarım.* (Istanbul: Yapı Kredi Yayınları, 2001).

Yalman, Ahmet Emin. *The Development of Modern Turkey as Measured by Its Press.* (New York: Columbia University Press, 1914).

Yardım, Mehmet Nuri. *Tanzimattan Günümüze Edebiyatçılarimizin Çocukluk Hatıraları.* (Istanbul: Timas, 1998).

Yavuz, İsa and Nezahat Yavuz. *Harfli Alfabe.* (Istanbul: Emek İş Yayınevi, 1973).

Yeni Yol.

Yu, Li. "Learning to Read in Late Imperial China," *Studies on Asia*, series III 1:1 (Fall 2004), 7–28.

Yücel, Tahsin. *Dil Devrimi ve Sonuçları.* (Istanbul: İyi Şeyler Yayıncılık, 1997).

Zeydanlioğlu, Velat. "Kemalism's Others: The Reproduction of Orientalism in Turkey." PhD Diss., Anglia Ruskin University, 2007.

Zorlutuna, Halide Nusret. *Bir Devrin Romanı.* (Ankara: Kültür Bakanlığı, 1978).

Zürcher, Erik J. *Turkey: A Modern History.* 3rd edn. (London: I B Tauris, 2004).

Index